Transport in the United Kingdom

Transport in the United Kingdom

D. Maltby
Reader in Civil Engineering,
University of Salford

H. P. White
Professor of Geography,
University of Salford

First published 1982 by
THE MACMILLAN PRESS LTD
London and Basingstoke
Companies and representatives
throughout the world

Typeset in 10/11pt Press Roman by
STYLESET LIMITED
Salisbury · Wiltshire

Printed in Hong Kong

ISBN 0–333–27826–7
ISBN 0–333–27827–5 pbk

Contents

List of Figures

List of Tables

Preface

We have written this book because we consider there is a need for a basic text for new or relatively new studnets of United Kingdom transport. We have in mind candidates for Chartered Membership of the Institute of Transport, undergraduates at universities, polytechnics, and other colleges of higher education reading transport as a minor or major subject, and postgraduates at universities and polytechnics attending courses of advanced study in transport, or conducting transport research. In addition, it provides background information for students of economics, geography, political science, and planning who wish to look at the relationship between transport and their own particular areas of interest. We also have in mind less formal students of this fundamental human activity with such widespread economic and social implications, such as politicians, journalists, members of environmental groups, or people who simply wish to increase their knowledge of transport in the United Kingdom for its own sake.

We have deliberately written the book, then, for a very disparate readership in terms of background, discipline and experience. At undergraduate level in universities and polytechnics, transport studies tend to have a minor role within such disciplines as civil engineering, economics and geography, although there is the exception of their forming a whole degree course at three universities and a subject in a joint degree at another, while they form courses of study leading to examinations for Corporate Membership of the Chartered Institute of Transport at other institutions of higher education. It is likely that most students on postgraduate courses in transport at universities and polytechnics have read transport as a minor subject in their undergraduate course, but some will be meeting transport studies formally for the first time. So the new or relatively new students of transport studies for whom we have written this book are to found throughout the spectrum of higher education.

The book is aimed primarily at the student of United Kingdom transport. We have written the book for a United Kingdom context for two principal reasons: firstly, our joint expertise based on study of transport over some 45 years relates primarily to the United Kingdom; secondly, it is very difficult writing international texts on transport because of national differences in policy, institutions, and methodology. None the less the main lessons of this book can be applied through parallel to countries with comparable political and economic frameworks to those of the United Kingdom.

The main reason why we think there is a need for a book such as this lies in the inter-disciplinary and complex nature of most transport problems on one hand, and the very wide spectrum of disciplines from which students of transport come, on the other. Although our basic disciplines are civil engineering and geography, respectively, we have only developed inter-disciplinary personal approaches to transport studies after many years of experience. Our main aim with this book is to speed up this process for new students. Thus the technologist on reading this book should become more aware of the social science dimensions of transport problems; equally the social scientist should become more aware of their technological dimensions. All readers should come to realise the complexity of most transport problems. Our second main aim is to provide that critical level of background knowledge which is essential for more advanced study, be this by courses of study or by research and investigation. Thus our book should contribute to the development of that broad understanding essential for significant advances in inter-disciplinary areas; we have provided comprehensive references to the literature to guide readers on their way to such advanced study.

There are six chapters in the book: chapter 1 on the transport sector; chapter 2 on the transport system; chapter 3 on trends in transport; chapter 4 on wider relationships between transport and socio-economic activity; chapter 5 on local transport problems and policies; and chapter 6 on national transport problems and policies.

Chapter 1 discusses the transport sector at national level in terms of such variables as employment, output, expenditure and external trade. There is some difficulty in defining the transport sector because of the pervasiveness of transport activity but a definition based on the Standard Industrial Classification is used. Thus the chapter considers specifically shipbuilding and marine engineering, vehicle manufacture, and transport and communications, transport in this context meaning transport operations. The chapter concludes by examining the importance of the transport sector for central government revenue and the way in which the transport sector features in public sector expenditure. The major contribution of this chapter is the way it inter-relates transport manufacturing, transport operations, and management of the economy by central government.

Chapter 2 discusses the characteristics of the transport system in the United Kingdom. Thus the emphasis of the chapter is on transport operations. It is structured by mode of transport with sections on the road network, private transport, public road passenger transport, road haulage, rail transport, air transport, water transport, and pipelines. It includes a final section on the organisation of transport in Northern Ireland, which differs in some measure from that of the rest of the United Kingdom.

Chapter 3 develops further the themes examined in chapter 2 and examines the main trends in the contributions by different modes of transport to transport operations. The chapter first considers overall trends in transport and notes that most transport modes are at different stages of development in a socio-economic and technological life cycle in which early expansion and growth in contribution to transport activity is followed by decline. The position of a particular mode of transport in this life cycle of development varies from country to country. It is in such a context that this book can contribute particularly to the study of transport in other countries. The chapter then considers trends in passenger transport with separate sections on domestic, and on international, passenger transport. The same structure is then applied to the examination of freight transport. The chapter concludes with a discussion of the relationship between trends in transport and technological change. This is an important chapter because it helps to explain trends in the contributions by different modes and how public policy has been used to affect such trends for reasons of social welfare. Such understanding is fundamental to the solution of future transport problems.

Chapter 3 having illustrated the complexity of many transport trends, chapter 4 is devoted entirely to wider relationships between transport and socio-economic activity. Transport in the general case is a 'derived' demand and so the solution to most transport problems lies in the wider relationships between transport and socio-economic activity. This chapter first considers that these relationships can be two-way; for example, increased economic activity can help to justify a new road but the road, once built, may result in even faster growth of economic activity. The chapter then considers the wider relationship between transport and economic development, between transport and social development, between transport and regional development, between transport and land-use activity, and between transport and communications.

The first four chapters of the book having been devoted to development of an understanding of transport, the final two chapters are devoted to a consideration of transport problems in the United Kingdom and ways in which they have been handled. Chapter 5 concentrates on local transport problems and policies. It argues, for example, that the underlying causes of local transport problems are general; urban scale only becomes important in the way these problems have been handled. Thus the chapter has sections on large cities, medium and smaller towns, and rural areas.

Chapter 6 is devoted to national transport problems and policies. It first makes the distinction between problem areas indirectly related to transport operation such as economic growth and regional development, energy, and transport manufacturing, and those directly related to the modes of transport operation. This determines the structure of this chapter. First there are sections on economic growth and regional development, energy, and transport manufacturing. Then there are sections on road, rail, air, and water transport, each dealing with the main national problems affecting these modes, and the ways and policies used to deal with them.

Four important themes run through the book. The first is the pervasive nature of transport activity. Most human activity has a transport element. It is because of this that it is impossible to define the transport sector in any definitive way, even though we have to do it in a more arbitrary way for the sake of analysis. It is also because of this that we must not draw the system boundaries too tightly in analyses of transport activity. The second is that transport should be dealt with as a system, with due consideration given to the effects on other modes of change in one mode, and to the inputs into the system from, and the outputs from the system to, the physical, social and economic environment. The third major theme concerns the concept of a life-cycle for any transport mode in socio-economic and technological terms; for example, private passenger transport may be now a dominant mode in domestic passenger transport but will this situation continue with increasing depletion of oil resources? The fourth important theme concerns the relative roles of the private and public sectors in the transport sector. At the time of writing the management of the United Kingdom economy by a relatively strict monetarist policy under the Thatcher Administration has brought into relief the whole question of the role of the public sector in transport manufacturing and transport operations. This is likely to continue to be a key area for debate in searching for solutions to transport problems in the future.

The book is the outcome of more than a decade of teaching transport studies over several courses at the University of Salford. It therefore reflects our teaching and research interests. But it also reflects the fact that many of our students, undergraduate and postgraduate, have had professional experience before taking up full-time or part-time courses or research. They have been responsible for our keeping abreast of many practical, everyday consequences of the transport objectives and policies dealt with in this book, and to them we owe a very great deal in the development of our thinking.

In particular we wish to thank Mr R. Chapman, for his help in the preparation of section 2.9 on the organisation of transport in Northern Ireland, and Mr P. N. Grimshaw, for the details of cement transport incorporated in section 4.2.2.

Finally, we wish to express our appreciation to colleagues at the University of Salford who helped in the preparation of the manuscript: to Mrs J. M. Bateson, Mrs L. C. Rycroft and Miss A. E. McDonnell for typing the manuscript; and to Mrs M. C. Warr, Mr G. Dobrzynski, and Mr R. Bennett for help in preparation of the artwork.

Statistical Sources

1. Annual Reports of:
    British Airways
    British Airports Authority
    Civil Aviation Authority
    British Railways Board
    London Transport Executive
    Provincial Passenger Transport Executives
    National Freight Corporation
    National Bus Company
    National Ports Authority
    British Transport Docks Board
    Individual ports
    Transport and Road Research Laboratory
2. British Road Federation, *Basic Road Statistics*
3. Central Statistical Office, *Annual Abstract of Statistics* (HMSO)
4. Central Statistical Office, *Monthly Digest of Statistics* (HMSO)
5. Central Statistical Office, *National Income and Expenditure* (HMSO)
6. Central Statistical Office, *Social Trends* (HMSO)
7. Central Statistical Office, *United Kingdom Balance of Payments* (HMSO)
8. Chamber of Shipping of the United Kingdom (after 1974, General Council of British Shipping), *British Shipping Statistics*
9. Civil Aviation Authority, *Monthly Statistics*
10. Department of Employment, *Employment Gazette*
11. Department of Employment, *Family Expenditure Survey* (HMSO)
12. Department of the Environment, *Passenger Transport in Great Britain* (HMSO)
13. Department of Trade and Industry, *Trade and Industry*
14. Department of Transport, *Transport Statistics Great Britain 1968–1978* (HMSO)
15. H.M. Customs and Excise, *Annual Statement of Trade of the U.K.*
16. National Ports Council, *Annual Digest of Port Statistics*
17. The Society of Motor Manufacturers and Traders, *The Motor Industry of Great Britain 1979*

1

The Transport Sector

This chapter considers the contributions of the transport sector to the UK economy. As a preliminary, it is first necessary to define 'transport sector'. This is done on the imperfect basis, which is subsequently qualified, of transport manufacturing and transport operations. Posts and telecommunications are generally included in the latter, mainly because of difficulties in distinguishing transport and communications separately in data sources; however, their inclusion also helps to emphasise the substitution possibilities between physical movement and telecommunications.

The chapter then considers in turn the contributions of the transport sector to national employment, output, and expenditure, and to the balance of payments. It concludes by considering the role of the transport sector in economic management of the United Kingdom.

1.1 Transport and Employment

In 1978, the total working population of the United Kingdom was some 26.4 million; civilian employees accounted for some 24.1 million, with 194 000 in shipbuilding and marine engineering, 793 000 in vehicle manufacture and 1 507 000 in transport and communication. So some 2 494 000, or 10 per cent, of civilian employees were in the transport sector, defining this for the moment on the limited basis of employment in shipbuilding and marine engineering, vehicle manufacture, and transport and communication.

Since the end of the Second World War, the number of men in the UK working population has hardly changed. The increase in the total working population over this period can be almost wholly ascribed to the increased number of women entering the labour force; for example, the total working population of some 23.3 million in 1948 included some 7.3 million women, while some 10.2 million women were in the 26.4 million working population of 1978. Other important changes in the working population over this period were the significant reduction in the numbers of people serving in the armed forces and the very marked increase in unemployment from the mid-70s. In the post-war period rates of unemployment in excess of 2.5 per cent were unknown before the 1970s, and substantially lower levels were quite common. However, unemployment rates have increased sharply beyond this level in the 1970s, particularly since 1975, reaching the very high rate of 6.2 per cent in 1977, some 1 484 000 registered unemployed, and declining slightly to some 5.7 per cent by 1979. At the time of writing it has increased once more to some 6.1 per cent, and significant increases beyond this are the subject of serious speculation, given continuing management of the economy by a monetarist policy.

In 1948, there were some 20.7 million civilian employees in the United Kingdom; of these some 343 000 were in shipbuilding and marine engineering, some 675 000 in vehicle manufacture, and some 1 797 000 in transport and communication, making a total of some 2 815 000, or 13.6 per cent, of civilian employees in the transport sector, substantially more than in 1978. There has taken place, then, a very large decline in employment in shipbuilding and marine engineering and a significant decline in transport and communication, while in vehicle manufacture employment increased up until the late 1950s—early 1960s to in excess of 900 000, only to decline thereafter.

The main explanation for this overall long-term decline in employment in the UK transport sector lies in output increasing at a slower rate than labour productivity (see section 1.2.2). An inspection of long-term trends in output and employment in different transport sub-sectors suggests three groupings: one in which both output and employment have declined, as in shipbuilding and marine engineering, motorcycle manufacture, rail transport, road passenger transport, and inland waterways transport; one in which output has increased but employment has declined, as in motor vehicle manufacture, road haulage, shipping, and communications; and one in which both output and employment have increased, as in air transport. An additional important point is that output in the UK transport sector has tended to increase at a slower rate than in the world as a whole, as in the cases of shipbuilding and marine engineering, aerospace manufacture, motor vehicle manufacture, and shipping.

There are many examples of labour productivity increasing through technological innovation: employment in shipping in the United Kingdom has declined with the trend to larger and specialised vessels; port employment has declined because the introduction of specialised vessels and facilities, particularly for containerisation, has increased the rate at which cargo can be handled; automatic signalling, mechanical track maintenance, and the replacement of steam locomotion by electric or diesel locomotion have all contributed to the substantial decline in railway employment; the introduction of one-man-operation (OMO) on buses has reduced labour costs and provided a partial solution to problems of labour shortage, although at the expense of lower service levels. Technological innovation also has implications for the United Kingdom's foreign trade; higher rates of innovation in other countries combined with more efficient working methods have contributed to the United Kingdom's declining share of world markets.

It is now useful to take a more detailed look at employment in the different parts of the transport sector. Figures 1.1 to 1.3 illustrate trends in employment in shipbuilding and marine engineering, vehicle manufacture, and transport and communication, respectively, in the United Kingdom since 1948. The decline in employment in shipbuilding and marine engineering is apparent, particularly between the late 1950s and mid-1960s. This has been reflected in rationalisation and closures of shipyards, and more recently, nationalisation of the major part

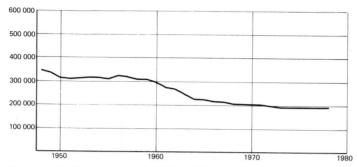

Figure 1.1 *Employment in shipbuilding and marine engineering*

of the industry. All this has been in response to the effects of increased
competition from overseas competitors, very often subsidised by their
governments: for example, over the 1959–74 period merchant ships under
construction in the leading non-communist shipbuilding countries increased
from some 7.2 to some 23.0 million gross registered tons (grt); corresponding
figures for the United Kingdom were 2.0 and 2.1 million grt, while activity
declined to a minimum of some 1.2 million grt in 1967. A further factor in the
1970s has been higher oil prices which have contributed to the recession in
world trade. This has affected particularly carryings of crude oil, resulting in
surplus capacity of oil tankers and attendant effects on shipbuilding activity.

   Employment trends in vehicle manufacture are more complex. They are
illustrated in figure 1.2 for total employment in this sector and in its sub-sectors,
motor vehicle manufacture and aerospace equipment manufacture and repair.

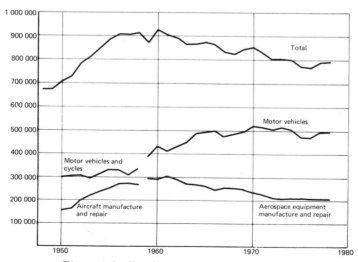

Figure 1.2 *Employment in vehicle manufacture*

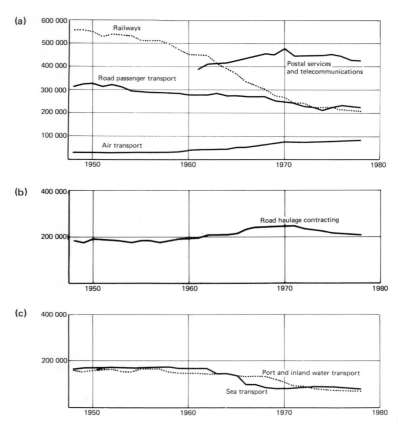

Figure 1.3 *(a) Employment in railways, road passenger transport, air transport, and postal services and telecommunications; (b) employment in road haulage contracting for general hire or reward; (c) employment in sea transport, and port and inland water transport*

Motor vehicle manufacture includes employment related to the production of parts and accessories for the motor-car industry. Employment in the aerospace industry increased up until around 1960 under the combined effects of expansion of air transport and a temporary technological advantage enjoyed by British manufacturers in the 1950s; for example, the ill-fated Comet and the very successful Vickers Viscount, both outcomes of the recommendations of the Brabazon Committee, were market leaders at this time.[1] Subsequently, aircraft manufacturing has been dominated by American companies despite a steadily expanding world market. Given the size of the US domestic market this is not surprising, but it has led to many operators standardising on American aircraft for reasons of efficiency in operation and maintenance; for example, even British Airways, the UK nationalised airline, follows this practice. These factors have added to the difficulties of the UK aerospace industry. As a consequence, employment in the industry has contracted since the early 1960s and rationalisation of manufacturing has taken place. As in shipbuilding, a major part of the industry has been nationalised, with British Aerospace being formed from the British Aircraft Corporation Limited, Hawker Siddeley Aviation Limited, Hawker Siddeley Dynamics Limited and Scottish Aviation Limited in 1977 by the Callaghan Administration[2] but 'privatised' in 1981 by the Thatcher Administration.[3] The government also owns the equity of the aero-engine manufacturer, Rolls-Royce Limited, which has an important share of the world market.[4] Defence contracts account for an important share of the output of the industry, which together with other contract or co-operative work, usually with European or American companies, has resulted in stabilisation of employment in recent years.

The European Airbus is a good example of such a co-operative venture. British Aerospace have a 20 per cent interest in it; they build the wings for the 250-seater A 300, and will do the same for the proposed 200-seater A 310. Both aircraft are wide-bodied and more fuel-efficient than their narrow-bodied predecessors. The A 300 is currently competing very strongly with the proposed Boeing 767 for the very large replacement market for medium-range jet aircraft. Co-operative ventures are vital for Rolls-Royce Limited. Currently, development of the RB211 jet engine depends on the success of the proposed Boeing 757, a narrow-bodied aircraft designed for denser medium-range routes, and for which British Airways is a leading customer.

Motor vehicle manufacture in the United Kingdom has four main activites: motor cars, commercial vehicles, buses and coaches, and parts and accessories.[5] Motor-car production is dominated by one state-owned company, British Leyland,[6] two American-owned companies, Ford and Vauxhall, and one French-owned company, Talbot — formerly Chrysler (UK). In addition, there are a number of small specialist manufacturers such as Lotus, Reliant and Rolls-Royce Motors Limited, the latter private company having been created in the reorganisation of the parent company in 1971.[4] The industry produced some 1.2 million vehicles in 1978, a total well below its production capacity, of which some 496 000, 41 per cent, were exported. British Leyland accounted for the greatest production volume, with some 612 000 vehicles in 1978, followed by Ford with some 324 000, Chrysler with some 196 000, and Vauxhall with some 84 000. British Leyland also makes the largest contribution to exports with some 248 000 vehicles in 1978, compared with some 132 000 from Chrysler, much of which is connected with a large contract for Iran, some 102 000 from Ford, and a mere 9000 from Vauxhall.

In 1978 the motor vehicle industry produced some 385 000 commercial vehicles, of which some 169 000, 44 per cent, were exported. As for motor-car manufacturing, volume production is dominated by British Leyland, with some 131 000 vehicles in 1978, Vauxhall with some 117 000, and Ford with some 102 000; so General Motors features more strongly in the United Kingdom in commercial vehicle rather than car manufacture. A special feature of this industry has been the existence of a small number of low-volume manufacturers such as ERF, Foden and Seddon Atkinson, alongside high-volume producers. They have been able to compete in the specialist vehicle market because the economics of production has favoured either small or high-volume operators; for example, new registrations of articulated commercial vehicles in 1978

included 2386 manufactured by Leyland Vehicles, 2051 by ERF, 2226 by
Seddon Atkinson and 2866 by Volvo. However, 1980 has witnessed the collapse
of Foden amidst worsening trading conditions for UK commercial vehicle
manufacturing generally.

Leyland Vehicles dominate bus and coach manufacturing with a major
proportion of their production facilities at the new factory in Workington, set
up jointly with the National Bus Company to manufacture the Leyland
National; for example, Leyland Vehicles accounted for 3734 of 5549 new
registrations of passenger service vehicles in the United Kingdom in 1978.
However, poor customer acceptance of the Leyland National and production
difficulties with the Titan have created suitable conditions for penetration of
this market by Seddon Atkinson, Metro Cammell Weymann, and Ailsa.[5]

The parts and accessories industry is the fourth part of the motor vehicle
industry. The motor-car industry in the United Kingdom, with perhaps the
exception of Ford, is unique for its dependence on 'bought-in' components;
it is for this reason that the future prospects for the parts and accessories
industry cannot be separated from those for vehicle manufacture.
Concentration of a major part of the motor vehicle industry in the West
Midlands adds to the significance of this interdependence.[5]

Employment in motor vehicle manufacture expanded under the impetus
of increasing car ownership in the United Kingdom up until the turn of the
1960s. Over this period the economies of scale of increasing production and
technical innovation, particularly in volume production of motor cars,
resulted in competitiveness in both domestic and foreign markets; for example,
the British Motor Corporation 'Mini' led this innovation. However, the picture
has changed significantly in the 1970s, with indications currently of impending
reduction in production capacity for motor cars at both British Leyland and
Talbot (Chrysler (UK)).

Many factors have contributed to this uncertainty about the UK motor-car
industry. They include world recession, increased oil prices, international
competition, particularly from Japan, failure to produce new models,
deteriorating labour relations, and rationalisations of production capacity by
multinational companies. One result is very high import penetration,
particularly of privately purchased vehicles.[7, 8, 9, 10]

A depressing feature of the UK vehicle manufacturing sector is the
similarity of employment trends for shipbuilding and marine engineering,
aerospace manufacture, and motor vehicle manufacture. In all three cases
contraction of employment has followed expansion, with rationalisation of
production facilities and an element of nationalisation taken under the threat
of foreign competition; yet world markets are still expanding.

Employment in the remaining parts of the vehicle manufacturing sector
has generally contracted since the Second World War. Some 179 000 people
were employed on the manufacture of railway locomotives, carriages, wagons
and track equipment in 1948; the corresponding total in 1978 was some 44 000.
This contraction reflects the decline in the use of rail transport over this period
and more effective use of assets.

Some 42 000 people were employed in the manufacture of motorcycles,
three-wheel vehicles and pedal cycles in 1960; by 1978 the total was some

15 000. For motorcycle manufacture, contraction in employment took place up until the early 1970s against the background of reduced domestic sales and virtual capture of this market by Japanese manufacturers.[11] The 'more expensive oil' era of the mid to late 70s has seen a revival in domestic sales but no weakening of the hold over the domestic market by foreign manufacturers. Similarly, domestic sales of pedal cycles declined up to the early 1970s, only to revive more recently, but in this case there is still a strong national industry.

Figure 1.3 shows that employment in the transport and communications sub-sector has contracted over all; however, this conceals expansion of employment in some cases.

Employment in communications expanded steadily to the late 1960s—early 1970s, remained at a fairly constant level to the mid-1970s, and then began to show signs of decline. This trend reflects many factors, but particularly the different nature of the 'posts' business on one hand, and telecommunications on the other. In both, labour productivity has increased as a result of investment in such facilities as automatic sorting equipment and automatic telephone exchanges. However, business has declined on the 'posts' side and expanded on the telecommunications side; for example, over the 1967—77 period the numbers of letters and parcels handled fell from 11 400 million to 9458 million, and from 217 million to 148 million, respectively, while the number of inland telephone calls increased from 7382 million to 16 656 million. So, the contractions in employment in the late 1970s reflect the combined effects of economic recession, a reduction in business on the 'posts' side, and very significant increases in labour productivity. These differences between the 'posts' and 'telecommunications' sides of the activities of the Post Office have found expression in the recent creation of two separate businesses.[12, 13]

Employment in road goods transport remained at a fairly steady level to the early 1960s. It then expanded modestly to the mid-1970s, since when there has been some decline, largely because of the general economic recession. This modest expansion in employment, in comparison with the very large growth in output in volume terms over the same period, illustrates the significant increases in productivity that have taken place, largely through more use of larger and faster vehicles.

Employment in air transport has expanded steadily since the Second World War in parallel with the growth of air transport. However, as for road goods transport, expansion in employment has been more modest because technological development, in this case investment in large aircraft, has raised productivity.

Elsewhere, contraction in employment has taken place as transport markets have declined. The most severe decline in employment has taken place in rail transport. In 1948 there were some 576 000 employees; the corresponding figure for 1978 was some 216 000. This decline also reflects a reduced demand for manpower as a result of investment in new technology: for example, the superior work capacity of electric and diesel locomotives has enabled a reduction in numbers of locomotives beyond that justified by decline in traffic alone; automatic signalling and area signal boxes have replaced mechanical signals and signal boxes at individual junctions; much track maintenance is now done mechanically, while track testing can be done automatically.

Employment in public road passenger transport has also declined significantly, but not as severely as for rail transport, with some 319 000 employees in 1948 and some 222 000 in 1978. In this case, employment has fallen in a series of steps, while traffic has fallen steadily since the peak of the mid-1950s, suggesting that employment has been fairly insensitive to traffic levels in the medium run. The result has been declining productivity as reductions in traffic have not been matched by declining service levels, and load factors have fallen accordingly. An important constraint on this output/ employment relationship has been the requirement to maintain minimum levels of service for social reasons. Widespread introduction of OMO since the mid-1960s has also affected these employment trends.

Employment in water transport has also declined since the Second World War. However, employment has continued to be distributed fairly evenly between sea transport on one hand, and port and inland waterways transport on the other: for example, some 165 000 people were employed in sea transport in 1948, and some 160 000 in port and inland waterways transport; the corresponding figures in 1978 were some 84 000 and some 75 000. In both cases employment remained at a fairly steady level up until the early 1960s. The remainder of the 1960s witnessed the most significant decline in employment. In the case of sea transport, a reduction in the share carried by the UK merchant fleet despite steady expansion in world trade, and trends to larger and specialised vessels, to containerisation, and to an emphasis on short turn-round times, all contributed to this contraction in employment; for example, over the 1960–70 period, the value of world trade increased some 150 per cent, while UK invisible earnings from shipping increased some 115 per cent.

The main reason for this contraction of employment in inland waterways transport over this period was competition from road haulage; for example, freight carried on the waterways of the British Waterways Board declined from 10.5 million tons to 4.2 million tons over the 1955–75 period, while staff employed by the Board declined from 5000 to 3181. A minor factor in the case of the London Area was less use of the canal system for distribution, as facilities at London Docks were phased out and those at Tilbury expanded.

Port employment, then, is the dominant component of the ports and inland waterways sub-sector, with concentrations at the largest ports, London, Liverpool and Southampton. It is at London and Liverpool that the problems over contraction of port employment have been most severe: at the former the transfer of major facilities to Tilbury have contributed to this problem; at the latter a continuing reduction in traffic has been a contributory factor. In general, though, rationalisation of port facilities, provision of modern handling equipment, and development of containerisation, all contributed to the decline in port employment in the mid to late 1960s and created conditions for reassessment of the port industry.[14] However, even though the nature of cargo handled changed over this period, its throughput in volume terms expanded; for example, over the 1960–70 period, foreign traffic through ports in Great Britain increased from some 157 million tons to some 240 million tons; another case of technological development affecting employment in a transport industry.

So much, then, for employment trends in the transport sector. However,

before leaving this topic it is worthwhile considering employment closely
related to transport, and employment in other sectors of the economy, perhaps
even employment overseas, which contribute to the output of the transport
sector.

Examples of employment closely related to the transport sector are
employment in motor repairers, motor vehicle distributors, garages and filling
stations, and employment connected with the planning and administration of
transport by central government and local government. Employment trends for
these three sub-sectors are shown in figure 1.4. Employment in motor repairers,
motor vehicle distributors, garages and filling stations has increased substantially
since the Second World War with the expansion of road transport, with some
239 000 people employed in 1948 and some 490 000 in 1978. The major
expansion in employment took place, as in motor vehicle manufacture, up
until the mid-1960s, with some 460 000 people employed in the sub-sector in
1966, but thereafter, employment has fluctuated in the 400 000s.

It is necessary to be cautious in examining trends in central government
employment because they might not be a reliable guide to central government's
involvement in the economy; for example, selling off parts of the scientific or
industrial civil service to the private sector will reduce the number of civil
servants, but need not reduce public expenditure. The general trend shows
central-government employment at similar levels in 1948 and 1978 with some
717 000 and 692 000 jobs respectively, but it declined to some 534 000 jobs
by 1960, and thereafter increased steadily. This reflected the increasing
involvement of government in a modern society, perhaps particularly under a
Labour administration. However, the present administration aims to reverse
this trend and reduce the size of the civil service significantly by the next
election as part of its measures to reduce public expenditure and, thereby,

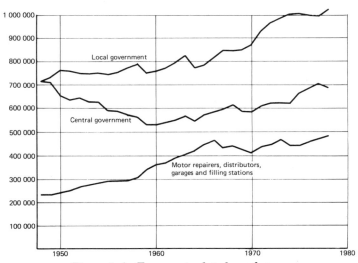

Figure 1.4 *Transport-related employment*

direct taxation. Since 1960 the number of civil servants in transport-related employment has increased with the general trend as central government involvement in transport has increased, with the latest example being support of the motor-car manufacturing industry.

Employment in local government was some 720 000 in 1948; however, it has steadily increased, particularly since around 1960, so that in 1978 it was some 1 027 000. As for central government, increases in employment in transport-related jobs have contributed to this general trend, with the distinction that the transport function in local government is limited to the administration

TABLE 1.1(a) *Sub-sectors (Transport, Non-transport and Imports) Accounting for at least 10 per cent of the Production Costs of Transport Sub-sectors in the United Kingdom in 1972**

Transport Sub-sector	Sub-sectors with Inputs $\geqslant$ 10 per cent
Shipbuilding	Shipbuilding Imports
Wheeled tractors	Iron castings Wheeled tractors Motor vehicles
Motor vehicles	Other iron and steel Other metal goods Motor vehicles Imports
Aerospace equipment	Electronics and telecommunications Aerospace equipment Imports
Other vehicles	Other iron and steel Other mechanical engineering Imports
Railways	Other vehicles
Road transport	Mineral oil refining Motor vehicles Rubber Road transport Miscellaneous services
Sea and air transport	Sea and air transport Imports
Communication	Electrical machinery, insulation wires and cables and other electrical goods Sea and air transport Communication Imports

of local roads and public passenger transport, car and lorry parks and, exceptionally, airports.

An industry-by-industry flow matrix of the United Kingdom will illustrate the interdependence of the transport sector and other sectors of the economy. Tables 1.1(a) and (b) are based on input–output tables for the United Kingdom in 1972.[15] Table 1.1(a) shows sub-sectors accounting for at least 10 per cent of production costs in transport manufacturing and transport operations sub-sectors. Two common characteristics are the integration of transport sub-sectors and their dependence on imports. The outputs of all the transport sub-sectors, with the exceptions of 'other vehicles' and 'railways', depend upon important inputs from within the sub-sectors: for example, the input from shipbuilding to the output of shipbuilding, the input from motor vehicles to the output of motor vehicles, etc. Imports make an important contribution to output in all the transport sub-sectors except 'wheeled tractors' and 'railways'; their contribution to sea and air transport is massive. Other important inputs are those which should be expected: 'other iron and steel' and 'other metal goods' into 'motor vehicles'; 'electronics and telecommunication' into 'aerospace equipment'; 'other vehicles' (principally rail rolling stock) into 'railways'; 'mineral oil refining' (fuel), 'motor vehicles', 'rubber' (tyres), and 'miscellaneous services' into 'road transport'; and 'electrical equipment' and 'sea and air transport' into 'communication'.

Table 1.1(b) shows those transport sub-sectors accounting for at least 10 per cent of the production costs of non-transport sub-sectors. Once again the results are not all that surprising: 'shipbuilding' makes an important contribution to the 'fishing' and 'petroleum and natural gas' sub-sectors; 'sea transport' to 'mineral oil refining'; 'road transport' to 'building materials' and 'distributive trades' sub-sectors; and 'communication' to 'miscellaneous services'. The last result emphasises the growing importance of communications in an economy becoming more service sector orientated. This latter analysis brings into view the general question of the sensitivity of output in different sectors of the economy to changes in transport cost.[16, 17]

TABLE 1.1(b) *Transport Sub-sectors Accounting for at least 10 per cent of the Production Costs of Non-transport Sub-sectors**

Transport Sub-sector	Non-transport Sub-sector
Shipbuilding	Forestry and *fishing*
Shipbuilding	Petroleum and natural gas
Sea and air transport	Mineral oil refining
Road transport ·	Building materials
Road transport	Distributive trades
Communication	Miscellaneous services

* Source: Input–output tables for the United Kingdom, 1972[15]

These analyses illustrate the difficulty in defining the transport sector. However, for the sake of structuring this book, the simple definition already proposed will continue to be used.

1.2 Transport and Output

1.2.1 Contribution to Output

Tables 1.2 and 1.3 show the contribution in 1975 of the different sub-sectors of the transport sector to gross domestic product*. The transport sector accounted for some 12 per cent of net output, of which shipbuilding and marine engineering contributed some 0.6 per cent, vehicle manufacture some 2.7 per cent, transport some 5.7 per cent, and communications some 3.1 per cent. Transport's share of 5.7 per cent is understated, because it excludes the considerable expenditure on private transport which, unlike fares for passenger transport or rates for freight transport, is included in the accounts of other sectors. Manufacturing accounted for some 28 per cent of net output. Within the manufacturing sector vehicle manufacturing's share of net output was the

TABLE 1.2 *Gross Domestic Product by Industry in 1975*

Sector	£ million
Agriculture, forestry and fishing	2541
Mining and quarrying	1535
Manufacturing	25641
Construction	6819
Gas, electricity and water	2987
Transport	5270
Communication	2832
Distributive trades	9253
Insurance, banking, finance and business services	6612
Ownership of dwellings	5593
Public administration and defence	7323
Public health and educational services	7183
Other services	12015
Total	95604
Adjustment for financial services	−3652
Residual error	555
Gross domestic product at factor cost	92 507

Source: National Income and Expenditure

* Since this is in factor cost terms, table 1.2 shows the contribution of the transport sector to final demand or total final expenditure after allowances for imports of goods and services, taxes on expenditure, and subsidies.

TABLE 1.3 *Gross Domestic Product by Manufacturing Industries in 1975*

Sector	£ million
Food, drink and tobacco	2900
Coal and petroleum products	387
Chemicals and allied industries	2101
Metal manufacture	1727
Mechanical engineering	3357
Instrument engineering	443
Electrical engineering	2400
Shipbuilding and marine engineering	533
Vehicles	2480
Metal goods not elsewhere specified	1684
Textiles	1461
Leather, leather goods and fur	110
Clothing and footwear	867
Bricks, pottery, glass, cement, etc.	1019
Timber, furniture, etc.	934
Paper, printing and publishing	2117
Other manufacturing industries	1121
Total	25 641

Source: National Income and Expenditure

third largest at some 9.7 per cent, and that of shipbuilding and marine engineering was the fourth smallest at some 2.1 per cent.

Table 1.4, which is based on the 1972 Input—Output Tables of the British Economy, illustrates the relative contributions of different sub-sectors in transport manufacturing and transport operation.[15] In 1972, motor vehicle manufacturing accounted for some 68 per cent of the total final output of transport manufacturing, and aerospace equipment for some 22 per cent. Air and sea transport accounted for some 76 per cent of the total final output of the transport operations sector, the remainder being equally shared by rail and road transport. Therefore, in terms of final output, 'motor vehicle manufacture' and 'air and sea transport' are dominant sub-sectors of the transport sector. An interesting result of this analysis is the modest contributions to final output of rail and road transport.

1.2.2 Trends in Output

Table 1.5 illustrates recent trends in the contribution to net output of the UK economy by the transport sector. Between 1968 and 1975, net output from shipbuilding and marine engineering, vehicle manufacturing, and transport operations, increased at a slower rate than the economy as a whole, with the trend for transport manufacturing following that for manufacturing generally; over this period, only the communications sector expanded at a faster rate than the economy as a whole.

TABLE 1.4 *Total Final Output of the Transport Sector in 1972*

Sector		£ million
Shipbuilding		546
Vehicle manufacture		
Wheeled tractors	241	
Motor vehicles	2428	
Aerospace equipment	795	
Other vehicles	118	3582
Transport		
Railways	372	
Road transport	376	
Other transport	2341	3089
Communications		921
Total final output		
grand total		65 855

Source: Input–output tables for the United Kingdom 1972[15]

A longer-term perspective is shown on table 1.6. It confirms these trends and shows that the structure of the economy has changed relatively slowly; for example, the contribution by manufacturing declined from 37 per cent to 29 per cent over the 1948–78 period, while that by transport and communications hardly changed at all, although expansion of the communications sub-sector has counterbalanced contraction of the transport sub-sector, as already indicated. Figure 1.5 illustrates these long-run trends in output in the transport sector in constant factor cost terms. Over the 1950–78 period, output in shipbuilding and marine engineering declined by some 10 per cent on this basis. Over the same period, output in vehicle manufacturing increased by some 90 per cent,

TABLE 1.5 *Gross Domestic Product by Industry in 1968 and 1975*

Sector	£ million			
	1968		1975	
Shipbuilding and marine engineering	268	(0.7)	533	(0.6)
Vehicle manufacturing	1187	(3.2)	2480	(2.7)
Manufacturing	12003	(32.1)	25641	(27.9)
Transport	2349	(6.3)	5270	(5.7)
Communication	813	(2.4)	2832	(3.1)
Gross domestic product at factor cost	37 411	(100.00)	92 507	(100.0)

Source: National Income and Expenditure

TABLE 1.6 *Gross Domestic Product by Industry in 1948, 1958, 1968 and 1978*

Sector	£ million			
	1948	1958	1968	1978
Manufacturing	3739 (37)	7019 (35)	11999 (32)	40690 (29)
Transport and Communication	880 (9)	1598 (8)	3162 (8)	11688 (8)
Gross domestic product at factor cost	10 210 (100)	20 130 (100)	37 411 (100)	141 999 (100)

Source: National Income and Expenditure

that in transport and communications by some 101 per cent, while gross domestic product increased by some 94 per cent. So, with the exception of shipbuilding and marine engineering, the output of the transport sector increased overall at a rate not too different from that for the economy as a whole. However, short to medium-run growth rates in the transport sector in some cases were quite different from those for the economy as a whole. This was to be expected in the case of shipbuilding and marine engineering, where output increased over the early 1950s to a peak in 1956, declined to the 1950 level by 1960, and thereafter remained about this level. Output in vehicle manufacturing increased at between two and three times the rate of the economy as a whole over the 1950–60 period, but thereafter has not exceeded the 1960 level by more than 16 per cent, and in 1978 was only some 4 per cent above this level.

So, in shipbuilding and marine engineering, and in vehicle manufacturing, changes in output were most marked before 1960. By contrast, the output of transport and communications has followed quite closely that of the economy as a whole, not altogether surprising in that both are, by and large, derived demands, as illustrated in figure 1.6. The only qualifications necessary in this case have been made already, namely that in recent years the output of

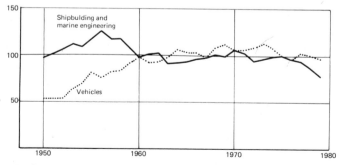

Figure 1.5 *Index numbers of output at constant factor cost: shipbuilding and marine engineering, and vehicles*

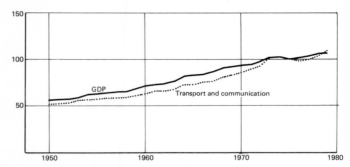

Figure 1.6 *Index numbers of output at constant factor cost: transport and communication*

communications has been increasing at a faster rate than that of the transport industries, although it should be remembered that official statistics neglect the contribution of private transport to the latter.

Figure 1.7 illustrates these long-run trends in output for the manufacturing sector. Over the 1950–78 period, output in the manufacturing sector increased by some 97 per cent, a rate of increase not too unlike that for gross domestic

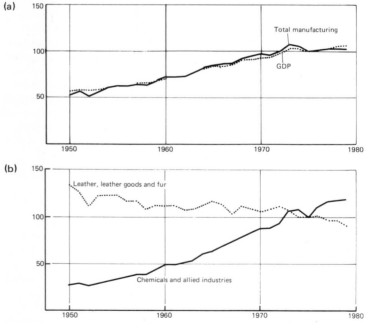

Figure 1.7 *Index numbers of output at constant factor cost: (a) total manufacturing; (b) leather, leather goods and fur, and chemicals and allied industries*

product. However, the contribution of this sector to gross domestic product declined in proportional terms, as illustrated in table 1.6, because of an increasing dependence on the import of goods and services. Furthermore, short and medium-run changes in output were not too unlike such changes in gross domestic product. Changes in output in different sub-sectors of the manufacturing sector varied considerably, and in some cases quite differently from those in transport manufacturing. Figure 1.7 also shows the long-run trends in output for the manufacturing sub-sector with the most severe decline in output over the 1950–78 period: leather, leather goods and furs; and for that with the greatest expansion of output: chemicals and allied products. Even though there were variations in output, the overall decline in the leather, leather goods and furs sub-sectors took place over the entire period rather than being concentrated as in the case of shipbuilding and marine engineering. Unlike vehicle manufacturing, growth of output in chemicals and allied products not only has been without equal, but has also been generally unfaltering.

These long-run trends in output in the transport sector should be viewed from the perspective of changes in the economy as a whole. It is in the service sector that output has increased at a significantly faster rate than the economy as a whole, while the opposite has taken place in the primary sector. Output in manufacturing has kept pace with expansion in the economy as a whole, but has varied considerably between sub-sectors, with very large increases in output in oil refining, the chemical industries, and instrument engineering, and very small increases or even decline in leather and furs, shipbuilding and marine engineering, textiles, metal manufacture, and clothing. These changes are reflected in the contributions by different sectors of the economy to gross domestic product, although allowance must be made for other factors, such as dependence on imports. Thus, the primary sector accounted for some 10 per cent of gross domestic product in 1948 and some 6 per cent in 1978, and manufacturing some 37 per cent in 1948 and some 29 per cent in 1978, while insurance, banking, finance and business services, public health and education services, and ownership of dwellings, accounted for some 8 per cent in 1948 and some 21 per cent in 1978.

1.2.3 Productivity

Productivity is an important issue in the transport sector. However, its measurement is difficult for technical reasons. Use of the simple output per employee ratio in table 1.7 shows that productivity in the UK transport sector has increased since the Second World War, as has productivity in the economy as a whole. These changes reflect, of course, changes in output and in employment over this period: for example, output in shipbuilding and marine engineering increased from the end of the Second World War to a peak in 1956, but employment did not increase significantly over this period (see figures 1.1 and 1.5). This suggests that increased output was made possible by improved productivity of both capital and labour. Output declined subsequently and after 1960 it did not vary greatly, but corresponding trends in employment were not evident until the mid-1960s, illustrating the

TABLE 1.7 *Movements in the Output Per Employee Ratio in the United Kingdom Taking 1975 As 100*

Sector	1950	1960	1970	1975
Shipbuilding and marine engineering	58	65	96	100
Vehicle manufacture	60	82	95	100
Transport and communication	46	60	84	100
All sectors	63	75	94	100

Source: National Income and Expenditure

constraints on matching employment with output because of the great problems in rationalising an industry in decline. Similar examples are provided by other transport sub-sectors. They all help to illustrate the superficiality of the output per employee ratio as a measure of productivity. For this reason, and because it conceals the different contributions to overall productivity of labour and capital inputs, its use in productivity measurement is justifiably criticised.

However, improved measures of productivity also have a number of weaknesses. The first is related to measurement of changes in output over a period of time. In principle it is necessary to trace change in net output or value added in real terms. One way of doing this is to estimate net output in financial terms at one point in time, for example, from a Census of Production, and then use a physical measure of net output as a volume index. However, this approach has two problems: value added per unit of production might vary with time; related to this, the units of production used as the volume index might conceal changes in the physical nature of output; for example, larger motor cars or longer journeys might account for differing proportions of net output with time.

The second weakness concerns treatment of labour and capital inputs; when measures of productivity combining labour and capital inputs are used it is necessary to be confident that they are not just mathematical artefacts.

One study of transport operations considered such problems for the United Kingdom over the 1952–62 period.[18] Productivity was measured for rail transport, road passenger transport, road haulage contracting, sea transport, port and inland water transport, and postal services and telecommunications. Labour productivity, defined as output per standardised labour unit hour, had an exponential rate of change in the transport sub-sectors of 2.34 per cent per annum over the period. Total factor productivity, defined as output per unit of total factor input, had a corresponding increase of 1.46 per cent per annum, indicating that capital input was rising relative to that of labour; this held for all the transport sub-sectors. However, there was considerable variation in productivity movements between the transport sub-sectors; for example, total factor productivity movements were highest in air transport at 5.47 per cent per annum and road haulage contracting at 4.46 per cent per annum, and lowest in railways at −0.64 per cent per annum and in road passenger transport at −1.25 per cent per annum. However, examination of these productivity movements over a ten-year period obscured important shorter-term movements: for example, on the railways, total factor productivity declined at 0.93 per cent per annum over the 1952−8 period, and much more slowly at 0.20 per cent per annum over the 1958−62 period; in road passenger transport, corresponding figures were a decline of 2.42 per cent per annum, followed by an increase of 0.50 per cent per annum; by contrast, air transport experienced fairly steady increases in total factor productivity of 5.21 per cent per annum, followed by 5.87 per cent per annum; sea transport, and port and inland water transport both experienced much larger increases in productivity in the last four years than in the first six years of the period, while road haulage contracting experienced the opposite.

This study also attempted to explain these productivity movements. It estimated, for example, that the effect of increasing capital per man accounted for up to less than about half, and in some cases much less than half, the labour productivity gain over the 1952−62 period. Thus, it was argued, the major explanation of these productivity movements generally lay in technical changes working in a number of ways: through the capital stock, through improved labour skills, through better organisational knowledge with regard to managerial and administrative skills, and through external factors such as institutional constraints.

A very recent study of the performance of a number of European rail systems recognised the problems of measuring total factor productivity.[19] It adopted a more pragmatic approach, and made comparisons simply on the basis of labour productivity for total operations, and passenger and freight operations separately for different staff categories. Over total operations the labour productivity of British Rail was shown to compare favourably with that of other European railways. However, more detailed examination showed that it compared unfavourably in passenger operations because of high staffing of stations on Inner Suburban Services in the London and South-East Area, and in freight operations because of continuing use of guards and/or drivers' assistants. Both of these shortcomings are related to capital investment: fewer station staff would be required in the first case if rolling stock with automatic sliding doors were used; the case for guards and for drivers' assistants on freight trains would be severely weakened if automatic braking systems were universally fitted and were absolutely reliable, although in this case there is strong union opposition to reduction of employment in itself; in both cases British Rail are pursuing investment policies which will resolve these technological constraints on higher labour productivity, but these are constrained by a shortage of investment funds.

1.3 Transport and Expenditure

Total final output of an economy is also referred to as total final expenditure. At market prices this is equal to the sum of the following

(1) consumer expenditure
(2) current expenditure by central and local government on goods and services

(3) gross domestic capital formation in fixed assets
(4) stocks
(5) exports of goods and services

To obtain gross domestic product at market prices it is necessary to subtract imports of goods and services from total final output, because gross domestic product is a measure of the output of the domestic economy, while transfers in total final expenditure at market prices, such as taxes or expenditure and subsidies, must be allowed for in obtaining gross domestic product at factor cost. It is also important to realise that some output is involved in the production of final output. This is usually referred to as intermediate output, is looked upon as a cost of production, and is excluded from total final output. The latter, therefore, is a measure of value added to the costs of production. This section will consider the transport sector within the context of total final expenditure and its components.

1.3.1 Total Final Expenditure

Statistics for total final expenditure at market prices in the United Kingdom are provided in table 1.8. In real terms, gross domestic product increased some 70 per cent over the 1958–78 period; however, growth over the second ten-year period was substantially below that for the first. In 1978, the major item of domestic expenditure continued to be consumer expenditure with a share of some 60 per cent, followed by general government final consumption with

TABLE 1.8 *Total Final Expenditure of the United Kingdom at Market Prices*

	1958	1968	1978
Consumer expenditure	15306	27481	96086
General government final consumption	3734	7640	32693
Gross domestic fixed capital formation	3569	8200	29218
Value of physical increase in stocks and work in progress	111	487	1528
Total domestic expenditure	22720	43808	159525
Exports of goods and services	4706	9010	47636
Total final expenditure	27426	52818	207161
Imports of goods and services	−4583	−9350	−45522
Gross domestic product at market prices	22843	43468	161639

Source: National Income and Expenditure

some 20 per cent, gross domestic fixed capital formation with some 18 per cent, and stocks, etc., with some 1 per cent.

The trend over the years has been for general government final consumption to increase relative to consumer expenditure; for example, consumer expenditure accounted for some 67 per cent of domestic expenditure in 1958 and some 63 per cent in 1968; corresponding proportions for general government final consumption were some 16 and 17 per cent. So general government final consumption has increased at a very much higher rate over the more recent ten-year period, illustrating the related political problem of a need for increased government revenue at a time of declining economic growth rates.

By comparison, gross domestic fixed capital formation's share of total domestic expenditure increased from 16 per cent in 1958 to 19 per cent in 1968, only to decline slightly over all over the second ten-year period to 18 per cent, partly a result of capital expenditure in the public sector being cut back as part of the answer to the problems of public sector financing in the late 1970s. There is emphasis on reductions in capital expenditure because of constraints on significant reduction of current expenditure in the public sector in the short run: for example, in 1968, gross domestic fixed capital formation by central and local government and by public corporations amounted to some 9 per cent, and by the private sector some 10 per cent, of domestic expenditure; the corresponding figures for 1978 were some 6 per cent and 12 per cent. Obviously, items such as expenditure on roads can be expected to feature significantly in such reductions.

Another important trend has been for the import content of domestic expenditure to change; for example, it accounted for some 20 per cent in 1958, some 21 per cent in 1968, and some 29 per cent in 1978. So the 1960s were quite different from the 1970s in terms of satisfying domestic demand by domestic output. This was particularly true of manufactured goods like motor cars.

Finally, in interpreting these trends in the shares of total domestic expenditure attributable to separate items, we must also bear in mind the increasing importance of the 'black economy', that is, economic transactions not recorded in official statistics; the trends for consumer expenditure might be understated because of this factor in particular.

1.3.2 Consumer Expenditure

Consumer expenditure is expenditure on goods and services by persons and non-profit making bodies, plus the value of income in kind. The majority of consumer expenditure (some 82 per cent in 1978) is expenditure by families, usually referred to as household expenditure and detailed in the Family Expenditure Surveys.

Household Expenditure

In 1978, expenditure on transport and vehicles in the United Kingdom amounted to some 13.6 per cent of total household expenditure. Major items were purchases of motor vehicles, spares and accessories, accounting for some 5.0 per cent of total household expenditure, and maintenance and running of motor vehicles, some 5.8 per cent. Other items were purchase and maintenance of other vehicles and boats at 0.2 per cent, railway fares at 0.7 per cent, bus and coach fares at 1.1 per cent, and other travel and transport at 0.8 per cent. These statistics illustrate the dominance of private road transport in consumer expenditure on transport.

Over the years, the share of total household expenditure on transport and vehicles has remained fairly stable: for example, between 1968 and 1978 it varied between 12.5 and 14.2 per cent. This suggests constraints on redistributing household expenditure significantly in order to accommodate large price increases in particular items such as fuel. However, it would be necessary to examine such a hypothesis for particular types of households over a period of time. This is difficult in practice because the characteristics of households change with time, and additional uncertainty would be introduced into the analysis by the use of an inflation index. Such problems illustrate the dependence of household expenditure on household structure; for example, household income tends to increase with size of household and with the number of members who are working, and to decrease with the number of members who are retired.

It is also interesting to examine the variation of expenditure on transport and vehicles with household income. Both total and itemised expenditure in this category tend to increase with household income. However, not surprisingly, significant expenditure on private transport tends only to take place when income is sufficient to permit entry into the private transport market: for example, in 1978, households in the £20 to £30 per week income group spent an average £0.45 per week on private road transport; those in the £30 to £40 per week group £1.66, and those in the £40 to £50 per week group £2.68.

Expenditure on public transport fares also increases with household income; on the face of it surprising, given the evidence of car ownership and car use increasing with household income. In this case, part of the explanation of this apparent anomaly lies with household structure: a household with several working members will have a high income but, of course, not all of them will necessarily have access to private transport.

1.3.3 General Government Final Consumption

This is current expenditure by central government and local government on goods and services. As already indicated, the trend has been for this item to account for an increasing share of domestic expenditure. In 1978, current expenditure on goods and services by central government amounted to £19 423 m.; of this, £160 m. was spent on roads and public lighting, some 0.8 per cent, and some £64 m. on transport and communication, some 0.3 per cent. The corresponding figure for expenditure by local government was £13 270 m., of which £791 m., some 6.0 per cent, was spent on roads and public lighting. So final consumption in the transport sector by local government is substantially greater than that by central government, although some 50 per cent is provided by central government through the Rate Support Grant. However, current expenditure by central government in the transport sector has increased at a faster rate in recent years as the trunk-road system has been extended and its maintenance costs increased accordingly. The latter form the single most important item of current expenditure by both central government and local government: for example, the 1979 Public Expenditure White Paper showed that road maintenance accounted for some £104 m. of current expenditure by central government in 1978–9 at 1978 survey prices, and some £573 m. of current expenditure by local government; total current expenditure by central government and local government on roads and public lighting in 1978 amounted to £160 m. and £791 m. respectively.[20] More recently, expenditure on road maintenance has generally been reduced as part of measures to restrain public expenditure; for example, the same White Paper showed total expenditure on road maintenance falling from £760 m. in 1973–4 to £641 m. in 1978–9, at 1978 survey prices, and assumed that it would remain around this level at least until 1982–3.

1.3.4 Gross Domestic Fixed Capital Formation

This is capital expenditure in vehicles, ships and aircraft, plant and machinery, dwellings, other new buildings and works, and net purchases of land and existing buildings. The transport sector is affected by such expenditure by virtue of investment in vehicles, production and servicing facilities, and transport infrastructure; it does not include purchase of vehicles in the personal sector.

As previously indicated, in the 1950s and 1960s the trend was for gross domestic fixed capital formation to account for an increasing proportion of total domestic expenditure. However, from a peak of some 20 per cent over the 1969–71 period it declined to some 18 per cent by 1978; it also declined in real terms from 1973 onwards, particularly in the general government sector. This worsening performance is the result of declining economic growth rates consequent upon such factors as increasing oil prices and associated government measures to reduce public sector expenditure. Most sectors of the economy have suffered from this overall decline in capital investment, particularly sectors like social and other public services, while reduction in roads capital expenditure has affected the transport and communications sector. The main exception is investment in the petroleum and natural gas sector related to North Sea oil, which increased some five-fold in real terms over the 1973–8 period.

The private sector has accounted for an increasing share of gross domestic fixed capital formation. This trend has been emphasised since 1973 by the very significant reduction in general government capital investment; for example, in 1978, gross domestic fixed capital formation in the private sector (the personal sector and private business) accounted for some 67 per cent. However, the importance of different sectors in capital expenditure varies considerably by type of asset, as shown in table 1.9: private business dominates capital expenditure on vehicles, ships and aircraft, and plant and machinery, and is very important regarding new buildings and works other than dwellings; the personal sector dominates capital expenditure on dwellings; public corporations are important regarding plant and machinery and new buildings and works other than dwellings; general government is important for capital expenditure on dwellings through local authority building programmes and on other infrastructure. So, private business is very important regarding purchase of transport manufactures such as fleet purchases of road vehicles; for example, in 1978, the contributions by different transport manufactures to a gross domestic fixed capital formation of £3656 m. in vehicles, ships and aircraft were: buses and coaches, £184 m.; other road vehicles, £2719 m.; railway rolling stock, £98 m.; ships, £544 m.; and aircraft, £111 m. These statistics illustrate once more the importance of motor manufacturing regarding demand for transport equipment in the United Kingdom; import penetration is a fairly robust measure of the success of domestic manufacturers in satisfying this demand.

The importance of public corporations and general government in gross domestic fixed capital formation varies considerably between types of assets. Public corporations are most important with regard to investment in plant and machinery and in other new buildings and works. General government is most important with regard to investment in dwellings, particularly in respect of local authority building programmes, in other new buildings and works, and in net purchases of land and existing buildings. Investment in roads is an important item of capital expenditure by the general government sector in other new buildings and works: for example, gross domestic fixed capital formation by

TABLE 1.9 *Gross Domestic Fixed Capital Formation by Sector and Type of Asset in the United Kingdom in 1978 (£ millions)*

Asset	Private Sector		Public Corporation	General Government	Total
	Personal Sector	Private Business			
Vehicles, ships and aircraft	458 (13)	2727 (75)	346 (9)	125 (3)	3656 (100)
Plant and machinery	847 (8)	7538 (67)	2426 (22)	423 (4)	11234 (100)
Dwellings	3037 (58)	36 (1)	287 (5)	1875 (36)	5235 (100)
Other new buildings and works	604 (7)	3601 (45)	1832 (23)	2035 (25)	8072 (100)
Net purchases of land and existing buildings	579	713	1	−272	1021 (100)

Source: National Income and Expenditure

central government in the United Kingdom amounted to £1227 m. in 1978, of which £416 m., some 33 per cent, was in roads, and £7 m. in other transport investment: the corresponding figure for local government was £3159 m., of which some £329 m. was devoted to roads and public lighting, some 10 per cent, while £32 m. was devoted to capital investment in trading services connected with road and rail passenger services, and £25 m. to the same for harbours, docks and aerodromes. So capital investment in roads accounts for a much higher proportion of central government capital investment than that of local government.

The trend in recent years has been for capital expenditure in roads to account for a declining proportion of general government capital investment; for example, the 1979 Public Expenditure White Paper shows it to decline from some £1180 m., at 1978 survey prices, in 1973–4, to some £691 m. in 1978–9, and that until 1982–3 expenditure would be above the 1978–9 level on trunk roads but remain at the 1978–9 level on local roads.[20] However, the present administration is unlikely to implement this planned increase in trunk road expenditure to the full.[21]

1.4 Balance of Payments and External Trade

1.4.1 Visible Trade

Over the past twenty years the general situation has been for the visible trade of the United Kingdom to be in deficit. A modest surplus was only obtainable in 1971, and since then the terms of trade turned even more against the United Kingdom; for example, the visible balances were –£722 m. in 1972, –£2383 m. in 1973, –£5235 m. in 1974, –£3333 m. in 1975, –£3927 m. in 1976, –£2278 m. in 1977, –£1573 m. in 1978, and –£3497 m. in 1979. The very large visible trade imbalance in 1974 reflected the effects of quadrupling of oil prices that year, as well as the related influence of inflation on a world-wide scale. Increasing exports of North Sea oil and the effects of economic recession on demand for imports are two factors which contributed to a surplus of £1177 m. in the visible balance of trade of the United Kingdom in 1980, but this conceals worsening competitiveness regarding trade in manufactured goods, particularly transport manufactures.

The main explanation for this deterioration in the visible trade balance of the United Kingdom lies in the fact that the average value of imports has increased relative to the average value of exports, because both imports and exports have increased at similar rates over all in volume terms. In the 1970s high price oil imports contributed to this trend, although increasing production of indigenous oil has worked in the opposite way in the late 1970s, and will do so even more in the 1980s; for example, in 1975 some 91 million tonnes of crude oil were imported into the United Kingdom and no indigenous crude oil was exported; in 1979 some 60 million tonnes were imported and some 39 million tonnes exported.

In addition, imports of finished manufactures and of machinery and transport equipment, particularly motor cars, have increased faster in volume terms than comparable exports; for example, over the 1971–8 period, imports of finished manufactures increased some 119 per cent, of machinery some 109 per cent, and of road vehicles some 184 per cent; corresponding figures for exports were 41 per cent, 25 per cent and 24 per cent. It is obvious that manufacturing in the transport sector features importantly in this deteriorating trading situation. Some commentators have referred to this apparent inability of UK manufacturers to compete in their home market as the 'de-industrialisation' of the United Kingdom. Now that the United Kingdom has a 'petro-currency', a 'strong' pound is worsening the situation.

Consider in more detail the importance of the UK transport manufacturing sector for the visible trade balance. In 1968, transport equipment accounted for some £924 m. of exports, a share of 14 per cent, while imports of transport equipment accounted for some £319 m. By 1978 exports of transport equipment were valued at some £4540 m., some 12 per cent of total exports, while imports of transport equipment were worth a comparable amount, some £4343 m.

A large part of the explanation for this changed situation lies in the performance of the UK motor manufacturing industry, which accounts for the major proportion of exports of transport equipment; for example, in 1978, exports by the motor industry amounted to £3867 m., some 85 per cent of all exports of transport equipment. The contribution to total UK visible exports by the motor industry has varied through the years. It advanced from around 12 per cent in the early 1950s to a peak of some 17 per cent in the early 1960s, from which it declined to around 10 per cent in 1979.

The composition of motor industry exports has also changed. In 1978, major items were cars and taxis (some 24 per cent by value), commercial vehicles (some 14 per cent), and parts and accessories (some 45 per cent). However, over the years the contribution of parts and accessories has increased at the expense of commercial vehicles and particularly of motor cars; for example, in 1952 the contributions were 34 per cent by motor cars and taxis, 24 per cent by commercial vehicles and 25 per cent by parts and accessories. It is for this reason that there is concern about the possible harmful effects on British parts and accessory manufacturing of a demise of indigenous motor-car manufacture; for example, the share of world exports in tyres held by the UK tyre industry is declining.

In value terms the balance of trade remains to the advantage of the United Kingdom for commercial vehicles, but has changed drastically to disadvantage for motor cars; for example, in 1978, exports of cars and taxis amounted to some £923 584 m., while imports were valued at some £1 764 681 m.; exports of commercial vehicles were worth some £553 651 m., while imports were valued at some £260 545 m. However, trends in volume terms are a cause of anxiety for the British commercial vehicle manufacturing: numbers imported in 1978 were some twelve-fold higher than in 1968; numbers of motor cars imported increased some eight-fold over the same period. The corresponding changes for exports, the lack of change over all for commercial vehicles, and a 31 per cent decline in motor cars, illustrate the problem starkly.

Several factors help to explain this deterioration in the visible balance of trade in motor cars, many of them interrelated.

(1) Foreign manufacturers are simply more efficient.

(2) Increasing numbers of consumers, particularly those making 'private' purchases, prefer a foreign car on the basis of price and quality.

(3) Doubts about the reliability and cost of servicing of foreign cars have been reduced with their increasing penetration of the market.

(4) The entry of the United Kingdom into the European Economic Community stimulated imports from member countries.

(5) Multinational companies have rationalised their production facilities in Europe with the result that some UK models are imported whole or in part and potential exports are also lost.

(6) Limited capacity for volume production in varying measures over the entire model range creates suitable conditions for import penetration.

(7) Rationalisation of dealerships in recent years, particularly by British Leyland, created supply outlets for imports.

(8) A combination of a 'strong' pound and a large cost inflation differential is making imports even more competitive on price.

Statistics from the Society of Motor Manufacturers and Traders illustrate the problem. In 1978, there were 1 591 941 new registrations in the United Kingdom, and 800 772 cars imported. The major supplier countries were Western Germany with 209 597, Japan with 168 188, France with 149 586, and Italy with 101 977. By comparison, exports of motor cars amounted to 466 382, with 17 688 destined for Western Germany, 2830 for Japan, 14 981 for France, and 7660 for Italy. In 1973, only 238 out of 375 215 Ford British models registered for the first time in the United Kingdom had been manufactured elsewhere in Europe; corresponding figures for 1978 were 138 125 out of 392 366. Major export markets for British cars tend to remain English-speaking countries; for example, in 1978, the United States accounted for some 19.5 per cent of exports by value, and the Irish Republic for some 6.9 per cent. Exports to the United States are principally from the 'top end' of the market, and there is also evidence of increased penetration by this type of car into more affluent European countries, like Western Germany and Switzerland. The one exception to this general pattern is Iran, which accounted for some 9.9 per cent of exports in 1978, a further factor that has contributed to the disadvantageous trade balance in motor cars for the United Kingdom.

Britain's future visible trade balance in motor cars can be improved by exporting a greater, and importing a lesser, value of motor cars. Expensive, quality-engineered models, such as Rolls-Royce, Jaguar and Land Rover, are still in strong demand in export markets. However, given the evidence of difficulty in expanding export markets generally, it is more likely that the future of the visible trade balance in motor cars will depend upon efforts of UK volume production manufacturers to compete on the home market. The role of British Leyland in this scenario is critical because it is the major exporter among UK manufacturers, and also, in the event of its demise, it is unlikely that other UK manufacturers will have the production capacity to resist the huge import penetration that would ensue. It is for this reason that the success of British Leyland's future models policy is critical for the company and the country.

1.4.2 Invisible Trade

The United Kingdom's balance of payments situation has been helped
considerably during these years of a worsening visible trade balance by an
improving performance in invisible trade. This consists of financial movements
on current account connected with payment of services or transfers of money;
for example, in 1978, the visible balance was −£1175 m., while the invisible
balance was £2207 m.

Major contributions to this invisible balance are made by interest, profit and
dividends earned by private sector and public corporations, financial services,
other services, and travel; for example, in 1978 these sectors made contributions
of £1292 m., £1488 m., £1366 m. and £955 m. respectively. Expenditure on
travel includes payments made abroad by UK residents for transport within or
between overseas countries, which would be classed as a debit to the invisible
balance, and payments in the United Kingdom by overseas visitors for transport
within the United Kingdom, which would be classed as a credit.

Civil aviation makes a more modest contribution to the invisible balance:
some £348 m. in 1978. The terms of trade for sea transport tend to be modestly
in credit or modestly in deficit; for example, it was in deficit to the extent of
£171 m. in 1978.

The general trend has been for the contributions of earnings from services to
the invisible balance to increase in real terms. There has been a steady growth in
the trade balance for civil aviation, with a very significant contribution from
carriage of passengers between countries other than the United Kingdom, which
illustrates the truly international character of British civil aviation. A credit in
1978 of some £1448 m. for civil aviation in the invisible balance also illustrates
the overall importance for the balance of payments of a competitive industry.

Trends in sea transport give more cause for concern. Whereas the contribution
of civil aviation to the United Kingdom's external trade has steadily expanded,
that by sea transport has declined since 1974. As in civil aviation, international
operations such as freight on cross trades make significant contributions to the
invisible balance. However, over the 1968–78 period the general situation has
been for the balance of trade in dry cargo to generally favour UK operators,
but in tankers to be always unfavourable to UK operators, mainly because of
payments for ships on charter. The invisible credit for sea transport in 1978 of
£3163 m. illustrates the potential threat to the United Kingdom's balance of
payments of a worsening performance of sea transport.

1.5 Central Government Management of the Economy

1.5.1 A Broad Perspective

Some indication has already been given of the effects of central government
management of an economy on the transport sector. Central government
normally seeks to satisfy objectives related to such criteria as economic growth,
employment, the rate of inflation, balance of payments, and the public
sector borrowing requirement. It is for this reason that such parameters are

used as the main regular indicators of economic performance and are also the major variable in models of the economy.[22] Central government also must concern itself with the balancing of its expenditure with its revenue, and in this connection the public sector borrowing requirement is of critical concern.

Management of an economy is difficult for a number of reasons. There are two main technical ones: firstly as the economic system is complex the main indicators of economic performance are interdependent, and it is therefore unlikely that we shall ever have a perfect understanding of how an economy works; secondly it is likely that any economy will be subject to external factors. It may also prove difficult to manage an economy for reasons related to institutional factors; for example, the combined forces of resistance to change and a desire to remain in office make it difficult for any democratic government to influence economic trends significantly.

It is normal to use a range of values for input variables to models of an economy, and to express output variables in the same way, in recognition of these difficulties; so interpretation of output requires considerable judgement. This rejection of single value forecasting has taken slightly longer to gain acceptance in forecasting travel, mainly because the models in use are more complex, and so it would be more difficult technically to use a range of values for the input variables.[23, 24]

A government can be most effective in its management of an economy in sectors where there exists a broad political consensus on the desirable policy and means of execution. A case in point is the road expenditure programme, which has not been the cause of major disagreement between the political parties in the United Kingdom since the inception of the motorway building programme. Not surprisingly, then, the present Conservative administration's road programme in broad terms continues the cut-back on road expenditure initiated by its Labour predecessor as part of reductions in public expenditure. On the other hand, there is severe disagreement between parties, if not between alternative administrations, about the right policy for restoring the fortunes of British Leyland, related primarily to the levels of state subsidy and employment on one hand, and use of import controls to protect domestic manufacturing on the other, which does not bode well for this policy objective.

There is, of course, one sector of the economy, the public sector, where central government might reasonably be expected to be effective in achieving its economic objectives.[25] It can do this through laying down criteria for investment and pricing, using cash limits when an economy is subject to monetary control, and guidelines when it is not, and through public expenditure programmes.[26] It is obvious that the transport sector is sensitive to such measures. Investment in transport infrastructure not only must satisfy the Treasury regarding rate-of-return criteria, but is dependent upon funds being available as part of public expenditure programmes. Pricing of transport operations, particularly where subsidy is involved, as in local bus and rail services, is also the subject of central-government control.[27] In principle, the cash-limits system acts as a constraint both on price movements and on employment. It is currently causing problems over pay and employment in the public sector generally, and in particular for the

British Railways Board, whose cash flow is so dependent upon the public service obligation grant.[28]

Central government is less successful in handling the institutional constraints on economic management in the public sector, particularly union opposition to the introduction of different, and usually more efficient, methods of working: for example, reducing manning on freight trains to levels common in other countries, rationalising local bus and rail services, as in the case of the Tyne and Wear Metro System, encouraging shifts from road to rail haulage, and the introduction of BACAT (barge aboard catamaran) systems for freight distribution between ports and their hinterland. It could be argued that such problems are the responsibility of transport management and not central government, but, of course, once central government intervenes it is difficult to define the limits of managerial responsibility.

Central government can foster higher economic growth rates by stimulating total final expenditure, directly through reductions in taxation and/or increases in public expenditure, and indirectly through creating conditions for lower real interest rates. The latter work in two ways: they encourage people to spend now rather than in the future; they might make investment in production more attractive, which would result in lower production costs for existing output, and the production of new output. This entire process would cause an increase in the level of employment over all. However, it has important constraints. The first is interest rates. Minimum Lending Rate (MLR) is a measure of the cost to government of financing its expenditure plans.* All other interest rates are influenced by MLR. It tends to be high when the government borrowing need, the Public Sector Borrowing Requirement (PSBR), is high, particularly under a strict monetary policy. Therefore a reduction in PSBR is needed for lower interest rates under a strict monetary policy; alternatively, faster economic growth is a prime requirement for increases in public expenditure in this context.

The second constraint is import penetration, which was a feature of periods of economic expansion in the United Kingdom in the 1970s. Inflation is a third constraint which was of major concern in the 1970s as well. In principle, it is caused by the money supply increasing at a faster rate than output, resulting in the phenomenon of 'too much money chasing too few goods'. However, understanding of the fundamental causes of inflation, like that of the economic system generally, is imperfect. The conventional Keynesian view is that money supply and output are interdependent variables, one justification for governments financing their borrowing requirements simply through 'printing money'. The monetarist interpretation is that this practice by governments has contributed to inflation because money supply is the dependent variable — control of this will bring inflation itself under control. So, in the 1970s monetarism has become the conventional economic wisdom of Western governments, which, having set targets for expansion of the money supply, try to achieve these through such instruments as calling on special deposits from the banking sector, using MLR to attract borrowing from the non-banking sector, and cash limits in the public sector. As already explained, PSBR is of central concern in all this; under a monetarist policy it must be

* The government stopped using MLR formally in 1981.

reduced to satisfy objectives of economic growth through tax reductions and low interest rates.

Balance of payments is a further measure of economic performance; put very simply, it depends upon the perceived relative prices for goods and services between foreign and domestic production. These will depend upon relative production costs and exchange rates. As the latter particularly are subject to external influences, they can act as a severe constraint on such objectives as rejuvenation of the transport equipment manufacturing in the United Kingdom.

This brief introduction to the principles behind management of an economy illustrates the complexity and interdependence of the factors concerned and, because of compatibility problems, the great difficulty in satisfying all objectives. It also provides a broad perspective for concern with the transport sector. There are, in addition, the complications of external factors. National growth rates and rates of inflation reflect those in the world, particularly in important trading partner countries. A currency may be important in international financial transactions, as is the case with sterling. Capital flows are the subject of international levels of interest rates, particularly when exchange controls are lifted, as occurred in 1979 in the United Kingdom. Patterns of trade may be influenced by trading agreements, a major objective of the European Economic Community, or by political unrest, as illustrated with oil by events in the Middle East since 1973.

1.5.2 The Importance of the Transport Sector for Financing Public Sector Expenditure

In the United Kingdom the public sector expenditure plans for the next financial year, and in outline for the next five years, are announced annually in the Public Expenditure White Papers. These are normally published early in the calendar year in which the next financial year commences.[21] Financing of these plans is detailed in the Budget, the principal one being at the very beginning of the financial year in question, namely in April. The main sources of central government revenue are income tax, national insurance contributions and taxes on expenditure. As some 10 per cent of employees in the United Kingdom in 1978 were in the transport sector, it is an important sector for the first two of these sources of revenue. Taxes on road transport expenditure amounted to £3509 m. out of total taxes on expenditure of £13 748 m. in 1978; in addition, £1108 m. was collected for vehicle and driving licences. Overall then, the transport sector is very important regarding the financing of public expenditure.

Specific taxes on road transport are fuel duty, vehicle excise duty, and car tax, while a more general motoring tax is value added tax (VAT) on vehicles and on fuel. It is estimated that all these will contribute about 11.4 per cent of central government taxation revenue in 1979—80. This figure excludes VAT on other expenditure on transport, such as on vehicle accessories, maintenance and insurance. Over the years this proportion has not changed significantly; for example, over the period from 1965—6 to the present day, the highest proportion was 11.8 per cent and the lowest 10.5 per cent.

Private motoring particularly makes important contributions to central government revenue; for example, it is estimated for 1979—80 that it accounted for some 53 per cent of specific motoring taxes, and its fuel duty for some 32 per cent. So, private motoring is an especially important consideration in economic management within the transport sector.

In recent years, related to controversy concerning financing of road and rail infrastructure, there has been much discussion about the basis of motor taxation. The first point that needs making is that there is no functional relationship between motor taxation and road expenditure; motor taxation was originally introduced to fund road expenditure, but the link was broken after 1926 and its only basis is historical precedent. However, it is essential to question whether contributions from different sections of motor transport are fair, whether the tax system is unduly complicated, and whether the level of taxation should be changed. It has been argued that the very heaviest road vehicles are currently under-taxed, when measured against the damage they inflict on road pavements.[29]

From the viewpoint of energy conservation, many commentators favour a system of taxation more weighted to vehicle use than vehicle ownership, because the former appears more sensitive to fuel price.[30] There is evidence that motoring has made a slightly reducing contribution to overall taxation on expenditure, because motoring-duty levels have fallen in real terms; for example, taxation represented some 70 per cent of the sale price for four-star petrol in the United Kingdom in 1970, but only some 44 per cent in July 1979, although the April 1980 Budget increase has reversed this trend temporarily. The basic problem is that fuel duty is not automatically adjusted with inflation. So, real trends in fuel duty have countered any objective regarding fuel conservation since the 1973 Arab—Israeli dispute.

1.5.3 Public Sector Expenditure on the Transport Sector

The share of public sector expenditure devoted to roads and transport has declined from some 5.5 to some 4.5 per cent over the 1970s, as first the Callaghan administration and then the Thatcher administration strove for lower levels of public expenditure over all. Public expenditure on roads and transport, particularly on road construction and maintenance, also fell in real terms, and by 1979—80 stood at some £3073 m. at 1979 survey prices. However, these trends exclude increasing public expenditure on transport manufacturing; for example, the 1980 Public Expenditure White Paper allows for £300 m. at 1979 survey prices to meet British Leyland's 1980 requirements.[21]

So transport is not a major expenditure sector. However, investment on new construction and improvement of roads, representing some 25 per cent of public expenditure in transport, is an inviting target for a government seeking cuts in public expenditure, particularly as there tend not to be major differences between alternative administrations on the roads programme. Consequently, the roads programme is particularly sensitive to economic management by central government.

Current expenditure by central government is dominated by expenditure on goods and services for military defence and the national health service, national insurance social security benefits, debt interest, and grants to local authorities. Important but less major items are housing subsidies and supplementary benefits. Transport is a very minor item of current expenditure on goods and services; for example, expenditure on roads and public lighting, and transport and communication, amounted in 1978 to some 1 per cent of current expenditure on goods and services, compared with the 77 per cent accounted for by military defence and the national health service. On the other hand, the transport sector features strongly in central government subsidies, particularly to British Rail, and is a subject of current grants to local authorities; for example, transport accounted for some 19 per cent of subsidies in 1978; even so, this only amounted to about 1 per cent of total current expenditure.

Local authorities depend for some 50 per cent of their current expenditure on grants from central government. Most of this money is not allocated to specific services but comes within the general provisions of the Rate Support Grant; however, a small proportion is specifically allocated through the Transport Supplementary Grant. Current expenditure on goods and services in local government is dominated by education, and to a lesser extent by social services and the police. However, spending on roads and public lighting is a more important item for local government than for central government, as indicated in section 1.3.3. Transport also features as an important subsidy item in current expenditure by local government, but in this case it is for fare support and concessionary fares mainly.

Road expenditure features more strongly in the capital expenditure than in the current expenditure of central government; for example, capital expenditure on roads in 1978 was some £416 m., some 33 per cent of total gross domestic fixed capital formation by central government, while current expenditure was some £160 m., some 0.8 per cent of total current expenditure by central government on goods and services. Both these items of expenditure were mainly concerned with the motorway network. By comparison, most other transport expenditure was channelled through local government, and supported by grants from central government. Gross domestic fixed capital formation by local government is dominated by the housing sector, while, in contrast with capital expenditure by central government, the transport sector is less important; for example, in the United Kingdom in 1978, roads and transport accounted for some £396 m., some 13 per cent, of gross domestic fixed capital formation in local government, compared with £423 m., some 34 per cent, in central government. Some 70 per cent of this capital investment in the transport sector by local government is financed by grants and loans from central government. So, central government has in principle a large degree of control over expenditure by local government, because it is the major source of funds and can also apply other sanctions on expenditure.

1.5.4 An Overall View of Public Expenditure on Transport

Table 1.10 illustrates public expenditure on roads and transport as proposed in the public expenditure plans for the 1980—81 financial year.[21] Spending

TABLE 1.10 *Public Expenditure Plans for Road and Transport in the United Kingdom for the 1980−81 Financial Year (£m)*

Motorways and trunk roads	
New construction and improvement	418
Maintenance	112
Total	530
Local transport	
Capital	
Roads − new construction and improvement	
Car parks	554
Public transport investment	
Current	
Roads − maintenance	600
Car parks	−15
Road safety etc.	8
Local-authority administration	175
Passenger transport subsidies	
British Rail	
Bus, underground and ferry services	226
Concessionary fares	116
Total	1664
Central-government subsidies to transport industries	
British Rail	
Passenger subsidies	393
Level-crossing grant	13
Replacement allowance	54
Pensions	36
Other subsidies	−
National Freight Corporation	7
Scottish Transport Group	4
New bus grants to nationalised industries and private operators	25
Other central-government support	9
Total	541
Ports and shipping	
Ports	61
Shipping	20
Total	81
Civil aviation	
Civil Aviation Authority	23
Capital expenditure by local authorities at local airports	16
Other civil aviation services	4
Total	43
Other transport services	
Roads and transport administration	32
Transport research and other services	20
Total	52
Total roads and transport	2910

Source: Command Paper 7841

on roads and transport in the United Kingdom reached a maximum in real terms in 1975–6. It was reduced from this level as part of reductions in public expenditure by the Callaghan administration, to deal with problems of economic recession worsened by significant increases in oil prices. The main burden of this reduction has fallen on road construction and maintenance. It is envisaged that total spending on roads and transport will fall even further over the next few years; so the Thatcher administration proposes to reduce expenditure further. This was reflected in the delay in publication of the 1980 Roads White Paper.[31] It is also likely that all expenditure subject to funding by central government will feel more harshly the constraints of cash limits. A Conservative administration might be expected to view subsidies more harshly, in particularly the major one under direct central-government control, the Public Service Obligation Grant to the British Railways Board. An important political constraint in this case may be that many loss-making rail services run through Tory constituencies, a possible explanation for the Callaghan administration expecting this grant to fall in real terms. Another item of increasing importance in public expenditure on transport could be support for concessionary fares in local transport.

The major items of public expenditure on transport are motorways and trunk roads, local transport, and central government support to the transport industries. The latter include British Rail, the National Freight Corporation, the Scottish Bus Group and the National Bus Company. These three items of expenditure accounted in 1979–80 for some 94 per cent of all public expenditure on roads and transport. Expenditure on ports and shipping, and on civil aviation, is modest by comparison, and expected to fall in real terms as port modernisation programmes require less priority and civil aviation grants connected with air traffic control services are reduced. However, increased capital investment by local authorities and the Civil Aviation Authority is envisaged in connection with improvements in airport capacity, particularly related to the proposal for the Third London Airport, although the British Airports Authority is expected to fund major development of the latter out of revenue.

Public expenditure on motorways and trunk roads amounted to some £519 m. in 1979–80 at 1979 survey prices, some 17 per cent of all public expenditure on roads and transport; some 78 per cent of this was on new construction and improvement. Public expenditure on local transport was the largest item at some £1761 m., some 57 per cent of all public expenditure on roads and transport. Its major sub-item was road maintenance, at some £599 m., while capital investment showed a declining emphasis on roads but maintenance of the level of investment in public transport. The latter includes investment in new rail facilities like the Tyne and Wear Metro and the Liverpool Loop and Link scheme, and in rail/bus interchanges, bus stations and bus garages. Other important items of local authority expenditure are fare support, concessionary fares, and the administration of all this expenditure. Fare support by one means or another has become a very significant characteristic of local public passenger transport, accounting for some 21 per cent of local transport expenditure in 1979–80.

So expenditure on public passenger transport at the expense of road expenditure is a feature of local transport expenditure in the United

Kingdom in the 1970s. There is little evidence that this intervention has halted generally the loss of patronage by local public passenger transport. However, the well-publicised introduction of 'low fares' policies by Labour administrations, such as in South Yorkshire in 1974 and in Greater London in 1981, resulted in increased patronage, although principally for off-peak services. It is not surprising, then, that not only the nature of intervention, but also its need, is in question. Because of this situation, success of the Tyne and Wear Metro, more than any other single scheme, is probably crucial for the future of public passenger transport as an instrument of intervention in local transport.

The distribution and intensity of local transport expenditure varies from one part of the country to another. Differences in distribution are not surprising in view of different needs: for example, in 1978—9 the Greater London Council devoted some 27 per cent of its expenditure on transport to fare support; Suffolk devoted some 4 per cent. Differences in the intensity of expenditure on local transport should also be expected to reflect local needs and priorities; using the same examples, the Greater London Council proposed to spend some £26 per capita at November 1976 survey prices on transport, Suffolk some £11 per capita. It is more difficult to reconcile significant differences in the intensity of central-government support through the Transport Supplementary Grant (TSG) entirely on the needs argument; for example, TSG had an intensity of £34 per capita at November 1976 survey prices in the 1978—9 financial year for Tyne and Wear; the corresponding figures for South Yorkshire, another conurbation county of similar population, was some £3 *per capita*. It could be argued that this comparison is atypical in as much as Tyne and Wear had a commitment by central government to its Metro System, while South Yorkshire was being penalised for intransigence over its fares policy, and that such differences would even out in the long run. Even so, differences between TSG of this order of magnitude provide grounds for some concern.

Central government subsidies to the transport industries amounted to some £616 m. in 1979—80 at 1979 survey prices, some 20 per cent of all public expenditure on roads and transport. The single largest item was some £391 m. to British Rail for the Public Service Obligation Grant, while central-government support to British Rail amounted to some £566 m. as a whole. British Rail is then an important factor in plans for public expenditure on transport, one reason for continuing speculation about the future size of the rail system. Other transport industries, by comparison, have modest roles. The National Freight Corporation, the Scottish Transport Group, and the National Bus Company, are all required in principle not to operate at a loss under the terms of the 1968 Transport Act.[32] The last two have done this with some success, although there is increasing need for subsidy of ferry services operated by the Scottish Bus Group, while both the Scottish Bus Group and the National Bus Company have received increasing fare support from local authorities for bus services. The National Freight Corporation has required considerable financial assistance in recent years because of problems with its cash flow, particularly in regard to the activities of its subsidiary, National Carriers Ltd. A recent change in its structure was the return of Freightliners Ltd to complete control by British Rail under the terms of the 1978 Transport Act: a return of its remaining activities to the private sector was initiated in Autumn 1981.[33,34,35]

References

1. Committee on Post-war Civil Aircraft (Public Record Office, 1943)
2. Aircraft and Shipbuilding Act 1977
3. British Aerospace Act 1980
4. Rolls-Royce (Purchase) Act 1971
5. Expenditure Committee, *Fourteenth Report – The Motor Vehicle Industry*, Session 1974–75, HC 617 (HMSO, 1975)
6. British Leyland Act 1975
7. *British Leyland: the Next Decade*, Report presented to the Secretary of State for Industry, Session 1974–75, HC 342 (HMSO, 1975)
8. Central Policy Review Staff Report, *The Future of the British Car Industry* (HMSO, 1975)
9. Department of Trade and Industry, *The British Motor Vehicle Industry*, Cmnd 6377 (HMSO, 1976)
10. Department of Trade and Industry, *Public Expenditure on Chrysler (UK) Ltd – The Governments Reply to the Eighth Report from the Expenditure Committee, Session 1975–76*, Cmnd 6745 (HMSO, 1977)
11. *Strategy Alternatives for the British Motor Cycle Industry*, A Report prepared for the Secretary of State for Industry, Session 1974–75, HC 532 (HMSO, 1975)
12. Department of Trade and Industry, *Post Office Review Committee Report*, Cmnd 6850 (HMSO, 1977)
13. Department of Trade and Industry, *The Post Office*, Cmnd 7292 (HMSO, 1978)
14. Ministry of Transport, *Reorganisation of the Ports*, Cmnd 3903 (HMSO, 1969)
15. Department of Industry Business Statistics Office, *Input–Output Tables for the United Kingdom 1972* (HMSO, 1976)
16. S. L. Edwards, Transport Costs in the Wholesale Trades, *J. Transp. econ. Pol.*, **III** (1969) 272–8
17. S. L. Edwards, Transport Cost in British Industry, *J. Transp. econ. Pol.*, **IV** (1970) 265–83
18. B. M. Deakin and T. Seward, *Productivity in Transport* (Cambridge University Press, 1969)
19. K. M. Gwillian, J. D. C. A. Prideaux, *et al.*, *A Comparative Study of European Rail Performance* (British Railways Board, London, 1980)
20. The Treasury, *The Government Expenditure Plans 1979–80 to 1982–83*, Cmnd 7439 (HMSO, 1979)
21. The Treasury, *The Government Expenditure Plans 1980–81 to 1983–84*, Cmnd 7841 (HMSO, 1980)

22. Treasury Short-term Forecasting Model and Simulations with the Treasury Model, Government Economic Service Occasional Paper 8 (London, 1974)
23. R. Lane, T. J. Powell and P. Prestwood Smith, *Analytical Transport Planning* (Duckworth, London, 1977)
24. A. G. Wilson, *Urban and Regional Models in Geography and Planning* (Wiley, London, 1974)
25. Expenditure Committee, *Seventh Report with Minutes of Evidence taken before the Public Expenditure (General) Sub-Committee, Appendices and Index: Public Expenditure and Economic Management*, Session 1971–72, HC 450 (HMSO, 1972)
26. The Treasury, *The Test Discount Rate and the Required Rate of Return on Investment*, Treasury Working Paper No 9 (HMSO, 1979)
27. Local Transport Grants, Dept of the Environment Circular 104/73 (London, 1973)
28. Railways Act 1974
29. Dept of the Environment, *Transport Policy – A Consultation Document Volume 2 Paper 6* (HMSO, 1976)
30. National Road Traffic Forecasts, Department of Transport Memorandum (London, 1980)
31. Dept of Transport, *Policy for Roads: England 1980*, Cmnd 7908 (HMSO, 1980)
32. Transport Act 1968
33. Transport Act 1978
34. Transport Act 1980
35. Slow Progress on Transport Assets Sale, *Transport*, **2/5** (1981) 9–13

2

The Transport System of the United Kingdom

In the previous chapter we have examined the place of the transport industry and of its ancillaries in the economy of the country as a whole. Some idea of the extent and the complexity of the British transport system has emerged incidentally. In this chapter, the structure of that system and the relative roles of the various transport modes are analysed. To do this it is necessary to break down the whole system into its component sub-systems. These may be regarded as being the various modes: road, rail, air, water (sea and inland), pipelines and innovatory systems.

Viewing road transport as a system, it is necessary to include both the organisation of the vehicles — cars, buses, trucks, etc. — and the provision of the infrastructure, the road network.

2.1 The Road Network

2.1.1 The Road Hierarchy

It is more correct to use the term *network* in connection with the roads of a country. The *system* would include not only the roads, but the vehicles and the passengers and freight carried by them, for the nature of the road network and the flows of vehicles, passengers and freight around it are all inter-dependent, and changes in any one of these factors will affect all the others.

In 1978 there were in Great Britain 336 543 km (209 119 miles)[1] of public road: 1.78 km per km^2 and 1 km per 155 persons. Both figures are very high by world standards. Because of an advanced economy and a dense population, the network is intense, save in the hillier and more remote areas. It is also universal in that virtually all dwellings and all industrial, commercial and agricultural premises have road access. Almost all minor roads are either surfaced with bituminous macadam, or at least sealed with tar or bitumen. In other respects the morphology and quality of the roads differ widely.

Trunk Roads

These are the roads which form the strategic national network, and as such are
financed by central government. The network includes roads classified as
motorways and those as non-motorway trunk roads.

(i) *Motorways*[2]   Their essential features are dual carriageways, grade
separation at all intersections with other roads, limited points of access, and
the complete exclusion of certain classes of traffic, notably pedestrians and
cyclists. Usually motorways are designated under the 1949 Special Roads Act,
though some sections of trunk roads have been built to motorway standards.
    A few of the older motorways had two-lane carriageways, but the present
tendency is to provide three lanes,* almost irrespective of traffic density. Such
a road consumes 39 820 m² of land per km of route, while up to 24.2 hectares
can be needed for an interchange. This represents considerable consumption of
land, especially in urban areas.
    The maximum permitted gradient is 3 per cent, but this can lead to congestion
on hills because of slow-moving lorries; a fourth, 'crawler', lane is sometimes
provided. Design limits on alignment mean heavy earthworks in broken
country.[3] Motorways thus involve considerable visual intrusion, and the design
of bridges and the amount of landscaping is important. To avoid at-grade
crossing, urban motorways have hitherto been elevated, as cuttings and tunnels
are extremely costly, partly because of the need to divert services, especially
sewerage. The Transport and Road Research Laboratory (TRRL) has recently
advocated a serious look at shallow tunnelling. This is partly because elevation
increases visual and audial intrusion and consequently increases the
compensation payable under the Land Compensation Act 1973.
    In 1978 there were 2307 km (1434 miles)[4] of motorway open. The map
(figure 2.1) shows the present and planned extent of the network. There is now
a continuous motorway between London and the Scottish Border (490 km)
through the industrial areas of the West Midlands and the North West, also
between London and South and West Yorkshire, and between London, Bristol
and South Wales. Continuous lengths are also open between Birmingham and
Exeter (254 km) through Bristol, and from Liverpool across the Pennines to
Leeds and on to North Cave, near Hull (157 km). For the rest, motorways are
mainly short stretches of longer trunk routes and short lengths of urban
motorways.
    Through great reductions in journey times, motorways generate large
volumes of short and medium distance traffic. In 1966, Evans showed that
only some 5 per cent of car traffic on the M1 was traversing the whole length
then open.[5] Raising average speeds also significantly reduces freight haulage
costs, many of which are time-linked. Traffic has been encouraged to such an
extent that the southern part of the M1 becomes severely overloaded at certain
times.

* Strictly there is no official policy other than 'the standard of road to meet the
  need'. But in borderline cases three lanes are preferred, while considerations
  such as cost of subsequent conversion and difficulties of undertaking major
  works without total closure on two-lane motorways are taken into account.

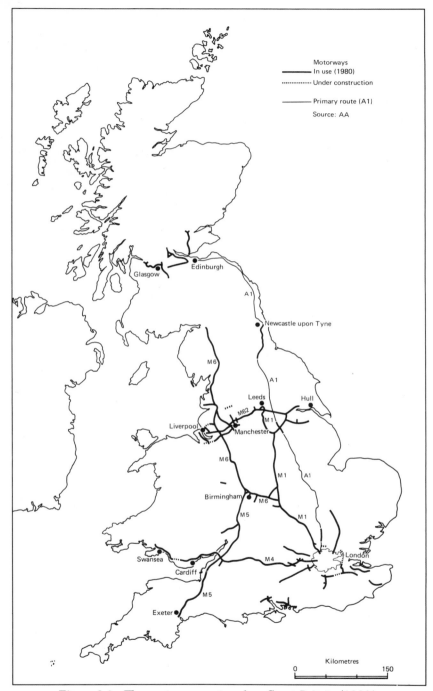

Figure 2.1 *The motorway network – Great Britain (1980)*

Motorways attract traffic from parallel roads. When there is little local circulation on these, they may now be little used, like the once congested A5 between Atherstone and Dunstable, where it closely parallels the M6—M1 but does not pass through any large town. On the other hand, feeder links may become overloaded, as is the A423 between Banbury and the M45—M6, or the A556, which provides the link between the M56 and M6 for southbound traffic from Manchester.

(ii) *Non-motorway Trunk Roads*   The major part of the trunk road network is not built to motorway standards, and accounted for some 12 560 km (7806 miles) in 1978. Since 1960 there has been considerable investment in upgrading the trunk road network, by provision of dual carriageways, reduction of access from minor roads, grade separation at major interchanges, and by-passing of towns and villages. The A1 has been improved in this way — including the by-passing of towns such as Stevenage, Stamford and Doncaster at motorway standards — virtually the whole way between Apex corner (North London) and Newcastle upon Tyne (418 km), as has the A74, from the end of the M6 to the M74 on the outskirts of Glasgow (138 km). But many trunk roads, such as the A49 from Warrington through Shrewsbury and Hereford to Ross-on-Wye (195 km), have had no more than minor improvements. The trunk road network is thus made up of roads of very varied standards.

Other Roads

These are financed by local authorities (see pp. 44, 146).

(i) *Other Main Roads in Rural Areas*   In 1975 these accounted for 32 640 km (20 400 miles). Many stretches carry heavy traffic. But though improvements have been considerable in number, the individual schemes are normally minor in character: the elimination of S-bends, widening the single carriageway, local by-passes, and minor improvements at intersections.

(ii) *Other Rural Roads*   There is a very large mileage of rural roads providing access to farms and isolated dwellings. Though many are little more than lanes, they are normally well maintained. Because of the very light traffic volume, the costs of maintaining the network in terms of vehicle-km per km of road are high, and these represent part of the social cost of providing rural areas with what are regarded as minimum levels of public services.

(iii) *Urban Roads*[6]   These are subdivided into a hierarchy of four classes.

(1) *Primary distributors*, which may be either radial or circumferential, and which may be built to motorway standards, but which are more commonly ordinary roads. Their function is to connect the major areas, usually referred to as landuse zones in official planning literature, within the city (see section 5.2.1); to provide access from inter-city routes to various parts of the city; and to provide by-passes for through traffic.

(b) *District distributors*, which connect local areas of the city or town to the primary distributors.

(c) *Local distributors*, within local areas.

(d) *Access roads*, which provide access to individual houses, shops and industrial premises.

One of the main problems is congestion, which usually occurs at peak periods, but which may also occur at certain spots, such as major intersections or in shopping streets, at other times, and which affects a large mileage of primary and district roads.

Another problem is that though roads higher up the hierarchy are classified according to their major function, they suffer from having to fulfil other functions as well. The majority are expected to provide access to the buildings which line them. Shops and public buildings attract large numbers of pedestrians, leading to further traffic conflict. They may also be used for parking, further limiting traffic flow and increasing accident risk.

A major planning objective is to reduce the access function of primary and district roads by building separate access roads to houses, regrouping shops into precincts, and providing off-street parking.

The close network of access roads can also provide a problem. In residential areas the environment can suffer when these become 'rat-runs', as peak-hour traffic seeks to avoid congested main roads. Planning objectives should aim at new access networks being designed to prevent their use by through-traffic. This can also be discouraged from older networks by one-way streets and physical obstacles, as has been done at Islington in inner North London.

2.1.2 Traffic Levels

In 1975 there were 53 vehicles for each kilometre of road in Great Britain. In 1955 there were 21 even though, apart from motorways and access roads to new development, total road mileage (as opposed to improvements) remained virtually static over the twenty years. But traffic levels vary greatly; for example, trunk roads accounted in 1975 for 5 per cent of the mileage of surfaced roads in Great Britain but carried 19 per cent of all road traffic while motorways accounted for a mere 1 per cent of road mileage but carried 9 per cent of all road traffic.

But even on motorways there is a considerable variation in traffic levels. The general pattern is very high traffic flows in the vicinity of the largest conurbations, high traffic flows on the parts of the network serving the central core of England, and a tendency to modest flows at the extremities of the network: for example, average 24 hour traffic flows in 1975 were in excess of 55 000 vehicles on the London approaches of the M1 and M4, at the junction of the M6 with the M5 in the West Midlands, and at the junction of the M61 with the M62 in Greater Manchester; they were in excess of 45 000 vehicles on the M6 between the M62 and the M5, and in excess of 50 000 vehicles on the M6 and M1 between the West Midlands and London; elsewhere on the central core of the network average 24 hour traffic flows varied between 20 000 and 40 000 vehicles; however, at the extremities of the motorway network, such as near Carlisle on the M6 or near Exeter on the M5, average 24 hour traffic flows were in the 10 000 to 15 000 vehicle range.[7]

The mix between cars and lorries also varies. On weekdays in 1975 26.2 per cent of the vehicles between junctions 2 and 3 on the M6 (near Coventry) were goods vehicles (not including light vans), but there were only 11.6 per cent on the A20 at Wrotham.

There are also great differences in traffic levels on the same roads at different times. Most urban roads suffer from diurnal peaking as a result of work journeys. A decision is thus needed for any road scheme as to what level of peak-hour traffice should be accommodated, as costly road space will be under-used at other times. Similar decisions are required for the approach roads to resorts, which become congested at week-ends and holiday periods, but not for the rest of the year. Rural roads in the National Parks and other beauty spots are also becoming congested at holiday periods. Finally, it should be noted that heavy flows of large lorries require more costly road foundations.

2.1.3 The Financing of Roads

In many countries, limited-access highways have tolls, which are not generally applied in Great Britain. Where distances are long, time savings considerable, and alternative roads bad or non-existent, the cost of the new roads can be recouped from the cost-savings of users. But in Great Britain the network of ordinary roads is so close and alternative routes so numerous, tolls would merely prevent the full use of the motorways, built to relieve congestion on those parallel roads. Access points are relatively close and so toll collecting points would be too numerous and costly to operate. However, where there is no practical alternative, notably across wide estuaries, tolls are levied on the use of bridges and tunnels, such as the Forth and Severn Bridges and the Mersey Tunnels (p. 177).

In 1978, direct expenditure on roads in Great Britain was £1513 m.[1] The Department of Transport meets construction and maintenance costs of the trunk road network. Design of trunk-road schemes costing more than £25 m. is carried out by their Road Construction Units (RCUs).* If the schemes cost less, design work is by the county councils, who also act as agents for the Department for maintenance.

Non-trunk roads are funded through the TPP system (see section 5.4.4). These roads, both rural and urban, are the responsibility of county councils, and are financed partly through rates levied by local authorities and partly through the Transport Supplementary Grants (TSG) and Rate Support Grants (RSG) from central government. Incidentally, the classification of roads in A, B and Unclassified, in connection with the road-numbering scheme, bears no relation to the financially based scheme just described.

2.2 Private Transport

2.2.1 Motor Cars

In 1978 there were 14 069 million private cars registered in Great Britain.[1] The geographical distribution of car ownership varies greatly, levels generally

---

* Schemes under £2.5 m. are the responsibility of the Regional Controller (Department of Transport) who usually works through the local authorities.

being higher in rural areas. In 1971, the average for England and Wales was
213 cars per 1000 people. In that year there were 286 per 1000 in
Montgomeryshire and 303 in Radnorshire, two of the remotest and least
urbanised counties. Conversely, ownership in the county boroughs of Bootle
(Merseyside) and Salford (Greater Manchester), two inner-city areas, was 102
and 97 respectively.[8]

Figures of car ownership are normally published in a highly aggregated form,
but these conceal important variations within large local authorities. More work
is necessary at this level. For an example Greater Manchester has been selected.
Table 2.1 shows car ownership in representative wards in one sector of the
conurbation. The aggregated figure of 97 cars per 1000 people for Salford
conceals differences such as 162 in Claremont ward and only 48 for Regent.

The number of households without a car is also important. In

TABLE 2.1 *Car Ownership Levels – Representative Wards in Greater
Manchester, 1971*

Area	Cars per 1000 Persons	Car-owning Households as % of Total Households	Remarks
Salford County Borough	97	27.6	
Regent Ward	48	14.9	–
Claremont Ward	162	45.4	–
Manchester County Borough	111	31.5	–
Moss Side East Ward	61	18.7	Inner-city area
Didsbury Ward	212	55.7	Inner suburban area
Benchill Ward (Wythenshawe)	116	37.1	Local authority housing
Altrincham Municipal Borough	199	54.4	–
Timperley No. 3 Ward	236	64.9	Private enterprise interwar housing
Hale Urban District	311	71.4	Outer suburban area
Mere Civil Parish	343	90.2	High proportion of commuters
Ashley Civil Parish	275	80.2	Rural area with some commuters
Great Britain	218	53.0	–

Source: 1971 Census

Montgomeryshire (1971) 33.2 per cent were without. In Moss Side East ward of Greater Manchester 81.3 per cent were without. Even in Hale, where the number of cars exceeded the number of households, 28.7 per cent of the latter were without. These households tend to be the poorer ones, which include those with large numbers of children and the more elderly.

Access to the household car is also important. When, as is most common in both rural and urban areas, the car is used for the journey to work, other members of the family are denied access during the day for journeys to work, school or shops. Conversely, family access for week-end shopping or leisure trips is much more common.

Most cars, whether bought new or second-hand, are financed through hire-purchase agreements, though a large proportion are paid for wholly or partly by the employer, not only because the employee uses the vehicle on business, but often as an emolument.

In the United Kingdom cars tend to be relatively small. In 1975, 46 per cent had engine capacities between 1000 and 1500 ccs, while only 7 per cent had capacities exceeding 2000 cc. Prior to the introduction of a flat-rate vehicle licence in 1947, taxation on private cars was based on engine size, and this encouraged small-engined vehicles (see section 3.2.1).

2.2.2 Motorcycles and Cycles

The rapid growth since 1950 of private car ownership has tended to reduce motorcycle ownership. In 1978, 1.2 million were licensed, compared with 1.6 million in 1965. Of those registered in 1975, half were under 50 cc and only 10 per cent over 250 cc. In the ten-year period, those under 50 cc increased from 500 000 to 546 000, while those over 250 cc declined from 205 000 to 111 000. The increase in light machines has probably been caused by the transfer from pedal cycles, and the decline in heavier ones because of the greater comfort of the car for the journey to work, and the greater ability to pay for that comfort. Between 1961 and 1971 the number of commuters entering Central London by motorcycle declined from 32 000 to 9000. Accident risk has also increased compared with car travel. The hobby element in ownership of cycles over 250 cc has probably become the principal motivation in ownership.

The use of pedal cycles has also declined for much the same reasons. There is a greater ability to afford cars for commuting and shopping, and a second car in the family has contributed to the decline. There has also been increased accident risk, especially among children. Although in 1961 the numbers of commuters entering Central London by bicycle was only 17 000 (out of 1.25 million), by 1971 the figure had fallen to a mere 3000.

However, with the increase in motoring costs since 1974, the trend may well be reversed, and more use will be made of light motorcycles and pedal cycles for short journeys to work and shop. The National Travel Survey[9] of 1975/76 contains some evidence to support this.

2.3 Public Road Passenger Transport

In 1978, 73 792 buses and coaches were licensed. They are legally Public

Service Vehicles (PSVs) if they carry passengers at separate fares. PSVs are subject not only to normal vehicle licensing, but require an annual Certificate of Fitness and a Road Service Licence from the Traffic Commissioners. There are four types of service,[10] and these provide a useful classification for this study.

(1) *Stage carriage services* These operate on a specified timetable and separate fares are payable. Within this definition works' buses are included if the employees are charged fares.

(2) *Express services* These are timetabled services on which separate fares are charged, subject to a specified minimum. Though applied to long-distance coach services, legally they are not defined by length or speed.

(3) *Excursions and tours* Services operated over a specified route at predetermined fares.

(4) *Hire or contract* In these operations separate payments are not made by the passengers, the contract being between the operator and a single hirer.

Table 2.2 illustrates the divisions of responsibility for the planning and operation of bus as well as rail services, and the enacting legislation.

2.3.1 Urban Stage Carriage Services

In Great Britain, buses provide the basic public urban transport, rail having a role in the larger conurbations (see section 5.2).

Under the 1968 Transport Act and the 1972 Local Government Act, Passenger Transport Authorities (PTAs) were set up in the major conurbations. The six metropolitan counties — West Midlands, Greater Manchester, Merseyside, South Yorkshire, West Yorkshire, Tyne and Wear — are PTAs, together with Greater Glasgow created under the 1973 Local Government (Scotland) Act. The PTA is the policy-making body with powers to plan and control all public transport within their area. Responsible to it is the Passenger Transport Executive (PTE), a body of professionals concerned with the direction of public-transport planning and the operation of the bus fleets.

The nucleus of the PTE bus fleets was the fleets operated by the former local authorities within the PTE areas. The PTEs have no powers of compulsory purchase but have bought out other operators and taken over their fleets. Thus, Greater Manchester PTE have bought out the services of the North Western Road Car Company (a National Bus Company subsidiary) within their area and those of Lancashire United Transport, then the largest independent operator in the country. On the other hand, the small private firm of A. Mayne & Son still provides the service between Central Manchester and Droylesden. Ribble and Midland Red (NBC subsidiaries) provide a large number of services within the Merseyside and West Midlands PTAs respectively, though service frequencies and fare levels are controlled by the PTAs.

The seven PTEs owned, in 1978, 10 950 buses, ran 517 million vehicle-km and carried 2012 million passengers. In that year the total figures for all PSVs in Great Britain were 73 792 vehicles, 3404 vehicle-km and 7305 million passenger journeys.[11]

TABLE 2.2 *Planning and Operation of Public Passenger Transport – England and Wales*

Authority	Is Authority Responsible for Public Transport Planning?	Responsibility for Operation	Enacting Legislation
Greater London Council	Yes	through LONDON TRANSPORT EXECUTIVE who own and operate Buses and Underground Railways. British Rail is operated and financed independently	1969 Transport (London) Act
Metropolitan County Councils	Yes	through their PASSENGER TRANSPORT EXECUTIVES who own and operate the bus fleets. They also determine fare levels and services wholly within the county, BR acting as agents.	1968 Transport Act 1972 Local Government Act
Non-Metropolitan ('Shire') County Councils	Yes – they also have powers to subsidise bus and rail services	None	1972 Local Government Act 1978 Transport Act
Metropolitan District Councils	No	None	–
District Councils in Shire Counties	No	Where bus fleets were formerly owned by Municipalities taken over by the District Council.	1972 Local Government Act
National Bus Company	No	Rural bus services and urban services if not owned by District Councils or PTEs. Operation by subsidiary companies such as Bristol Omnibus Company, Crosville, Southdown.	1968 Transport Act
British Rail	No	All local services outside PTEs – these form part of the Public Service Obligation network and are subsidised directly by Central Government and in a few cases individual services are subsidised by shire counties. In the PTEs they act as Agents for the PTE.	1972 Local Government Act 1974 Railways Act

The London Transport Executive owns and operates all buses within the area of the Greater London Council (GLC). With 6322 vehicles in 1978 it is easily the largest fleet operated as a single unit.[12] Under the 1962 Transport Act an independent London Transport Board was created, responsible directly to the Minister of Transport. But under the 1969 Transport (London) Act the Board was dissolved and its assets taken over by the GLC with the Executive responsible for operation. The objective of this was similar to that behind the creation of the provincial PTAs. In 1978 the fleet ran 278 million vehicle-km in service and there were 1032 million passenger journeys.

The major towns and cities, and many of the smaller ones as well, have traditionally operated their own passenger transport systems. These were originally tramways, but later bus fleets were added, and until the 1950s these were largely profitable enterprises. Profits were used either to relieve the rates or to hold down fares. Many councils co-ordinated their transport and land-use planning, providing services at low fares to slum-clearance areas on the peripheries of their areas. In 1968, prior to the creation of the PTAs, there were 92 municipal bus fleets, varying in size from Birmingham's 1477 vehicles to Colwyn Bay's 5. Uniquely, Blackpool also operates a fleet of trams. In 1978 the remaining 52 municipal fleets consisted of 5905 vehicles which ran 212 million vehicle-km and carried 1052 million passengers.

All towns and cities over 150 000 operate their own fleets, except Stoke-on-Trent. But below that figure there is considerable variation. Chester has a municipal fleet, Oxford and Cambridge, of similar size, do not. In these and in most of the small towns, urban services are provided by the National Bus Company.

2.3.2 Rural Bus Services

In the 1920s a very close network of stage services[13] grew up, both between towns and connecting villages with market towns. By 1939, rural bus services were better in terms of extent and frequencies in the United Kingdom than in virtually any other country. The institutional organisation depended on the policies of the licensing authorities set up under the 1930 Road Traffic Act. The larger companies, mainly controlled by two holding companies, Thomas Tilling and British Electric Traction, were given protective monopolies on the more lucrative inter-urban routes, on condition that they maintained, by cross-subsidisation, services to isolated villages. These companies are known as Territorials and are still household names in the areas they serve, names such as East Kent, Southdown, Crosville. Under powers authorised by the 1930 Act, the railway companies invested heavily in the Territorial companies, though they never instituted any degree of road–rail co-ordination.

Under the 1947 Transport Act, railway investment was transferred to the British Transport Commission, which soon acquired the Tilling Group's bus interests. Although a Bus Executive was planned, there was no central policy exercised over the nationalised Territorials. In 1967, British Electric Traction sold out to the government, and under the 1968 Transport Act the National Bus Company and the Scottish Bus Group were created. The subsidiary companies were now controlled far more strictly through centrally imposed financial targets. Outwardly this new centralisation is shown by the NBC and SBG 'house symbols' and the limitation on vehicle liveries.

In addition to the generally large Territorial companies, there were also, at any one time, a large number of independent operators. They varied greatly in size. At the time of the 1968 Act, which inaugurated such extensive changes in the bus industry, Barton Transport of Nottingham had 335 vehicles. But many owned only a few vehicles and operated perhaps a single route as a subsidiary activity to their main ones of express and private-hire work. In 1968, Parish's Motor Services operated two or three stage services centred on Oswestry (Shropshire) and owned a total of eight coaches and a minibus. The 1968 Act made little change in the position of independent operators.

Prior to 1955 many independents sold out to the Territorials, but the latter became less interested in acquiring new services in the following years of decline. Under the 1968 Act and the 1972 Local Government Act the shire counties became responsible for the planning of rural services and for the subsidisation of those services considered to be socially necessary. Since independents often have lower running costs than Territorials there is now a tendency for the county councils to prefer contracting with them to operate subsidiary services.

As will be seen in chapter 5, the picture is of continued decline in rural passenger transport. The provision of rural services is no longer economic, except of inter-urban routes through relatively densely populated areas.[14] Any innovations must be designed to reduce subsidy rather than to eliminate it. In 1978 the NBC fleet of 18 162 vehicles provided 1075 million vehicle-km and carried 1825 million passengers. The SBG figures were 212 million and 351 million respectively. It must, however, be remembered that many services of both groups were in fact urban. The vehicles of independents covered 1017 million km and carried 764 million passengers. The 5800 independent operators owned 28 574 vehicles, but the majority were engaged in activities other than stage carriage, and these figures reflect the private-hire sector.

2.3.3 Express Coaches

Like the stage carriage services, express services developed mainly during the inter-war years.[15] Most Territorial companies ran express services, and there were also BET/Tilling subsidiaries such as Royal Blue, which specialised in express services. Some independent specialists, such as Yelloway, also emerged.

Without infrastructure, and with minimal terminal requirements, there could be great flexibility in planning services and in altering them to meet changing traffic demand. Not only were services provided between all large and medium sized towns, with stops in the larger intermediate villages, but there was a network of seasonal services linking the industrial areas with coastal resorts. The post-1930 licensing system limited the number of coaches per day on any route.[16] This meant the companies were unable to aim at capturing the total market, and thus were not worried by having to cater for peaks. This, coupled with low fares, ensured constant high load factors, which in turn were the principal factor in maintaining low fares.

After 1968, for the first time, the NBC consolidated the Territorial express services into a unified network. A marketing package with the brand name of National Travel was introduced, though the coaches are operated by the subsidiaries. Independents still maintain a minority of the scheduled routes, one of the larger firms being Yelloway Motor Services of Rochdale.

The express-coach market is mainly passengers to whom cost is more important than time; that is, holiday makers, pensioners, and students. At this end of the market National Travel is not in real competition with British Airways. But competition with British Rail's Inter-City services is strong, and it is no coincidence that the latter have introduced travel cards for pensioners and students entitling them to 50 per cent reductions except on peak days. The 1980 Transport Act greatly eased entry into stage carriage work and almost completely deregulated express work (pp. 150, 174).

Tours, excursions and private hire are of growing importance. The market is shared by most operators. It is an important sector of National Travel's activities. The PTE's are also concerned with it as a subsidiary activity. Greater Manchester Transport owns three subsidiaries engaged in this activity, Charterplan, Godfrey Abbot, and Warburtons, while also using their stage carriage fleet for private and contract hire. There are also numerous independents everywhere concerned with this work. This market, which includes contract hire to firms providing journey-to-work transport for their employees, and to local education authorities for the transport of children to and from school, is the only sector of PSV (Public Service Vehicle) transport to show growth in recent years. In 1974, express services covered 187 million vehicle-km and carried 58 million passengers. Excursions and contract hire accounted for 821 million vehicle-miles and carried 573 million passengers.

2.3.4 Vehicle Design in Relation to Operation and Economics

Under the 1930 Road Traffic Act all PSVs are subject to annual inspection by the Department of Transport (DTp). If this is satisfactory a *Certificate of Fitness* is issued. No vehicle can be operated without one. The design of PSVs is thus subject not only to economic considerations, such as fuel and maintenance costs, and to passenger capacity and comfort, but also to safety standards and maximum dimensions imposed by the DTp.[17, 18]

For the past ten years all new buses have been designed to allow One Man Operation (OMO). This once-and-for-all cost reduction was achieved by the Territorial operators in rural areas during the 1960s, though it had long been common among independent operators. In 1966, OMO became legal for double-deckers and it began to be introduced to urban services. But until the mid-1970s the operators were slow to introduce suitable tariff structures and fare collection systems, which are necessary concomitants of OMO in urban conditions. Without them, loading times increase over those of conductor operation, to the detriment of general traffic flow at peak periods, and to journey speeds in particular.

Efforts have been made in recent years to reduce costs by introducing unorthodox vehicles, though normally without conspicuous success. Drivers' wages account for nearly 60 per cent of operating costs, thus the use of mini or midi-buses normally presents no real savings in rural areas. First cost is lower, but vehicle life is much shorter. The introduction of mini-buses by the GPO for the carriage of passengers on mail delivery routes has been more successful, as there is little addition to crew costs.[19] It remains to be seen whether schemes by the NBC to provide and maintain mini-buses for villages which are driven by local volunteers will be successful. Independents frequently use either second-hand vehicles to reduce capital costs or coaches between private hires.

In urban conditions battery-powered electrically driven buses have been experimentally introduced. Pollution is reduced and under certain conditions fuel costs may be lower, but existing batteries are costly and heavy, and the designer must also choose between speed and range between rechargings.

2.4 Road Haulage

2.4.1 Industrial Structure

As will be seen in the next chapter (section 3.4.1), the great majority of freight is transported by road, and in 1977 this mode accounted for 82.7 per cent of the tonnage carried.

Disaggregation of the total figures is not easy.[20] But in the first place a large proportion of the work done is in *local delivery*. In 1978, general goods vehicles of 1.5 tons or less, unladen weight, accounted for 67.5 per cent of the fleet, and covered 20 800 million vehicle-km against 19 200 million by the 32.5 per cent of heavier vehicles. Since most of the light vehicles are engaged in delivery, distances covered in the working day are small. Drivers' wages are therefore high in terms of ton-km, as the activity is characterised by small consignments in small vehicles.

A second distinction is between *public haulage*, the operations of professional carriers, and *own-account* carriage, that is, in vehicles operated by the firms owning the goods carried, be they manufacturers, distributors or retailers. In 1974, of the 1537 million tons of freight lifted, 831 million were carried by public hauliers and 706 million on own-account.

The 1933 Road and Rail Traffic Act made an absolute distinction between the two. The own-account operator could obtain a 'C' licence on demand, but the holder could only carry goods in connection with his business. This distinction was abolished by the 1968 Act, but subsequently there has been only a slight trend towards own-account specialists carrying goods for 'hire and reward'. A notable exception is Speedy and Prompt Deliveries (SPD), until 1968 the own-account fleet engaged in distribution of Unilever products, but which has since moved into the general distribution of foodstuffs. In 1974 own-account operators' share of carryings was 45.8 per cent, compared with 57.9 per cent in 1964. The proportion carried on own-account tends to fall with increase in length of haul. For distances of less than 50 km, in 1977, 51 per cent of the tonne-km achieved were in own-account vehicles, but for distances over 300 km, only 17 per cent.

A third distinction is between *parcels* and *full-load* operations. The parcels carrier has a number of central depots, on which are based the vehicles engaged in collection and delivery of less-than-full-load items. At the depots the parcels are bulked for trunk haul by larger vehicles. Parcels operators covering the whole country are Roadline and National Carriers, wholly owned subsidiaries of the National Freight Corporation. But there are a number of private firms engaged in parcels work in more restricted areas. Full-load operators, the norm in road haulage, convey direct single consignments from origin to destination.

Fleet size varies greatly, but a feature of the industry is the small average size. The industry is by no means highly capitalised, and this, together with the need to retain flexibility, of management and in customer contacts, tends to outweigh any scale economies.[21] In 1974 there were 138 000 operators. Of these, 74 800 (53.1 per cent) owned a single vehicle and a further 46 500 (33.4 per cent) owned between two and five. On the other hand, there were only 400 (0.3 per cent) with fleets of over a hundred vehicles.

The 1947 Transport Act nationalised public haulage on distances over 25 miles, but this was reversed under the 1953 Act, which not only permitted private firms to apply for licenses, but empowered the British Transport Commission to sell off its fleet of 41 000 vehicles. In the event, they were unable to find buyers for all the vehicles and were allowed to retain and operate a fleet of 7000. From 1956 onwards a number of private firms have been taken over, many of which still operate under their old names. Under the 1962 Transport Act British Road Services and the other nationalised fleets were transferred to the *Transport Holding Company*, and under the 1968 Act to the *National Freight Corporation*. The 1980 Transport Act, however, legislated for the sale of NFC assets to the private sector and the abolition of the Corporation — this sale was initiated in Autumn 1981.

The 1933 Road and Rail Traffic Act instituted a licensing system which limited entry to the public haulage industry, a *quantitative* system, which remained essentially unchanged until 1968, whereby licenses were issued after public hearings before the Traffic Commissioners in each of the appropriate traffic areas into which the country was divided. There were thirteen of these, and in each the Commissioners were also responsible for PSV licensing.

The original intention of the 1968 Act was to introduce qualitative licensing for all light vehicles (under 3.5 tons gross laden weight) and most short and medium distance haulage. This meant that any operator could obtain a license for himself and each of his vehicles, and retain them, provided his fleet was properly maintained and he was not convicted of offences such as overloading. Quantitative licensing was to be retained for heavy vehicles employed on hauls of over 100 miles (160 km), and for certain bulk loads such as coal and aggregate for any distance. In the event, no Minister has activated the powers given him to impose quantitative licensing. Consequently, Great Britain has now the most liberal entry conditions into public haulage of any EEC country. At the time of writing, monitoring of maintenance and overloading has been far from effective.

Public haulage is highly competitive. The quotation of rates, and the provision of vehicles when and where wanted, is highly flexible and the subject of constant negotiation with customers. Large concerns, including the

National Freight Corporation, must decentralise decision-making to local managers. Profit margins are fine and bankruptcies among small hauliers frequent.[22]

There is evidence that many own-account operators are not very cost conscious, and that many operate vehicles for reasons other than lower running costs. These reasons include convenience, control over schedules and the advertising value of company liveries. Policies of large firms vary greatly. Tate & Lyle rely entirely on their own fleet; Cadbury Schweppes use public haulage and rail between factory and area distribution depot, and their own fleet for local delivery; and on the other hand Woolworth's do not own any of their own vehicles.

2.4.2 Trends in Vehicle Size and Design

Light vehicles (under 3.5 tons gross laden weight) are mass-produced by large British and foreign manufacturers in the same way as private cars. They are almost wholly used for short-distance work. Of heavy lorries (over 3.5 tons glw) two large groups can be distinguished. In 1978, 44 per cent were in the range of 3.5–11 tons glw. Most of these have standard bodies on mass-produced chassis, though some have custom-built bodies. In contrast, there is also a concentration at the upper end of the permitted weight range. With constant relaxations of the latter (the present limit, 1976, is 32 tons glw) there has been a trend towards larger vehicles. In 1975, 82 600 (15 per cent) exceeded 24 tons glw, whereas in 1965 only 24 000 (4 per cent) exceeded 8 tons unladen weight.[1]

Bodies for larger vehicles are invariably custom built on chassis made by smaller manufacturers as well as by Leyland. The trailer units in articulated sets are normally built by specialised firms. There has also been a trend towards specialised vehicles, either skeleton frames for containers or adapted for the bulk carriage of particular commodities, with savings on handling costs being traded off against loss of backloads. The carriage of petrol and milk in tankers is of course of long standing. But nowadays the majority of cement, even for local delivery to contractors' sites, is carried in bulk. Other commodities include vegetable oils, sugar, flour and animal feed. The use of semi-trailers, which can be readily attached to and detached from tractor units have grown in popularity. In 1975, 70 900 vehicles over 24 tons were articulated. Legislation has restricted the use of trailers attached to ordinary lorries.[23]

2.5 The Rail System

Unlike road systems, rail systems are under unified control by a single authority for infrastructure (track, stations and signalling), rolling stock, and commercial operations (freight and passenger). In 1978 the British Railways Board owned and operated 17 869 route-km, 3581 km for freight only, and a further 1117 km only for passenger traffic.[24] The number employed in 1978 was 243 264 or 13.6 per route-km. Using this as a measure of productivity and taking into

account traffic density, British Rail is one of the more efficient systems in
Europe.[25] In addition to the BR system, London Transport operates 383
route-km for specialised urban passenger traffic. There are also a number of
minor specialised systems operated by port authorities, the National Coal Board,
Greater Glasgow PTE, etc. The growth of railway-preservation societies has
meant that by 1976 a significant total of 257.5 route-km of line were operated
by twenty-seven societies.[26]

2.5.1 Passenger Traffic

Traditionally, freight provided the principal source of revenue for railways in
Great Britain. But in 1971, for the first time, receipts from British Rail's
passenger traffic exceeded those from freight. In 1979, passenger-km totalled
31 900 million, a figure last exceeded in 1961, when the network was 30
per cent larger.
 British Rail divide their passenger business into four sectors

(1) Inter-City
(2) London and South East
(3) other provincial services
(4) PTE services

Inter-City

The main features of the national inter-city network are: (i) the density of the
network and the frequency of service and (ii) the three sub-networks, rail, air
and coach. For the most part, these are operated by nationalised concerns in
fierce competition for traffic and investment funds, and without vestige of
co-ordination and co-operation.
 The major share of the inter-city market, as far as public transport is
concerned, is taken by British Rail. The Beeching Report of 1963[27] identified
this sector as being 'part of the total requirements of the country for which they
(the railways) offer the best available means'. Since then, the development of
those services marketed as *Inter-City* has been one of the principal objectives
of the British Railways Board, and there has been considerable investment in
upgrading main lines and their services. This must be seen against technological
advance, which has allowed increased speeds without fundamental change in
'orthodox' rail technology, that is, steel flanged wheels on steel rails. Thus, in
the 1950s, top speeds of about 120 km/h (75 mph) allowed start-to-stop
schedules of 96 km/h (60 mph), no significant improvement over speeds in
1914. But in the 1960s these were generally increased to 160 km/h (100 mph)
and 128 km/h (80 mph) respectively. In 1976 the High Speed Train (HST) with
maximum speed of 200 km/h (125 mph) was introduced between Paddington
and Bristol/South Wales, and in 1978 between King's Cross and Edinburgh. It
is also expected that an electric version of the Advanced Passenger Train (APT)
will be in service between Euston and Glasgow in 1982. This has a design speed
of 240 km/h (150 mph) but will initially be restricted to 200 km/h in service.

As always, increased speed incurs increased power output and energy consumption.

Improvement in speed has been accompanied by increased service frequencies. In 1962 there were four departures from Euston to Glasgow between 0700 and 1900, and in 1975 these had been doubled. There is now an hourly service between London and most major provincial centres in England and South Wales, and a half-hourly one to Birmingham.

Upgrading of the lines has been achieved by (i) electrification of the Euston—West Midland—North West—Glasgow route (ii) renewal of track, including elimination of the worst curves (iii) resignalling (iv) rebuilding of stations.

All this has been the basis of an aggressive marketing policy,[28] which also includes the 'Inter-City' brand image, effective advertising, and a flexible fares policy based on charging what the traffic will bear. In 1977 the second-class single fare on the prime London—Manchester route was at the rate of 5.493 pence per mile, but between Liverpool and York only 3.985 pence. Attention is also paid to the selling of off-peak capacity through reduced fares.

There is still considerable variation in speed and passenger comfort between express services on the other Regions and those of the Southern, where the distinction between inter-city and outer suburban has no real validity. Development of secondary services has also been uneven. The Glasgow—Edinburgh service, 76 km between centres with a combined population of 2 million, has been constantly upgraded, while those between Manchester and Liverpool, with a combined population of nearly 4 million, and 56 km apart by rail, have stagnated since the diesel service was introduced in the early 1960s.[29]

But generally it has been a success story. Passenger traffic has increased steadily on the prime routes, and the Inter-City network in 1979 not only covered its operating costs, but 40 per cent of the gross revenue was available as a contribution to track, signalling and other fixed costs.[30]

London and South East

Because of its size, the concentration of over one million jobs in the central area, and the length of journey to work, Greater London is heavily dependent on rail transport (chapter 5).[31] In 1977, 16 per cent of arrivals into Central London between 0700 and 1000 were by car, 13 per cent by bus and 70 per cent by rail.

British Rail provides an extensive network of suburban services, which in 1978 conveyed the greater proportion of commuters. In addition, the average length of journey is greater than on London Transport trains. For the most part, these suburban services share tracks with Inter-City expresses and freight trains, and therefore are not technically *rapid-transit*.[31] A few services, such as Broad Street to Richmond, and those to Crystal Palace, are entirely within the GLC area. But generally it is impossible to distinguish between inner suburban services and those to places such as Guildford, Purley, Sevenoaks, the Medway Towns, Southend and Bletchley.

It is, however, possible to distinguish between the Southern Region, with its intensive electrified services extending to all the coastal towns between Ramsgate and Bournemouth and its traditional specialisation in long-distance commuting, and the outer suburban services of the other Regions. With the exception of those radiating from Liverpool Street, which have similar characteristics to those of the Southern, those on other lines are of less complexity and represent only a part of the traffic.

In 1978, the daily average arrivals (Monday—Friday) between 0730 and 1000 at the fifteen main-line terminals were 409 000, of which 263 000 arrived at the seven Southern Region ones. Though short-distance commuting has declined in recent years, long-distance commuting has increased considerably, aided by faster trains and a pronounced 'taper' on season-ticket rates.

Services are also provided by London Transport, which operates 383 route-km of rapid-transit lines with 249 stations. The system is called by both operators and users the 'Underground', but though lines in the central area are all in tunnel, most of the subsequent extensions are on the surface. These extensions are either new lines, such as those to Stanmore, Uxbridge and Cockfosters, or they are lines taken over from the former Companies or British Rail and converted to rapid-transit.

London Transport lines extend out to Ruislip in the west, Cockfosters in the north and Upminster in the east. For historical reasons, however, there are few lines penetrating far into the southern suburbs, except that to Morden.[32] In 1978, London Transport operated 4323 rail-cars, normally in trains of six to nine cars. They provided 48 million train-km, conveying 546 million passengers. [33] In comparison there were 1374 million bus passengers. Journeys by Underground tend to be longer on average than those by bus, km against km. This obscures the important function of the Underground in conveying short-distance passengers within the central area.

Other Provincial Services

These are of lesser importance than the previous two sectors. In 1979, receipts grossed £53 m., against £390 m. from Inter-City and £311 m. from London and South East. But direct operating costs attributable to these services amounted to £95 m. Their provision therefore involves a heavy subsidy.

Though British Rail do not disaggregate them, we can identify four sub-sectors.

(1) Outer suburban services in the large conurbations in which the inner services are maintained under contract to the PTEs. These are not nearly as important in terms of distance, service frequency or passengers carried as those of London and South East, but they can be of local importance. An example is that over the 61 km between Manchester (Oxford Road) and Chester, the first 14 km to Hale being within the PTE area. Beyond, ten stations are served by a basic hourly service, augmented in peak periods.

(2) Suburban services in the few cities which have them, but which do not have PTEs. Cardiff is the best example, where the services are well

developed, compared with Bristol of similar size but where they have declined (chapter 5).

(3) Services of a trunk nature, but which are not included in the Inter-City network, by virtue of speeds, frequencies and lower-grade rolling stock.[34] They amount to a considerable route mileage and include all lines in the Highlands beyond Glasgow and Inverness, the Crewe—Shrewsbury— Hereford—Cardiff service, and that between Birmingham and Norwich via Leicester, Peterborough and Ely. Between 1963 and 1968 these suffered continuous rundown, but more recently they have benefited from stock 'cascaded' from the Inter-City network and from improved schedules.

(4) Purely rural services. It is doubtful whether rural rail operations ever were economic; it is likely they were only possible through the writing-down of capital investment and by cross-subsidisation. But after 1925 the situation was exacerbated by loss of passengers to the buses. Parallel services were established almost everywhere, quite unlike the situation in many European countries where this was not permitted. Withdrawals of rural rail services began on a relatively small scale in the 1930s, though the main period of withdrawals was 1955–68.

As far as possible, costs of secondary lines have been reduced by singling of double track, simplification of signalling, reduction of stations to 'bus-stops' and the issuing of tickets on the trains by guards.

PTE Services

With the exception of South Yorkshire, the urban areas controlled by the PTEs have a well-developed suburban network. In Greater Manchester there were 255 km (159 miles) of route carrying suburban services and stations in 1979. While the proportion of total trips made by rail in the provincial conurbations is small (chapter 5), the share of traffic along the corridors of movement that have rail lines is significant.

With the setting up of the PTEs after 1968 they became responsible for rail as well as bus services. At the same time, road congestion had led to a revival of interest in the part rail could play in urban transport. Rail patronage in PTE areas has remained at a constant level during the 1970s, at a period of decline in bus patronage. Nevertheless, revenue does not cover operating costs. In 1979 the former was £47 m. and the latter £59 m.

The authorities' responsibilities are both short and long term. The former include which services should be retained, service levels and fares policies. This involved financial and operating agreements with British Rail. In some PTEs 'brand images' have been created for marketing purposes, such as 'Merseyrail' and 'Clyderail'.

In the long term the PTEs are responsible for the planning of rail services as part of a co-ordinated transport system. The 1968 Act also allowed rail infrastructure to be eligible for the same grant levels as for roads, and investment in urban railways is now included in TPP applications. In Birmingham an intensive service is being provided for the first time on the Bristol line out to Longbridge, with new stations at the Five Ways office complex, the University/Hospital complex and the Leyland plant, hitherto all without rail access. In Liverpool, suburban lines have been extended in tunnels under the Central Business District (CBD). In Newcastle there has been an innovation for Great Britain, the conversion of a run-down BR suburban network to rapid-transit and its extension under the CBD. Because this involves transfer of the lines to the PTA, this has met considerable institutional and union opposition. There has also been investment in suburban car—bus—rail interchanges, such as the one at Altrincham (Greater Manchester) (chapter 5).

2.5.2 Rail Freight

We must be aware of two conflicting trends; firstly, a long-continued decline in rail's share of total carryings; and secondly, basic technological and operational innovations.[35]

Between 1965 and 1978 carryings fell from 229 million tons to 172 million, though ton-km fell only from 24.64 thousand million to 22.80. The decline was the result of a number of factors.

(1) The growth of road haulage with its greater flexibility and ability to move loads from door to door. This allowed it to capture almost all the traffic from the growing 'light' industries since 1950.

(2) The decline of traditional 'heavy' industries which were more dependent on rail. The principal loss was in coal, which declined from 151 million tons in 1963 to 94 million in 1978. The greatly increased carryings of petroleum and other bulk traffics did not compensate.

(3) The policies advocated by the Beeching Report of 1963 and subsequently adopted.

(4) Lack of investment in freight facilities as well as conscious disinvestment.

In 1963 freight traffic could be divided into four groups.

(1) Wagonload traffic, which formed the great bulk. Wagons were forwarded from 2221 public terminals, and from large numbers of private sidings, by trains which ran short distances between 558 marshalling yards, where they were split up and re-formed.

(2) 'Sundries' or less-than-wagonload traffic. This was dealt with at the majority of terminals, though there was increasing emphasis on concentrating these on large depots with longer road collection and delivery.

(3) Trainload traffic passing direct from origin to destination, though, as yet, there were few of these 'block trains'.

(4) Parcels by passenger train.

The Beeching Report stressed the major losses incurred by Sundries, and British Rail ceased to invest in facilities and to seek traffic. Under the 1968 Act the business was transferred to a new body, *National Carriers Limited*, controlled by the National Freight Corporation. NCL forwards traffic by trainloads between a few principal depots and to a considerable extent by

Freightliners, of which they are a principal customer, but they trunk-haul smaller flows themselves to the extent of 66 per cent of their carryings in 1976.[36]

British Rail also began to run down wagonload traffic and close large numbers of freight terminals and private sidings. In 1978 the numbers of depots and marshalling yards had been reduced to 458 and 38 respectively. In addition, Great Britain has only 13 private sidings per 100 km of route, compared with 25 in France and 39 in Western Germany.

The British Railway Board concentrated investment and marketing on trainload traffic and on containerisation. Both systems involved reduced numbers of highly specialised terminals, much more intensive utilisation of rolling stock, and elimination of marshalling yards.

The trainload policy met with considerable success, based on cost reductions achieved by bulk handling methods and intensive utilisation of equipment. In addition, high capacity wagons with low empty (tare) weights were introduced. On major routes a 25 ton axle load is permitted, so that four-axle wagons with a 100 ton glw can be used. A typical example, a bulk cement wagon, has a tare weight of 22.25 tons and a payload of 77.75 tons. A typical two-axle aggregate wagon has a tare of 12.25 tons and a payload of 37.75. Trainload traffics include coal to power stations, steel plants and domestic coal concentration depots, and petroleum, aggregates and other minerals. They also include manufactured goods such as cement, steel, motor cars, chemicals and fertilisers, mainly between factory and regional distribution depot.

The use of containers was introduced on a countrywide basis in the 1930s. But the Beeching Report envisaged the use of much larger ISO containers with very low tare/payload ratios and trains of special wagons shuttling at high speeds between pairs of terminals — the *liner train*. Marketed as the Freightliner system, it had an initial success, but never achieved the major transfer of traffic from road envisaged by Beeching. In fact, the main growth came from a direction he did not anticipate: deep sea, Continental and Irish shipping containers, which now account for nearly half of those carried, which in 1978 totalled 843 000 TEUs (twenty-foot equivalent units).[37]

Under the 1968 Act, the terminals and the collection and delivery fleet were transferred to Freightliners Ltd, 51 per cent of the capital held by the National Freight Corporation and 49 per cent by the British Railways Board. With the NFC the controlling voice, it was possible to discern a lack of long-term interest by them in Freightliners Ltd and an unwillingness to invest in new terminals at important centres such as Bristol, Stoke-on-Trent and Preston. However, other organisations have established terminals. These include the Containerbases (owned by consortia of shipping firms, port authorities and British Rail) at both ports and inland sites, and those owned by port authorities, British Steel, London Brick Company, Ford Motor Company and two London boroughs (for containerisation of town refuse). Under the 1978 Transport Act, however, Freightliners Ltd was transferred back to British Rail, who have maintained it as a wholly owned subsidiary.

But over much of the system there was insufficient traffic for trainloads or for freightliner terminals. British Rail was forced to reverse its policies and to

invest in a modernised fleet of general, as opposed to specialised, wagons.[38]
By the end of 1977, trains of modern, air-braked, high-capacity wagons
conveying wagonload traffic were running on twenty-nine services marketed
as 'Speedlink'.[39]

Considerable attention was also paid to parcels traffic,[40] which in 1975
accounted for £53.4 m. of the total freight revenue of £318.4 m. The trend in
organisation is to move parcels between a reduced number of terminals by
special trains of cans 'in circuit' in set trains. Parcels are handled in unit loads
in BRUTEs (British Rail Universal Trolley Equipment), which can themselves
be loaded into the vans.

2.5.3 System Change

The system of British Rail had undergone fundamental changes since the
publication in 1963 of the Beeching Report. Some of these have been mentioned,
but they can be summed up briefly as follows.

(1) *Simplification of the system.* This was achieved by the reduction of
the 27 171 route-km open in 1963 to 18 878 in 1975, about 30 per cent. In the
same period, 45 per cent of the passenger stations and 89 per cent of the freight
depots were closed. These closures were as common on main lines remaining
open as on closed lines. Thus only Lockerbie remains open (for passengers) on
the 117 km between Carlisle and Carstairs, while on the 378 km between
Hitchin, the outer limit of the London area, and Newcastle upon Tyne there
are now only thirteen intermediate stations. Such simplifcation is illustrated
in figure 2.2.

(2) *Upgrading of track and signalling.* This has been achieved by the
laying of heavier track and elimination of curves and other speed restrictions,
and by the extension of colour-light signalling centrally controlled. This has
enabled trains to be operated at higher speeds and more frequent intervals.
Labour inputs have been greatly reduced by mechanisation of track
maintenance and elimination of small signal boxes.

(3) *Motive power and rolling stock.* 3434 route-km (19 per cent) of the
system was electrified by 1977, rather a low proportion compared with other
EEC rail systems. But the busiest routes have been converted and 46 per cent
of the passenger-train-km were electrically hauled. There are two main
systems: 750 Direct Current third rail (1760 km) almost wholly on the
Southern Region, and 25 000 volt Alternating Current overhead (1758 km)
adopted as standard by other regions for main-line and suburban purposes.
For the rest, all trains are diesel hauled. Passenger trains are hauled either by
locomotives or are electric or diesel *multiple-units* (EMU and DMU), in which
two to six cars are permanently coupled into units, which are self-propelled
and capable of being driven from either end. When traffic is heavy, two or
more units can be coupled together and driven by one man. The advantage is
that power increases in proportion to train weight. More attention is being
paid to coaching stock design. On long-distance trains the traditional
compartment stock has given way to open coaches, though increased comfort
has been achieved without increasing tare weight. Attention has also been paid

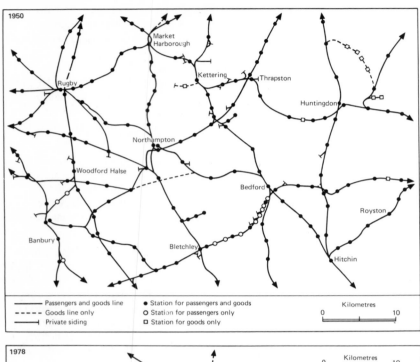

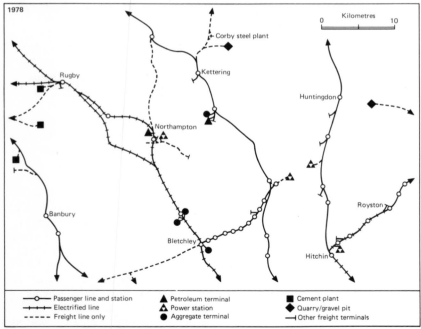

Figure 2.2 *The simplification of the British Railway system*

to design of freight wagons, the aim being for all stock to be capable of running in trains at 120 km/h (75 mph).

2.5.4 Urban Rail System Design

This includes the spacing of stations.[17, chapter 5] A compromise must be reached between access requirements for close spacing and the maintenance of reasonable average speeds. Location is also important; a badly placed station will not attract passengers. But hitherto this factor has not received the attention from planners it deserves. Experience in Toronto,[41] however, has proved how land-use has altered around stations on newly opened subways. Service frequency is also important, being closely related to distance travelled as well as to potential traffic volume. In central areas rapid-transit services should be at intervals of five minutes or less, whereas outer-suburban frequencies of thirty or sixty minutes are reasonable.

Electrification is imperative for underground lines, and important if services are frequent, stations closely spaced and average speeds high. But if traffic volumes on surface links do not warrant investment in electrification, diesel-powered trains are possible. In spite of work on alternative technologies such as monorail systems, the orthodox railway (*duorail*) remains the most technically satisfactory.

All London Transport lines were electrified prior to 1939, as was virtually the whole of the Southern's suburban network. Since 1945 there has been large-scale investment in electrification of the inner and outer suburban lines of the other Regions serving London. With the completion of the current St Pancras–Bedford scheme, the only diesel-hauled services will be from Paddington and Marylebone. In the 1960s there was considerable investment in electrification of the Glasgow suburban system and this is currently being extended. In Manchester and Birmingham, electrification of individual services was mainly a by-product of track-electrification schemes.

2.5.5 Rail Financing

Until the mid-1950s total receipts covered both direct operating costs (sometimes called 'escapable' costs) and the fixed costs of track, signals and stations (sometimes called 'system' or 'inescapable' costs). But thereafter the gap between costs and receipts widened and began to alarm the government. The 1962 Transport Act and the Beeching Report of 1963 both attempted to maintain a self-financing position, by identifying services which failed to cover even direct operating costs and then ceasing to provide them.

However, because of political pressure to maintain some passenger services, the British Railways Board were left with conflicting objectives. The Minister of Transport refused them permission to close some loss-making lines and at the same time expected them to cover costs. The 1968 Transport Act introduced the concept of subsidising 'socially necessary' passenger services. At first, individual services were identified and grants paid. But the 1974

Railways Act replaced this method by a single block grant paid on the *Public Service Obligation* (PSO) *network* (outside the PTE areas) of a size agreed between the government and the British Railways Board.

All along, freight traffic was expected to pay its way. After 1974, freight-only lines had to cover all costs out of revenue. Freight traffic on lines within the PSO network was expected to pay for its direct costs and a notional 'rental' for use of the track.

2.6 Air Transport

The overwhelming majority of international passenger traffic to all areas other than the EEC is by air, 86 per cent of the 10.87 million in 1977. Only on cross-channel services to Europe and Ireland is there competition for passengers by surface transport, and in 1977 air's share of the 11.6 million passengers to and from the EEC was 38.2 per cent. Air cargo accounts for a significant proportion by value of exports and imports, 19.7 per cent and 17.6 per cent respectively in 1978 (p. 101). On the other hand, largely because of the short distances, air traffic accounts for a very small proportion of domestic traffic: 0.5 per cent of passenger-km in 1978.[1]

2.6.1 Domestic Services

Inter-city air services, marketed as 'Inter-Britain', represent a small part of British Airways operations and a small proportion of total inter-city movement. In 1978 there were 6.4 million passenger journeys by domestic flights of all airlines, compared with 38.9 million by international services.

Domestic operations in the United Kingdom, because of short sector-lengths, tend to be higher cost than long-hauled operations. Aircraft speed, also, is not of great importance in short hauls, as time in the air is a small part of city-centre to city-centre transit times. Of more importance is reduction in time spent reaching the airport and time spent before take-off. The former can only be achieved by improvement in the road or rail ground links. The latter is only possible through simplification of check-in procedures and the elimination of delays through weather, made possible by improved navigation aids. The introduction of the *Shuttle* services, first between London and Glasgow in 1975, and between London and Edinburgh, Belfast and Manchester, have greatly increased the attraction of domestic air travel. These employ on-board ticket sales and the guarantee of a seat for all passengers arriving at least twenty minutes before the scheduled time of departure, even if an extra aircraft is thus needed.

The main competition with rail is in the business-travel market, and in the 320–620 km radius. The air has a large share of the traffic between London and Edinburgh, Glasgow and Newcastle. But the London–Manchester/Liverpool market, with frequent and high-speed rail services and virtually no difference in overall transit times, favours the rail, and the major air traffic is of passengers travelling by air on from London. On the other hand, rail provides little competition (apart from overnight services perhaps) in the London—Aberdeen market. Air also has a very great advantage where a water crossing is involved, particularly from Belfast to London and other major centres, to and from Orkney/Shetland where traffic has grown considerably with the development of the oil fields, and the Channel Islands, a major tourist centre.

Licences for all routes are issued by the Civil Aviation Authority, who control competition and fare levels. Previously it was the policy to provide British Airways (and its predecessor, British European Airways) with a monopoly of the major routes. But since the report of the Edwards Committee[42] in 1969 licenses have also been granted to the 'second-force' airline British Caledonian, which now operates between Gatwick Airport and Glasgow, Belfast, etc. 'Third-force' operators include wholly owned subsidiaries of British Airways such as Cambrian, and independent operators such as British Midland and Air UK, a consortium of small operators formed in 1979.

The main domestic routes (figure 2.3) radiate from London to major provincial centres. Of lesser importance are those connecting provincial airports. Finally there are the services maintained with direct government subsidy for social reasons between Glasgow and the Western Highlands and Islands.

2.6.2 International Services

These are divided into two sectors, scheduled and chartered. Scheduled services are concentrated on the three London airports, and Manchester and Prestwick. They are operated by the nationalised airline, British Airways, by the second-force airline Caledonian Airways, and to a much lesser extent the third-force operators which, until February 1982, included the innovative Laker Airways, and by foreign operators.

Chartered services have grown in importance over the last twenty years with the growth of *Inclusive Tour* holidays, popularly known as 'package tours'. The flights are operated by smaller airlines, British for the most part, under charter to the tour operators, though one large tour-operator, Thompson's, operate a wholly owned subsidiary, Britannia Airways. These operate to major tourist areas, particularly to Spain, but also to Italy, Yugoslavia and other European countries. In recent years, longer-distance flights, including ones to the United States, are increasing in numbers. Scheduled airlines, including British Airways, who have a wholly owned subsidiary organising inclusive tours, also charter surplus capacity on scheduled flights or charter aircraft.

In 1977, charter flights accounted for 174 192 of the 759 111 air-transport movements at UK airports. They tend to be concentrated into seasonal peaks. They also use a wider range of airports than scheduled flights.

Air cargo is carried on both scheduled and chartered services. Scheduled flights are mainly *combination* flights, the cargo being carried in the holds of passenger aircraft. Scheduled *all-cargo* flights tend to be confined to North Atlantic and European routes. The introduction of jumbo-jets, with very large hold capacities has tended to check their development. Charter flights are

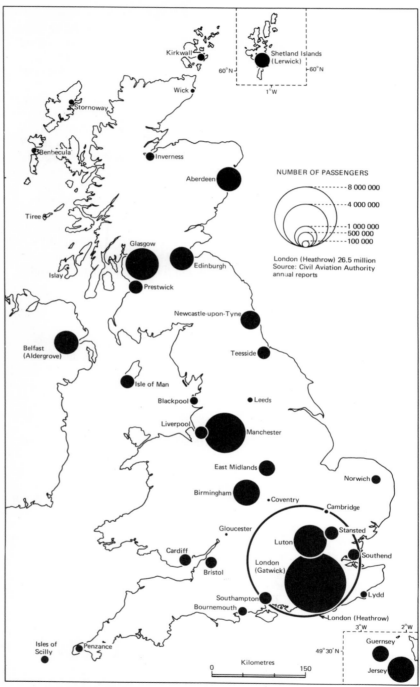

Figure 2.3   *Airports and passenger traffic – United Kingdom (1978)*

mainly provided by smaller airlines using older aircraft, whose value has been considerably written down and bought secondhand. The brokers of the Baltic Exchange in the City of London, originally set up to arrange shipping charters, also specialise in air chartering.

2.6.3 Aircraft Development[43]

In the years since 1945, aircraft development has been continuous and has been occurring at an accelerating pace. Development has included increased capacity, from 21 passengers carried by the DC3, an almost universal use in the late 1940s, to the 300–350 passengers carried by Boeing and Douglas jumbo-jets. Speeds have also increased from about 250 mph (400 km/h) to the 1200 (1920 km/h) of Concorde. At the same time, piston engines have been replaced by turbo-propeller and then by jet engines. All this has resulted in economy of scale. Larger aircraft are less costly per unit of carrying capacity, faster aircraft achieve more seat-km or capacity-tonne-km over unit time, and the size of flight crew does not increase with size of aircraft.

The consequence has been, in real terms, a continuous reduction in seat-km and capacity-tonne-km costs. To this must be added the value of time saved by passengers and cargo-shippers. To some extent, because of control over fare levels (see section 6.6.1), this reduction has not been fully reflected in fares, though in recent years, with the introduction of competition on the North Atlantic, fares have fallen dramatically. In 1979 it cost as much to travel to Copenhagen from London as it did to Los Angeles.

2.6.4 Airports

The siting of airports must inevitably be a compromise between conflicting considerations.[44] Commercial considerations require them to be sited as near as possible to the city they serve, while operational ones require the approaches to be as free as possible from buildings. Land requirements bring airports into competition with other land-uses, while noise pollution must be taken into account. Conflicts in connection with airport siting are well illustrated by the protracted enquiries preceding the choice, still unsettled, of the Third London Airport.[45]

It is also considered desirable that there should be some central planning of the hierarchy of airports. The United Kingdom lacked any such plan until 1978, when a White Paper on Airport Policy[46] appeared. As a result, the three London airports, and Manchester and Prestwick, were designated *Gateway Airports*. These are airports where international traffic will be developed.

Competition between airports is severe. Smaller airports tend to suffer from proximity to others with a wider range of destinations and more frequent services. Liverpool (Speke) and Leeds/Bradford suffer from too close a proximity to Manchester (Ringway), which has a wider range of services and thus attracts more passengers and, in turn, the major investment.

With improved surface communications, Birmingham (Elmdon) is too near London (Heathrow).

Airports are controlled by a number of authorities.

(1) *The British Airports Authority*, which is a nationalised body and which controls three of the airports in the London area, Heathrow, Gatwick and Stansted, and the major Scottish ones, such as Glasgow (Abbotsinch).

(2) *The Civil Aviation Authority* owns the eight Highlands and Islands airports. Sunburgh (Shetland) and Kirkwall (Orkney) have experienced large traffic increases with North Sea oil, but those in the Western Isles are simple airstrips maintained for social reasons.

(3) *Local Authorities*, either singly or as consortia, have established a large number of local airports, often more for prestige than for economic reasons. But some have been successful and have grown considerably. Manchester (Ringway) is owned and operated by Greater Manchester County and Manchester City Council, each with equal representation and with an alternating chairmanship. East Midlands Airport (Castle Donington) is controlled by a number of local authorities.

(4) *Private Companies* The only commercial airport owned by a private company is Southampton (Eastleigh).

(5) *The Northern Ireland Government* is the authority controlling Belfast (Aldergrove).

Air traffic control at all airports, as well as elsewhere, is the responsibility of the Civil Aviation Authority. The central government makes grants for approved developments of runways and terminals. Manchester Airport is often claimed to be 'profitable'. Income exceeds direct operating costs, but recent large-scale improvements have been financed by interest-free grants. The major airports are concerned with both scheduled and charter flights. But many airports are more specialised in the traffic. Luton, the fourth busiest, and local authority owned, specialises almost wholly in charter flights. In 1976, 1.78 million international passengers were dealt with, and only 25 000 on domestic flights. Southend is mainly concerned with cross-channel air cargo flights, and Southampton with passenger traffic to the Channel Islands. In Scotland, Glasgow (Abbotsinch) deals with domestic traffic, and Prestwick with international, particularly transatlantic.

London (Heathrow) has by far the largest traffic. In 1978 there were 268 800 aircraft movements (32.5 per cent of the total for the United Kingdom) and 24.97 million passengers. Gatwick came second with 99 007 movements and 5.4 million passengers. Stansted, the third BAA London airport, is comparatively unimportant and is concerned mainly with long-distance charter flights. Manchester was the busiest provincial airport with 50 969 movements and 3 million passengers.[47]

2.7 Water Transport

2.7.1 Seaports

The nature of a port and the extent of its hinterland depends on many factors.

In general terms, low-value imports, which cannot easily bear transport costs, tend to be destined for a restricted hinterland, while higher-value exports tend to originate from a wider one. For example, in 1966 it was found that imports were carried an average distance of 58 km to their final destination, while exports were carried an average distance of 106 km from their place of origin.[48] Thus, port hinterlands, by and large, are fairly restricted. Classic cases for imports are oil refineries and steelworks on coastal sites. Milford Haven with its three associated refineries and pipeline to a fourth, Llandarcy (near Swansea), is an example of the former, and the specialised iron ore terminals of Port Talbot (South Wales) and Hunterston (Lower Clyde) of the latter.

Britain being an island means that seaports are vital to the economy, and the port industry is thus an important sector of the transport system.[49] The Rochdale Report (1963)[50] provided a good landmark for starting a study of the modern industry, and identified fifteen major ports which handled the great majority of UK overseas trade, and of these, London and Liverpool were dominant. The period since has been one of fundamental change, which can be summarised as follows.

(1) Responses by the ports to technological innovation in shipping, notably the development of unit-loads and of increasing size in bulk carriers. This has taken the form of container and roll-on-roll-off berths and bulk-loading equipment.

(2) The drastic reduction in the labour force as a consequence, which has caused further labour difficulties in the major ports, already beset by them.[51]

(3) The relative decline of the major ports, especially of Liverpool, and the increasing importance of the 'minor' (that is, non-Rochdale) ports.

The 'minor' ports include

(1) The new specialised bulk-loading ports, especially petroleum ports, of which Milford Haven is the leader. The tonnage of vessels entering this port is now second only to that of London.

(2) Ferry terminals such as Harwich, Dover and Holyhead, which have benefited from the introduction of roll-on-roll-off facilities for both lorries and accompanied cars, as well as from containerisation and increasing trade with the rest of the EEC.

(3) General cargo ports which have benefited from innovative management and good labour relations. Examples are Ipswich and Shoreham, while Felixstowe has been a leader for the whole industry in the adaptation to containerisation after 1966.

Port Ownership and Organisation

There is a wide variety of port authorities.

(1) *Port Trusts* — statutory authorities with membership composed of local government, user interests, and Department of Transport nominees: for example, Port of London Authority, Tyne Commissioners, Dover Harbour

Board. The Mersey Docks and Harbour Boad, after a financial crisis in 1972, was reconstituted as a limited company.

(2) *British Transport Docks Board* — set up by the 1962 Transport Act and the inheritors of the large investment by the railway companies nationalised in 1947. This includes the major ports of Southampton, Hull and South Wales, as well as the minor ports of Fleetwood and King's Lynn.

(3) *Local Authorities* — Bristol is the only major port, but there are numerous minor ports, such as Preston.

(4) *British Rail* — owns and operates rail-connected ferry terminals such as Parkeston Quay (Harwich), Folkestone, Stranraer and Holyhead.

(5) *Private Companies* — Manchester is the one major port in company ownership, but there are a number of minor ports including Felixstowe, Sheerness and Cairnryan (Stranraer Loch).

The Rochdale Report recommended the setting up of a *National Ports Authority* to allocate and control investment. The government, however, created the *National Ports Council*, a purely advisory body.[52] An attempt to nationalise the whole industry failed in 1976 when a government bill was defeated.

The port authorities have control over the installations and approach channels, though pilotage and navigation aids are provided by Trinity House. Dock labour, that is, *dockers*, who work cargo on the quay, and *stevedores*, who work it on the ships, are employed by the authorities in some ports, for example, Manchester, Felixstowe and the British Rail terminals, but in some of the major ports such as London, by independent employers.

Table 2.3 shows the rank order of the thirty largest British ports. It will be noted that, in addition to the fifteen ports regarded as 'major' by the Rochdale Commission, Milford Haven, Immingham, Medway, Felixstowe and Dover are included. Apart from Felixstowe, a general-cargo port, the others are specialised petroleum, iron ore and ferry ports. London, by virtue of its importance as a petroleum importer maintained its premier position, but Liverpool, in spite of still being second for 'other cargoes' had declined from its traditional second place to sixth.

2.7.2 Deep-sea Shipping

The British merchant fleet is important as an earner of foreign exchange. In 1977, a total of 72.2 million deadweight tons (dwt) were registered under the British flag, the third largest fleet.[53]

In deep-sea operations there have been fundamental changes which can be summed up as follows.

(1) The decline in passenger traffic, which has led to the withdrawal of almost all passenger and passenger-cargo liners. The only work remaining for passenger vessels is cruising and some summer North Atlantic sailings by the *Queen Elizabeth II*.

(2) The consequences of the 'Container Revolution' which could be said to have begun in 1966. Containerisation was first introduced in the North

TABLE 2.3 *Rank Order of 30 British Ports, 1976*

	Total Cargo Handled[‡]	Fuels[‡]	Other Cargoes[‡]
London[†]	1	2	1
Milford Haven	2	1	30
Tees and Hartlepool[†]	3	4	3*
Southampton[†]	4	3	12
Immingham	5	6	4*
Liverpool[†]	6	7	2
Medway	7	5	15
Manchester[†]	8	9	5
Forth[†]	9	8	11
Clyde[†]	10	10	6*
Swansea[†]	11	11	8*
Hull[†]	12	19	9
Felixstowe	13	22	7
Bristol[†]	14	14	13
Tyne[†]	15	12	20
Dover	16	26	10
Cardiff[†]	17	13	16
Harwich	18	24	14
Ipswich	19	17	18
Newport[†]	20	15	21
Shoreham	21	16	24
Goole	22	20	19
Plymouth	23	18	25
Fleetwood	24	27	17
Great Yarmouth	25	21	28
Grimsby	26	29	22
King's Lynn	27	23	26
Preston	28	25	27
Boston	29	30	23
Holyhead	30	28	29

Source: Annual report — National Ports Authority
[†] defined as a 'major' port in the Rochdale Report (1963)
* major importer of iron ore
[‡] by cargo tonnage handled

Atlantic, and later into the Australasian, Far Eastern, and South African trades. This has led to great increases in size of vessels. 'Break-bulk' cargo-liners are limited in size to about 10 000 to 15 000 dwt because of the time taken to load and unload, a process taking up to fourteen days. But a container vessel takes hours rather than days, so there are no limitations on size other than the ability to enter the ports on the route. Container vessels are thus being built with tonnages of 30–40 000. Because of increased size and radically reduced turn-round times, fewer vessels are needed to handle a given tonnage over unit time.[54]

(3) The increasing size of oil-tankers. With expanding world trade in petroleum there was also expansion in size of vessel, as considerable economies of scale can be achieved. With increased capacity, the cost per ton of construction falls, as a 50 per cent increase in linear dimensions results in a 95 per cent increase in capacity. Crew costs also do not increase in proportion to size. During the Second World War large numbers of standard T2 tankers were built of 12 500 dwt. By the early 1950s, 50 000 tonnes became common. The closure of the Suez Canal in 1956 accelerated the process, and soon 100 000 tonnes became common. By 1970, 250–300 000 tonnes were in general use. At the time of writing, the largest ship registered is the *Batillus*, 553 000 dwt.[55]

(4) Bulk carriers became far more common for the carriage of iron-ore, fertilisers, grain, etc. Similar economies of scale became possible, though bulk carriers have not been built as large as the VLCCs (very large crude carriers), and 150 000 dwt is regarded as large.

The increasing size, and therefore gross cost, of vessels has led to financing by consortia. The principal British container lines are ACT (Associated Container Transport) and OCL (Overseas Containers Limited) both of which are consortia of the major shipping lines. The oil companies have invested in British VLCCs, but they and British Steel also rely on chartering.

2.7.3 *Coastal Shipping and Ferry Services*

Traditionally, coastal shipping has played an important role in domestic transport. But it has tended to remain static in recent years, fluctuating between 110.0 million tonnes in 1967 and 100.3 million in 1977. This has been due to the decline in coal movements, from 32.6 million tonnes to 10.4 million in the period. The other major commodity is petroleum products (77.4 million tonnes in 1967), though there is increasing competition from inland transport, rail and pipeline. Since 1978, a proportion of North Sea oil is brought ashore by ship.

Ferry services are of great importance, both across the Irish Sea to Northern Ireland and the Republic of Ireland, and to continental ports. In recent years, with the development of roll-on-roll-off (ro-ro) facilities, first for tourist cars and since the mid-1960s for lorry traffic, and of trade with the EEC, they have assumed an increased importance.

They may be classified as follows, though it should be remembered that many vessels are designed for more than one function.

(1) *'Classic' Ferries*, that is, passenger-carrying vessels run in conjunction with rail services to ports such as Dover, Harwich and Holyhead.

(2) *'Ro-ro'* for tourist cars and lorries. In addition, ferries operating between Dover–Dunkirk and Harwich–Zeebrugge and Dunkirk convey railway wagons.

(3) *Cellular container vessels* which have also increased in importance.

(4) *Hovercraft* operating between Dover–Calais/Boulogne and Ramsgate (Pegwell Bay)–Calais. Although only five units are operational at the time of

writing, they convey some 10 per cent of tourist cars and some 30 per cent of those conveyed on the shorter routes across the Straits of Dover.

The number of terminals and routes have multiplied in recent years. Apart from traditional terminals, such as Harwich, Dover and Stranraer, new ones at Felixstowe, King's Lynn, Portsmouth, Plymouth, Newport (Gwent), Fleetwood and Cairnryan, as well as many more, have developed. In the same way, organisations participating have increased. British Rail (operating through a wholly owned subsidiary, *Sealink*) and continental partners SNCF and SNCB (French and Belgian Railways) operate classic ferries, ro-ro, and container services from the terminals they own or have been traditionally associated with. On the Irish Sea, the British and Irish services, bought by the Irish government from Coast Lines, compete with the Sealink services, while DSDF (Danish government) and Fred Olsen (a Norwegian firm) operate between Esbjerg–Harwich and Bergen–Newcastle. There are also a number of private firms; examples are Townsend–Thorensen, an Anglo-Norwegian firm operating from Dover, Portsmouth and Southampton, and P & O Ferries, which represent deep-sea interests moving in. The latter not only operate passenger and cargo ro-ro services from Dover and Southampton, but cargo services between Fleetwood and Northern Ireland.

2.7.4 Inland Waterways

Technically, inland waterways may be divided into (a) *navigations*, which are improved natural waterways, rivers and lakes, and (b) *canals*, which are artificial cuts. There are some 2600 km of navigable waterway. But by 1960 commercial traffic had ceased over most of the network. In 1978, six stretches (three canals and three navigations) were recorded as carrying 5.4 million tonnes of freight: 2.6 million tonnes were conveyed on the Aire and Calder Navigation, which, with the South Yorks Navigation and the River Trent Navigation (below Nottingham), feed into the Humber ports: The Weaver Navigation (Cheshire), the Lee Navigation (East London), and the Gloucester and Sharpness Canal were the other three.

The 'narrow' canals of the English Midlands are now maintained as 'cruiseways' for pleasure traffic, which is rapidly growing in volume. The whole network is controlled by the Inland Waterways Board, set up under the 1962 Transport Act.[56]

2.8 Pipelines

If water and gas are included, the pipeline network is extensive, and the traffic is of very large volume. However, excluding these, petroleum and petroleum products are the main traffic (figure 2.4). In 1978, 82.0 million tons were moved, compared with 26 million in 1965. Because of the coastal location of British refineries, crude pipelines are short, though there is a trend to increasing length as deeper water terminals have to be developed to accommodate VLCCs. Thus, there is a 121 km pipeline from the Amlwch

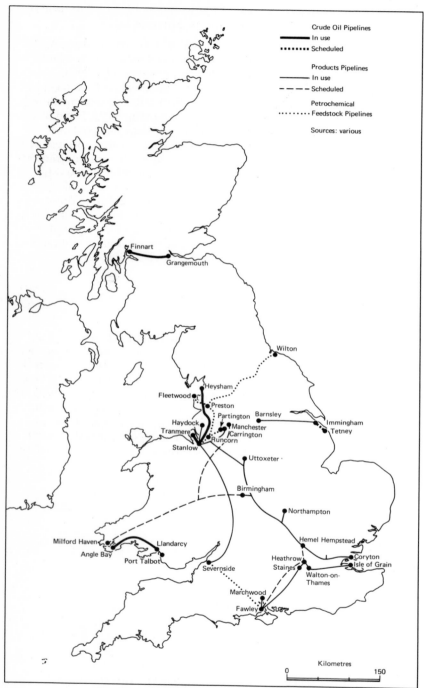

Figure 2.4 *Pipelines – Great Britain (1978)*

(Anglesey) terminals to the Stanlow refinery on the Manchester Ship Canal. Others have been constructed from terminals where North Sea oil is brought ashore, such as the 212 km line from Cruden Bay to Grangemouth.[57]

The major refineries are also connected with large inland distribution depots, such as those at Northampton and Rowley Regis (West Midlands), which are used to transport the lighter fractions. Heavier residual oils, which account for some 45 per cent of output, are too viscous and are transported by rail. The chemical complex at Avonside, and other major consumers, such as Heathrow Airport, are also linked with the network, which is financed and operated by a consortium of oil companies.

If suspended in water, solids can be transported by pipeline. Chalk is moved in this way from Totternhoe Quarry (near Dunstable) to cement-plants at Rugby and Southam. But the low trainload rates offered by British Rail have prevented further development.

2.9 The Organisation of Transport in Northern Ireland

Since 1922, many aspects of internal affairs have been devolved from Westminster to the Government of Northern Ireland. As a result, the legal framework, and methods of government intervention into and control of the transport sector, have differed in detail from those in the rest of the country. It is convenient therefore to summarise the position in Northern Ireland at the time of writing.

Stage carriage bus services throughout the Province, including urban services in Belfast and rural services elsewhere, are operated by *Ulsterbus*, a company wholly owned by the Government of Northern Ireland. Express services are operated by *Ulsterbus Express*, a division of Ulsterbus. Ulsterbus and private operators engage in excursions and contract and private hire.

The organisation of road haulage is similar to that pertaining in Great Britain since the 1968 Transport Act. Entry is equally free, and there is no restriction on the number of licenses granted, and no distinction between own-account carriage and that for hire and reward. Most haulage firms are small, but in addition there is the government-owned *Northern Ireland Carriers*. Since an important aspect of transport is that connecting with the Irish Sea ferry services, there are special arrangements with BRS and British Rail for the haulage of semi-trailers and containers to and from the ferry ports of Belfast and Larne.

The residual rail system is operated by *Northern Ireland Railways*, another government-owned company. In 1978 there were 318 km of line in operation. Passenger services may be divided into the longer-distance ones from Belfast to Londonderry/Portrush, Larne, and the cross-border one to Dublin, and the Belfast suburban services, principally to Lisburn and Bangor. The service to Dublin is operated in conjunction with CIE (Irish Transport Company), both administrations providing trains which run over the other's tracks.

Because of the short distances involved, no internal freight services are provided. There are, however, two terminals, at Belfast and Londonderry, to which trains from the CIE are worked. The Londonderry terminal is the railhead for County Donegal, containers and bulk petroleum being taken on by lorries of CIE as well as by those of the privately owned Londonderry and Lough Swilly Railway, which ceased rail operations in 1953. These two companies and the CIE also provide cross-border stage carriage services.

The ferry services for passengers, private cars, lorries and containers, are concentrated on Belfast and Larne, the latter having grown very considerably since 1960 with the development of ro-ro and container services to Stranraer, Cairnryan, Fleetwood and Heysham. The operators include Sealink (the British Rail subsidiary), P & O Ferries and Townsend—Thoresen.

Public ownership was introduced at an early date. In 1935, the Northern Ireland Road Transport Board was set up to take over not only all bus services, other than those of Belfast Corporation, but all road haulage as well. The experiment was unsuccessful, and eventually private entry to road haulage was allowed and accounted for virtually the whole of post-war expansion. In 1948 the NIRTB assets were transferred to the Ulster Transport Authority, which also took over the bankrupt Belfast & County Down Railway. With the establishment of the British Transport Commission, the Northern Counties Committee railway, owned by the London Midland & Scottish Railway, was taken over. The cross-border Great Northern of Ireland was left in private hands until 1953, when the governments of Northern Ireland and Eire took over, setting up a joint Board. But in 1958 the assets were shared between the UTA and CIE. In 1968 the UTA in turn was dissolved and its assets shared among the various government-owned companies.

References

1. Department of Transport, *Transport Statistics* (HMSO, annual)
2. J. Drake, H. L. Yeadon and D. I. Evans, *Motorways* (Faber, London, 1969)
3. For design details see: Ministry of Transport, *Roads in Urban Areas* (HMSO, 1966); Department of the Environment, *Roads in Urban Areas—metric supplement* (HMSO, 1974); Ministry of Transport, *Layout of Roads in Rural Areas* (HMSO, 1968); and appropriate Dept of Transport technical memoranda
4. British Road Federation, *Basic Road Statistics* (BRF, annual)
5. E. W. Evans, Intercity Travel and the London Midland Electrification, *J. Transp. econ. Pol.*, 3 (1969) 69—95
6. Ministry of Transport, *Roads in Urban Areas* (HMSO, 1966), Section 2.1, p. 9
7. Central Office of Information, *Annual Abstract of Statistics* (HMSO, annual)
8. Office of Population Censuses and Survey, *Census 1971: Availability of Cars* (HSMO, 1973)
9. Department of Transport, *National Travel Survey 1975/76* (HMSO)
10. W. Lamden, *Bus and Coach Operation* (Iliffe, London, 1969)

11. Government Statistical Service, *Passenger Transport in Great Britain* (HMSO, annual)
12. London Transport Executive, *Annual Report*
13. J. Hibbs, *The History of British Bus Services* (David & Charles, Newton Abbot, 1968)
14. J. Hibbs, Maintaining Transport Services in Rural Areas, *J. Transp. econ. Pol.*, 6 (1972) 10–21
15. J. Hibbs, *The Bus and Coach Industry*, (Dent, London, 1975)
16. K. M. Gwilliam and P. J. Mackie, *Economics and Transport Policy* (Allen & Unwin, London, 1975). But note the 1980 Transport Act permitted considerable freedom of entry
17. P. R. White, *Planning for Public Transport* (Hutchinson, London, 1976) p. 55
18. Public Passenger Vehicle Act 1981
19. D. Turnock, The Postbus: a New Element in Britain's Rural Transport, *Geography*, 62 (1977) 112–18
20. An attempt to do so on a geographical basis has been made by M. Chisholm and P. O'Sullivan, *Freight Flows and Spatial Aspects of the British Economy* (Cambridge University Press, 1973)
21. S. L. Edwards and B. T. Bayliss, *Operating Costs in Road Freight Transport* (Department of the Environment, 1971)
22. For background see: R. G. Bassett, *Road Haulage Management and Accounting* (Heinemann, London, 1976); G. W. Briggs, *Road Haulage Management* (Butterworth, London, 1975)
23. The Motor Vehicles (construction and use) Regulations, Statutory Instrument No 1017 (1978) p. 100, section 136
24. British Railways Board, *Annual Reports*
25. European Economic Community, *Annual Transport Statistics* (Statistical Office of the EEC, Luxembourg); British Railways Board, *A Comparative Study of European Railway Performance* (British Railways Board, 1980)
26. P. N. Grimshaw, Steam Railways: Growth Points for Leisure and Recreation, *Geography*, 61 (1976) 83–8
27. British Railways Board, *The Reshaping of British Railways*, (Beeching Report) (British Railways Board, 1963)
28. R. G. Harman, BR Passenger Services, a New Approach to Marketing, *Modern Railways* (March, 1974); J. G. Smith, Passenger Business Planning of Inter-City Services, *Modern Railways* (Nov., Dec., 1975)
29. C. J. Allen, Decline on Liverpool–Manchester Services, *Modern Railways* (Nov., 1972)
30. British Railways Board, *Annual Report*, 1979
31. H. P. White, London's Rail Terminals and their Commuter Traffic, *Geographical Review*, 54 (1964) 347–65
32. H. P. White, Greater London, Vol. 3 in *A Regional Railway History of Great Britain* (David & Charles, Newton Abbot, 1971)
33. London Transport Executive, *Annual Report*, 1979
34. H. P. White, High-speed Rail Pulls in the Passengers, *Geographical Magazine*, 50 (1978) 601–4
35. D. H. Aldcroft, *British Railways in Transition* (Macmillan, London, 1968)

36. National Freight Corporation, *Annual Reports*
37. G. F. Allen, Freightliners Comes Home a Changed Company, *Modern Railways* (June, 1979)
38. The Future of Wagon-load Traffic, *Railway Gazette International* (May, 1971)
39. G. F. Allen, Railfreight Presents Speedlink, *Modern Railways* (Nov., 1977)
40. P. A. Lord, The Future of Parcels and Sundries Traffic, *J. Chartered Inst. Transp.*, **33** (1970) 542–50
41. G. F. Allen, Railroads Give Toronto a New Heart, *Modern Railways* (Dec., 1969)
42. Committee of Inquiry into Civil Air Transport (Edwards Committee), *British Air Transport in the Seventies*, Cmnd 4018 (HMSO, 1969)
43. A. H. Stratford, *Air Transport Economics and the Supersonic Era* (Macmillan, London, 1973); K. R. Sealey, *The Geography of Air Transport* (Hutchinson, London, 1966)
44. K. R. Sealey, *Airport Strategy and Planning* (Oxford University Press, 1976)
45. Commission on the Third London Airport (Roskill Commission), *Report, Papers and Proceedings* (HMSO, 1971)
46. Secretary of State for Trade, *Airports Policy*, Cmnd 7084 (HMSO, 1978)
47. British Airports Authority, *Annual Reports*; Civil Aviation Authority, *Annual Statistics*
48. McKinsey & Co., *Containerisation: the Key to Low Cost Transportation*, a Report to the British Transport Docks Board (London, 1967)
49. J. Bird, *Seaports and Seaport Terminals* (Hutchinson, London, 1971)
50. Committee of Inquiry into the Major Ports of Great Britain, *Report*, (Rochdale Report) Cmnd 1824 (HMSO, 1962)
51. M. Mellish, *The Docks and Devlin* (Heinemann, London, 1972); M. P. Jackson, *Labour Relations in the Docks* (Saxon House, London, 1973)
52. National Ports Council, *Annual Reports*, Occasional Papers
53. General Council of British Shipping, *British Shipping Statistics* (annual)
54. G. van den Berg, *Containerisation* (Hutchinson, London, 1975); K. M. Johnson and H. C. Garnett, *The Economics of Containerisation* (Allen & Unwin, London, 1971)
55. A. D. Couper, *The Geography of Sea Transport* (Hutchinson, London, 1972)
56. Inland Waterways Board, *Annual Reports*
57. R. T. Frost, Pipeline Development in the United Kingdom, *Geography*, **54** (1969) 204–11

The best single source for the institutional history of the British transport system is, D. H. Aldcroft, *British Transport Since 1914* (David & Charles, Newton Abbot, 1975).

For details of recent legislative, institutional, operational and technological developments the following journals are useful

Coaching Journal	*Fairplay*
Commercial Motor	*Flight*
Containerisation International	*Railway Gazette International*
Dock & Harbour Authority	*Modern Railways*

3

Transport Trends

This chapter examines trends in domestic passenger and freight transport, and in international transport to and from the United Kingdom, concentrating principally on the period since 1945. This timescale is chosen on a number of counts: significant transport legislation just after the end of the Second World War,[1] very large increases in prosperity over this thirty-year period compared with the one up to the beginning of the Second World War; and the fact that thirty years hence significant developments in transport might reasonably be expected, particularly in connection with depletion of the world's oil resources.

In addition, where suitable statistics are available, a longer perspective is developed in recognition of the facts that most transport infrastructure has a very long life, and that time-lags between conception and completion of technological developments in transport can be very long.

The chapter concludes by discussing the importance of technological change for trends in transport.

3.1 Overall Trends in Passenger Transport

Important trends are shown in figure 3.1. In general, they can be classified in terms of either continuing growth or growth followed by decline; for example, population, number of private vehicles, and air transport passenger movements, fall into the first category, while journeys by rail, tramway, trolley bus, bus and coach, and possibly number of motorcycles fall into the second.

Consider first of all the trends of expansion. The population of the United Kingdom 38 million in 1901, 56 million in 1978, has steadily increased at an average rate of around 5 per cent every decade. It increased at a higher rate over the 1951–71 period, but more recently there have been signs of population increasing at a lower rate. The numbers of private vehicles and of passengers carried by air transport have shown quite considerable increases since the Second World War. In 1946 there were some 1.8 million private cars and vans in the United Kingdom; the corresponding figure in 1978 was some 14.4 million. In 1946 some 0.4 million passengers were carried by air transport to and from the United Kingdom, while 0.2 million were carried on domestic scheduled air services; corresponding figures for 1978 were 38.9 million and 6.4 million.

Now consider the trends of expansion followed by decline. Travel on the

(a)

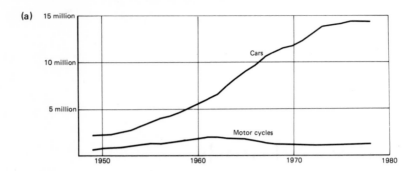

(b)

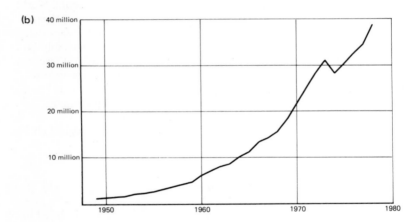

(c)

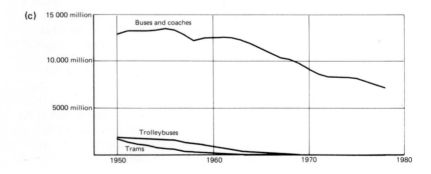

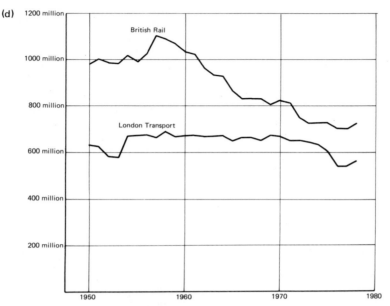

Figure 3.1   *Trends in passenger transport: (a) cars and motorcycles with licences current in the United Kingdom; (b) passengers carried on aircraft flights between the United Kingdom and abroad; (c) passenger journeys by public road passenger transport in Great Britain; (d) rail passenger journeys by British Rail and London Transport*

British Rail network was at similar levels just before the First World War and just after the Second World War, while traffic reached a peak of some 2186 million passengers in 1920. However, patronage declined from some 1266 million journeys in 1946 to some 724 million in 1978, although 1979 witnessed a slight increase as a result of aggressive marketing of inter-city travel. As temporary reversals in this long-term trend of decline have taken place in the past, it remains to be seen whether 1979 is heralding the onset of a period of increasing patronage. It is also interesting that since 1950 the volume of rail travel in terms of passenger miles has barely changed, despite this fall in the number of journeys, because the average length of journey has increased; for example, commuting by rail, particularly in the London and South East area, has been drawn progressively more and more from outer suburbs, while inter-city rail travel has become more competitive for medium journey distances to London, in which rail travel offers a time advantage over both travel by car and air.

Development and expansion of both tram and trolley bus services preceded their decline and virtual extinction this century in the United Kingdom. In comparison, other European countries have been more successful in retaining tram systems, while it is ironic that energy considerations have renewed

British interest in trolley buses. Patronage of trams was highest between the two World Wars with 1119 million journeys in Great Britain* in 1901, 2795 million in 1911, and 3778 million in 1933, but declined during the 1930s and withered away very rapidly after the Second World War, with 1462 million journeys in 1951, 104 million in 1961, and 10 million in 1971, when only Blackpool's system survived. Trolley buses, a later development on lighter-density routes, with 254 million journeys in Great Britain in 1933, carried their maximum traffic just after the Second World War, with 2005 million journeys in 1949. Thereafter, patronage declined rapidly to some 756 million journeys in 1961, and 15 million in 1971; today none is in operation on public routes.

Major development of the London Transport railways took place between the World Wars. Patronage trends show 492 million journeys in 1938, 570 million in 1946, and 624 million in 1951. Thereafter, patronage developed more slowly, never quite managing to exceed the 700 million mark, with 675 million journeys in 1961, 654 million in 1971, and a peak of 692 million in 1958. More recently patronage has reduced significantly with 569 million journeys in 1978.

In most cases services provided by trams and trolley buses were taken over by conventional buses. This was reflected in bus patronage, which increased from 5424 million journeys in Great Britain in 1933 to 13 270 million in 1951. However, bus patronage reached a peak of 13 520 million journeys in 1955, since which date it has steadily declined, with some 7305 million journeys being made in 1978.

The general picture, then, is that patronage of local public transport reached a peak in the 1950s; thereafter, largely because of the increasing use of private transport, it has fallen steadily.

Motorcycles provide another example of a trend of expansion followed by decline, but in this case there are signs of expansion again; for example, the numbers of motorcycles, scooters, and mopeds registered in the United Kingdom increased from some 0.5 million in 1946 to a peak of some 1.8 million in 1961; thereafter, it declined to some 1 million by 1972, only to subsequently increase to some 1.2 million by 1976, at which level it has remained. It would be easy to ascribe this recent expansion to more expensive petrol, but factors such as trends in car prices and in young peoples' earnings, and factors related to lifestyle are also likely to be involved.

3.2 Trends in Domestic Passenger Transport

Any discussion of trends in domestic passenger transport in the United Kingdom must first recognise the dominance of private transport. It must then make a necessary distinction between local and non-local travel as a preparation for a discussion of trends in the use of public transport.

* The official practice of presenting statistics on domestic transport for Great Britain rather than the United Kingdom will be followed where appropriate.

3.2.1 The Dominance of Private Transport

The single most important development since the Second World War has been
the growing importance of private transport in the patterns of passenger
movement: for example, by 1978 it was accounting for some 81 per cent of
motorised passenger movement in Great Britain; by comparison, corresponding
figures for bus and rail transport were 11 and 7 per cent, and air transport a
mere 0.5 per cent. This dominance of private transport can largely be attributed
to the growth in car ownership: for example, total car registrations in the
United Kingdom in 1946 were 1.8 million, representing a car ownership level
of 0.07 cars per capita; in 1978 the figure was 14.4 million, 0.25 cars per capita.
It is envisaged that car ownership might increase to between 0.40 and 0.47 cars
per capita by 2010.[2]

However, annual new car registrations have varied significantly over the 1970s;
for example, these increased steadily to the mid-1960s, remained around the
1 million level in the late 1960s, and then increased sharply to some 1.7 million
in 1972 and 1973, the two years preceding the last major Arab—Israeli dispute
and the first major monopolistic action by the OPEC cartel; new registrations
subsequently fell to some 1.3 million in 1974 and 1.1 million in 1975, from
which level they climbed again to some 1.6 million by 1978.

So in the medium run the volume of new car registrations does not appear
to have been affected by the large increases in petrol prices; one reason for this,
of course, is that current petrol prices are little different from those in 1973 in
real terms.

Neither is there evidence of significant changes in purchasing patterns, such
as a greater demand for smaller cars. Cars in the 700—1000 cc engine size
category did increase their market share temporarily in 1974 at the expense of
cars in the 1000—2000 cc class, but subsequently the opposing longer-run trend
has continued.

It is likely that an important factor in this connection in the United Kingdom
is company cars. These form a major proportion of new registrations and tend
to predominate in the 1500—2000 cc engine size category. They are also a
major source of vehicles for the secondhand car market.

The overall effect of these increases in car ownership has been for the
proportion of households without a car to decrease; for example, this proportion
fell from 59 per cent in 1965 to 43 per cent in 1978 in Great Britain. However,
car ownership spread less rapidly in the 1970s than in the late 1960s, and it
remains to be seen whether this reflects the effects of such limits on car
ownership as the proportion of the population eligible and competent to drive,
or the more temporary effects of economic recession.

Private transport has also become more dominant because, with the
exception of a temporary reversal in 1973—4, annual mileage has steadily
increased through cars being used more frequently and for longer journeys.
However, this is a relatively minor factor compared with the increases in the
actual number of cars.

Growth in private transport has been mainly through serving new travel
demands rather than replacing existing ones; for example, over the 1955—75
period, travel by private transport increased by some 243 thousand million

passenger-km in Great Britain, while there was, in contrast, a much smaller
decline of some 29 thousand million passenger-km in travel by bus and train.
But increased use of private transport has had serious consequences for public
transport, particularly on local services; for example, some 59 per cent of
commuters travelled by car in Great Britain in 1975—76, compared with some
54 per cent in 1972—3 and some 35 per cent in 1965.[3] However, other
journey purposes form a major and increasing share of travel by private
transport; for example, journeys to and from work by private transport in Great
Britain increased from 1.31 to 1.71 *per capita* per week over the 1965—73
period, while other journeys by private transport increased from 2.85 to 5.13
per capita per week.[4] So, the largest increases in travel by private transport
have been for less essential journeys, and those less readily undertaken by
public transport, such as journeys connected with shopping, social visits, leisure
and holidays, all of which tend to take place at times and in areas not well
served by public transport. This illustrates, of course, the fundamental dilemma,
that public transport serves such journeys poorly because demand is low, and
there is low demand because services are poor.

3.2.2 Local and Non-local Travel

It is necessary to be careful in generalising about trends in travel because
characteristics vary so much between different modes, geographical areas, and
journey purposes. A useful starting point is to attempt to distinguish between
local and non-local travel because they are so different in terms of sizes of
markets, average journey distance, and travel purposes. An initial difficulty is
satisfactory definition of local, and non-local, travel. An official approach has
been to simply define non-local travel as journeys over 25 miles in length; this
has obvious limitations for areas like South East England where commuting
over long distances is common, but nevertheless provides a useful definition.[5]
This and subsequent sections will rely on data from the 1975—6 National
Travel Survey and the 1977—8 Long-distance Travel Survey, both of which have
been already referenced.
    The most important distinction between local and non-local travel is in the
disparate sizes of their markets; for example, journeys of 25 miles or more
accounted for only some 3.3 per cent of all passenger journeys in Great Britain
in 1975—6. They are also very different from the viewpoints of travel purpose
and mode of travel; for example, for journeys under 25 miles the most common
journey purposes in 1975—6 were shopping and personal business, which
accounted for some 29 per cent of these journeys, and commuting, which
accounted for some 23 per cent; for journeys of at least 25 miles, the most
common journeys were for commuting and social purposes, which accounted for
some 20 per cent and 19 per cent of these longer journeys, respectively.
However the pattern changes significantly if one considers journeys over very
long distances; for example, for journeys longer than 100 miles in Great Britain
in 1977—8 the most common journeys were for unspecified non-business
purposes, to and from holiday, and in the course of work; these accounted for

some 40 per cent, 20 per cent, and 19 per cent of such journeys respectively.

This variation with distance in the importance of different journey purposes also illustrates the different natures of markets for local and non-local travel. The local travel market is likely to be less subject to temporal variation, because it is a very much larger market and includes the steadying influence of commuting. On the other hand, non-local travel markets have marked seasonality because of the important contribution of holiday travel.

There are also interesting variations in the contribution made by different modes of travel over different journey distances. Stage carriage bus services accounted for some 11 per cent of all journeys under 25 miles in length in Great Britain in 1975—6 but made no contribution to longer journeys; rail services accounted for some 1 per cent of all journeys under 25 miles and some 11 per cent of longer journeys; travel by car accounted for some 37 per cent of all journeys under 25 miles and some 69 per cent of longer journeys.

It is worthwhile to examine in more detail the variation in the contribution of different modes of travel over these longer distances. Commuting accounted for some 21 per cent of journeys longer than 25 miles in Great Britain in 1977—8; the major mode of travel was car, which accounted for some 49 per cent of these commuting journeys, followed by train with some 35 per cent, while bus services accounted for a mere 4 per cent, largely on express coach services. Only a small minority of commuting journeys were in excess of 50 miles. However, a higher proportion of commuting journeys by train than by car were over 50 miles long, mainly related to commuting in the London and South East areas. Commuting journeys by bus in excess of 50 miles were almost negligible.

For the remaining majority of journeys over 25 miles unrelated to commuting, travel by car was the dominant mode; it accounted for some 82 per cent of these journeys. Travel by train accounted for some 10 per cent of journeys, bus some 3 per cent and air less than 1 per cent. However, travel by train and particularly by air featured more strongly over the longest distances than travel by car; for example, some 27 per cent of rail travel and some 90 per cent of air travel were over distances in excess of 100 miles, compared with some 13 per cent of car travel. Most of this air travel was journeys in the course of work. None the less, similar numbers of journeys were made by train, air, and car, even over distances in excess of 200 miles because of the dominance of travel by car over all.

Contributions to travel by motorcycling and cycling are relatively minor and largely limited to local travel; for example, journeys by motorcycle accounted for some 1 per cent of all journeys in Great Britain in 1975—6, and cycling some 3 per cent. However, walking makes an important and often overlooked contribution to travel; it accounted for some 56 per cent of all journeys under 5 miles in 1975—6, and some 44 per cent of all journeys.

Other public transport modes are works and school buses, and buses used for excursions and tours. These accounted for some 1 per cent and 0.5 per cent, respectively, of journeys in Great Britain in 1975—6, compared with some 10 per cent by stage carriage bus services. Works and school bus services tend to operate over longer distances than stage bus services but seldom in excess of 25 miles while not surprisingly, a significant proportion of the market for excursions and tours is for journeys in excess of 25 miles.

3.2.3 Public Transport Trends

Now that a necessary distinction has been made between local and non-local travel it is appropriate to consider trends in public transport. First of all, local travel by bus and by train, and innovations in local public transport, are considered, then non-local travel by rail, bus and air.

Local Travel by Bus

As just indicated, stage carriage bus services account for most journeys by public transport in this country; by comparison, the number of journeys by rail are modest, and those by taxi even more so.

There are, of course, regional emphases: in 1975—6 residents of the 'London built-up area' made the same proportion, some 17 per cent, of all journeys by rail (on British Rail and London Transport services) as by stage carriage bus services; elsewhere, the proportion of journeys by stage carriage bus services tended to decline with size of urban area, from a maximum of some 23 per cent for urban area populations in excess of 250 000 to some 8 per cent for urban area populations between 3000 and 25 000, while it was some 7 per cent in rural areas. By comparison, it is interesting that works and school buses tended to account for an increasing, albeit modest, proportion of journeys in the progression from large to small urban areas, and to be more important in rural areas.

The structure of public road passenger transport has been described in section 2.3. Over the 1968—78 period the number of passengers carried in Great Britain declined some 29 per cent, largely on local stage carriage services. The decline was general for all public sector operators, and ranged from 25 per cent for London Transport to 40 per cent for the Scottish Bus Group. By comparison, carryings by private operators increased some 36 per cent, mainly indicating growth in the contract and private-hire market.

The general picture, then, is significant decline in local travel by stage carriage bus services. There are local variations: for example, a 5 per cent increase in patronage in Oxford in 1974 was associated with the introduction of comprehensive traffic management, although subsequent fare increases reversed this temporary trend;[6] the 'low fares' policy in South Yorkshire in recent years has slowed decline in peak patronage and increased off-peak patronage.[7] The general evidence is that peak period patronage of stage carriage bus service has declined at a faster rate than off-peak patronage; for example, journeys to work by stage carriage bus services declined by some 47 per cent over the 1965—76 period compared with some 33 per cent for all stage carriage journeys. This partly reflects the fact that school services have become a major consideration in stage carriage bus services.

Local Travel by Rail

The structure of rail transport has been described in section 2.5. The main local rail services are currently provided by British Rail, the London Transport

Executive, and in a much more limited way by the Greater Glasgow Passenger Transport Executive, although it should be emphasised again that British Rail acts as an agent for the six English Passenger Transport Authorities.

The normal division by British Rail of its passenger market into the four business sectors, Inter-City, London and the South East, the Passenger Transport Executives, and other Provincial Services, all of which carry local rail travel, conceals the growing emphasis on commuting from outer suburbs, not only in London and the South East but also in the provincial conurbations; so, a static market in terms of passenger mileage for local rail travel probably reflects a decline in journeys. In recent years, because of the high cost of rail fares, there has been some indication of this emphasis reducing in the London and South East area as rail commuters have sought less distant employment.

Commuting is a more important element of travel by rail than travel by bus, and so trends in commuting provide a reasonable guide to patronage trends of local rail services.

Commuting by rail has declined at a significantly lower rate than commuting by bus. This is reflected in a comparison of National Census results for 1966 and 1971. The proportions of commuters travelling by train in England and Wales barely changed from 6.7 per cent in 1966 to 6.6 per cent in 1971, while the proportions travelling by bus reduced significantly from 29.5 per cent to 23.8 per cent. London and the South East area is by far the most important for rail commuting, accounting for some 1.21 million rail commuters in 1971, some 82 per cent of all rail commuters in Great Britain. In contrast, the Passenger Transport Executives (with the exclusion of South Yorkshire) accounted for 0.14 million rail commuters, around 9 per cent, and the remainder of Great Britain, 0.12 million rail commuters, some 8 per cent. This dominance of London and the South East on rail commuting patterns is not shared with commuting by bus. In this case the Passenger Transport Executives and the remainder of the country are much more important, with, in 1971, around 1.7 and 2.6 million commuters respectively, or 30 and 45 per cent, while the share of the South East region was around 1.4 million, 25 per cent.

Trends in rail commuting showed small declines between 1966 and 1971 in West Yorkshire (5810 commuters in 1971), SELNEC (31 010 commuters), Merseyside (22 570 commuters) and West Midlands (13 580 commuters), and small increases in Tyneside (13 540 commuters), and Central Clydeside (49 200 commuters). By comparison, rail commuting showed a very significant increase of around 29 per cent in the South East region (1.21 million commuters in 1971) over this period. It appears that the market for rail commuting has been fairly steady since 1971. One study has shown that the market for rail commuting on Merseyside was at a similar level in 1975 to that in 1971, and had only showed small variations around this level.[8] The market might be increasing slightly in the conurbations, as indicated by British Rail's recent statistics, because the joint responsibility for bus and rail services of the PTEs has encouraged some diversion of bus passengers to rail services as a result of rationalisation of bus services and fares policies. However, trends in patronage are problematic outside the conurbations because, not only are demand levels low, but also there is not a comparable administrative framework for rationalisation of bus and rail services, particularly between British Rail and the National Bus Company within the shire counties, and British Rail and the Scottish Bus Group in the Scottish regions.

The problem of providing rail services has been most acute in rural areas, and areas containing small urban settlements outside the commuting influence of London and the major provincial conurbations. This has been reflected in the high rate of closure of such lines over the past fifteen years, and the introduction of measures such as unstaffed stations and 'paytrains' to reduce costs. The problem was recognised in the 1968 Transport Act, with the introduction of subsidies for the retention of rail lines that were considered 'socially necessary' (p. 63). Some lines are also subsidised by local authorities in their Transport Policies and Programmes (pp. 157, 160).[9,10]

The other major local rail service in this country is that operated by the London Transport Executive, with some 569 million journeys in 1978 compared with 724 million journeys by British Rail. As already indicated, its market remained fairly steady, slightly below the 700 million journeys-per-year level, for some two decades up to the early 1970s, but has fallen significantly subsequently. The most important extensions to the system in recent years have been the Victoria Line, completed in July 1971 and linking Brixton and Walthamstow Central Station via Central London, providing a fast connection between Victoria, Euston, King's Cross and St Pancras Stations, and the extension of the Piccadilly Line to Heathrow, which was opened in December 1977. The Jubilee Line was opened between Baker Street and Charing Cross in April 1979, the trains from Stanmore being diverted over it. There are now serious doubts about the completion of its planned extension to Lewisham via Docklands. There is obviously close interaction in terms of patronage between some of British Rail's inner London suburban services and London Transport's bus and underground services; for this reason it is necessary to be cautious in interpreting trends in patronage. However, it is evident that patronage of underground services has reached a 'plateau' in recent years, and it will be interesting to note whether the recent significant extensions to the system alter this situation. There is a limited underground rail system in Glasgow, while the first section of the new rapid-transit system in Newcastle upon Tyne (pp. 36, 59), in which high hopes are placed, was open in August 1980.[11]

Innovations in Local Public Transport

Recent years, then, have witnessed a more significant decline in local travel by bus than by rail. Rail services have benefited from having a separate way, from serving commuting over distances for which journey times by rail compare favourably with those by car, and from being based largely on commuting to city centres to which access by car has been made more difficult by traffic restraint. Innovations in public transport services, particularly in bus services, have been introduced to stem the decline in patronage. There is little evidence that they have had a significant effect but, equally, without them decline in patronage might have been more severe. Such innovations have affected fare levels, quality and type of services, and traffic restraint.

Innovations with fare levels have included maintenance of fares at the same level over a long period, fare reductions, the use of differentials between peak and off-peak fares, and the offer of the concessions through limited-period travel tickets purchased, in the main, 'off the vehicle'. Maintenance of fare levels is equivalent in real terms to a reduction in fares relative to other prices. The most recent general example was limitation of fare increases in the price restraint policies of the 1971–4 Heath administration. A specific example has been maintenance of fare levels by South Yorkshire County Council as part of their transport policy, which defied central-government policy that fares levels should increase at a faster rate than costs in order to reduce subsidies.[7] (pp. 36, 150) An example of reduced fares policy was the ill-fated initiative by the GLC in October 1981. The general evidence is that demand for off-peak services is more responsive to fare reductions than demand for peak services.[12] Differentials between peak and off-peak fares are an established characteristic of local rail services. Their basis is that the marginal cost of carrying off-peak passengers, when there is usually spare capacity on the system, is very small. They were used temporarily with bus services in the early years of the SELNEC (now Greater Manchester) Passenger Transport Executive with the objective of generating demand for off-peak services.[13]

There is increasing interest in offering fare concessions through limited-period travel tickets; examples are the Traveller, and (now withdrawn) Bus Economy Tickets, sold by Merseyside PTE, and the Saver Seven Tickets sold by Greater Manchester PTE. The main advantages to the passenger of these tickets is that unlimited local travel is made available at about the fare cost that the traveller is already paying; so, in real terms they represent a reduction in travel cost over all. Advantages for the operator are increased purchase of travel 'off-the-vehicle', which particularly helps one-man operation (OMO) of buses, as well as integration of bus and train services, and increased cash flow. Their main effect as regards patronage is in encouraging existing travellers to make fuller use of public transport facilities, rather than generating demand from new travellers. However, in the West Midlands PTE the use of such a facility with a significant fare reduction has generated considerable patronage for local rail services.

Concessionary fares for schoolchildren and old age pensioners (OAPs) should not be described as innovatory. However, they have become a serious subsidy consideration for bus services, particularly for OAPs, who in recent years not only have increased in number but also have benefited from a general recognition that they should enjoy improved social benefits. There is some concern that the costs of concessionary fares, which now can represent a considerable item in local transport budgets, are currently largely borne by local authorities and not by appropriate contral-government departments. It is also being argued that concession schemes should be standardised throughout the country; for example, there can be severe anomalies between schemes for OAPs operated by different district authorities in shire counties, compounded in this case by there not being a single public transport operating authority.[14]

The carriage of children to and from school is a major peak period capacity consideration for bus operators, particularly in the morning, when the commuting demand must also be served. There has been talk over the years of delaying school starting times to reduce this combined demand for bus services, but the constraints are such that little progress has been made. It is possible that totally comprehensive state education and falling school rolls will ameliorate the problem. But other factors, such as school size and integration on single campuses, not to mention problems of social and ethnic mix, could also be pertinent. Proposals in the 1980 Education Bill to remove the obligation of education authorities to provide the transport for pupils living more than a certain distance from school could have had significant consequences in rural areas, but did not survive its passage through Parliament.

Fare levels represent only part of service quality. Equally important are such factors are frequency, reliability and punctuality, not to mention the general condition of rolling stock and other facilities, and accessibility to the public transport system. In recent years these other factors have become major considerations for local bus services, in order to offset the harmful effects of traffic congestion. Introduction in recent years of OMO to save labour costs has compounded these problems, because it has resulted in longer 'stop' times for fare collection, while implementation of bus priority schemes has been generally too piecemeal for significant improvements in patronage. There has only been limited progress in improving service performance through monitoring by radio. There is some evidence that off-peak demand for bus services is more sensitive than peak demand to service frequency, possibly because off-peak frequency is generally so much lower anyway.[12] In practical terms an advantage of increasing off-peak frequency to boost patronage is that it could be done without calling for an increase in overall fleet size. However, such measures should generate sufficient revenue to cover additional labour and other marginal costs.

Increased patronage of peak period bus services depends on reduction in traffic congestion which critically affects quality of service. It is very difficult, however, to see how such reductions can be obtained, given the limited capacity of the existing road system. The implications for patronage of separate ways for buses, as at Runcorn New Town, seemingly a logical solution to the problem, are not quite clear, because the evidence to date indicates that improved service performance has not resulted in significant transfers of car travellers to the bus system, partly because release of road space by buses on the general road system has made travel by car more attractive.[15]

Improvements in components of service levels other than fares have not been of the same concern for local rail travel, mainly because rail systems enjoy the benefit of their own right of way. A distinction should be made between improvements in journey times achieved through higher operating speeds and reducing the number of stations served by particular services, and service improvements through increased frequency. It is principally commuting services in the South East, where journeys can be long, that have benefited from higher operating speeds. Electrification of services into Euston, Liverpool Street and Fenchurch Street Stations in the mid-1960s resulted in significant improvements in journey times, and contributed to the large increase in rail-commuting into London between 1966 and 1971. It is also possible that the superior punctuality and cleanliness of electric rolling stock contributed to the increase in patronage. However, a severe constraint on increasing commuting by rail at present is a need to refurbish a large part of EMU and particularly DMU rolling stock. This is regarded as difficult in a financial situation where heavy subsidies are required to maintain services, as, for example, in all the principal areas of rail commuting, and in a market which for social reasons is not suitable for an aggressive pricing policy. Most rail commuting is on local services. However, wider introduction of the High Speed Train (HST), and introduction of the Advanced Passenger Train (APT), will widen the catchment area of people who for reasons of journey time alone can contemplate longer-distance commuting.[16]

There have been many innovations in types of public transport services. These include: 'bus and ride', 'kiss and ride', and 'park and ride' facilities at suburban railway stations; city-centre bus services, often linking railway stations; 'park and ride' bus services; 'dial a ride'; and rural transport experiments. There is little evidence that any of these innovations have resulted in significant transfers from travel by car to travel by public transport. The main effects are changes in existing patterns of travel by public transport for facilities at suburban railway stations, and generation of new off-peak travel for 'park and ride' bus services, 'dial a ride', and rural transport experiments.[17, 18, 19] Traffic restraint has not generally yet been applied rigorously in this country to halt the decline in public transport patronage. A comprehensive traffic management in Oxford resulted in increased patronage of bus services in 1974.[6] However, the Nottingham 'zone and collar' traffic scheme, albeit applied only to one sector of the city, was unsuccessful in gaining patronage from car commuters.[20] It is likely that more rigorous traffic restraint will have most success in increasing patronage of public transport in London, on account of such factors as longer commuting distances and more limited road capacity.[21]

Non-local Travel

This takes place in many ways by public transport: by scheduled services; by private hire; by excursions on coach and train services; by contract on coach and air services; and by charter air services. Travel by rail and air in the United Kingdom is mainly by scheduled services, although travel at reduced fares is possible on these. However, travel by other than scheduled services is very important for coach travel; for example, excursions and tours, and private hire and contract work, are the most buoyant parts of the bus travel market.

The structure of non-local public passenger transport has been described in chapter 2. Section 2.3.3 deals with express bus services, section 2.5.1 with rail passenger traffic, and section 2.6.1 with domestic air services.

The relative importance of different modes of transport in non-local travel has already been indicated. Travel by car retains its dominance for longer journeys, rail transport become more important, and travel by air becomes significant over the longest distances. However, market shares on particular routes can vary considerably from this general picture; for example, market shares for travel between London and Manchester in 1968 were estimated at 37.5 per cent for car, 50.0 per cent for rail, 3.1 per cent for bus, and 9.4 per cent for air.[22] More recent data from the Long-distance travel surveys over the 1974—7 period show the market shares between Greater Manchester County and the London

Metropolitan Area as, car 43 per cent, rail 38 per cent, bus 13 per cent and air 6 per cent; so, with necessary reservations on account of differences in definition of catchment areas, the relative importance of the different modes has possibly changed to favour travel by car and by bus at the expense of travel by train and by air.

General indications are that travel by inter-city rail services has been increasing significantly, travel by express bus services has declined, while travel by domestic air services has reached a fairly steady level after increasing very significantly up until the mid-1960s. However, it is necessary to qualify such general indications.

The inter-city rail market varies quite considerably in terms of quality of service, with important distinctions between electric and diesel-hauled services. and between London and non-London based services. The BRB in their planning policy have emphasised the revenue-earning capacity of increased speed, which has led to concentration on 100 mph electric-hauled West Coast Route services and Deltic diesel-hauled East Coast Route services.[16] APT services were to be introduced on the West Coast Route in 1981/2, while HST services were introduced on the East Coast Route in 1978, having been in scheduled operation on Western Region services between Paddington and South Wales. There has also been an emphasis on frequency of service, with, for example, at least hourly services between London and most provincial cities, and on 'all-class' trains, unlike the Continent where premium services are common. Not surprisingly, then, the highest London-based flows are of the order ten times the magnitude of the highest non-London-based flows, a situation which has a bearing on British Rail's inter-city fares policy of changing what the market can reasonably bear, with unit fares on London-based routes generally much higher than on non-London-based routes. The latest development in pricing policy has been to compete with the longer-distance coach travel market by offering concessionary fares to groups, like OAPs and students, which traditionally have travelled by coach, a good example of the application of marginal cost pricing by British Rail to maximise revenue; for example, travel by express bus services declined very significantly in 1977 and 1978 with the introduction of these concessions.

Major London-based flows are those connected with long-distance commuting into London (Brighton 1.63 million journeys in 1973, Oxford 0.74 million, Cambridge 0.71 million, Colchester 0.64 million), or with travel to and from the major provincial centres (Birmingham 1.26 million journeys in 1973, Manchester 0.94 million, Liverpool 0.71 million, Glasgow 0.28 million). Non-London-based flows show important links between major provincial centres (Birmingham—Manchester, 0.15 million journeys in 1973), or more locally (Manchester—Leeds, 0.22 million, Darlington—Newcastle upon Tyne 0.21 million).

A major effect of reduced journey times has been generation of new travel; for example, extension of electrification of the West Coast Route to Glasgow in 1974 resulted in a 50 per cent increase in London traffic, 10 per cent diverted from air travel and mainly first-class passengers, and 40 per cent new traffic and largely second-class passengers. Attracting traffic from other modes is then an important if not necessarily major effect of improved quality of service. The earlier electrification of the West Coast Route in 1966 reduced significantly the importance of Birmingham Airport for domestic flights to London, and made inroads into the Manchester to London air-travel market.[23] On the other hand, introduction of 'air-shuttle' services between London and Glasgow and London and Manchester has captured some of the rail market on those routes. Travel by car is a potential market for rail travel in as much as a small decrease in such a large market would result in a very significant increase in rail travel. Even though rail travel cannot compete so well in terms of accessibility, it can offer more comfort and less travel stress, two factors which are emphasised in marketing travel by rail.

Journeys by express bus services declined some 41 per cent in Great Britain over the 1968—78 period, from 74 to 44 million journeys per year. This decline was greater than that for bus services over all, 29 per cent, and for stage carriage services, 32 per cent, over the same period, and has taken place at a faster rate recently with the wider introduction of concessionary fares by British Rail. Previously there was only limited competition between inter-city rail and bus services because they tended to serve quite different markets; rail services generally served passengers who valued travel time highly, while express bus services served those for whom fare cost was a major consideration. It is unlikely that travel by express bus will offer major competition to rail services for long-distance travel to London, because not only is the rail service level much superior, but also further improvements are expected through introduction of HST and APT services. In contrast, with the motorway network substantially completed, travel by express bus will not be able to enjoy comparable savings in journey time. However, express bus services provide sterner competition for non-London-based rail traffic, particularly over shorter distances where the journey time advantage of rail services is at a minimum.

Domestic air services increased their traffic considerably to the mid-1960s, with 527 000 passengers in 1951, 2 834 000 passengers in 1961 and 5 123 000 passengers in 1966. Thereafter, traffic increased to 6 513 000 passengers in 1973, but declined to 5 755 000 in 1975 with the effects of the 1974 oil price increases and the related economic recession; it has subsequently increased again to around the 1973 level. Market shares are greatest over longer distances; for example, London—Manchester around 10 per cent, and London—Glasgow around 40 per cent.

Heathrow is the major airport, with some 3.1 million domestic traffic passengers in 1974, followed by Glasgow (1.4 million), Manchester (773 thousand), Edinburgh (734 thousand), Gatwick (676 thousand) and Newcastle (357 thousand).[24] This is predominantly scheduled traffic, fairly evenly divided in volume between London and non-London-based routes; but London dominates the pattern of these movements. The main airports for services to and from London are Glasgow, which had some 821 thousand passengers on these services in 1974, Edinburgh (577 thousand), Manchester (398 thousand) and Newcastle upon Tyne (255 thousand).

Domestic air services are in a similiar situation to express bus services in that, unlike rail services, they cannot look to technological development to provide competitive advantage. Introduction of 'short take-off and landing' (STOL), and 'vertical take-off and landing' (VTOL) aircraft on commercial routes might make it possible to site airports nearer to urban centres and so shorten access time, a critical factor in domestic air travel. However, while these developments are distant prospects, air transport must rely on other means to expand markets, such as easier booking facilities and more frequent services, as exemplified in 'air shuttle' services.

3.3 Trends in International Passenger Transport

International passenger traffic to and from the United Kingdom has grown at a very fast rate; for example, total movements increased from some 25.2 million in 1968 to some 59 million in 1978. Air travel has made the major contribution to this large increase in international travel, reflecting particularly the increasing popularity of charter holidays; for example, movements by air increased from 15.7 million in 1968 to 38.8 million in 1978, some 147 per cent, while those by sea increased from 9.5 million to 19.9 million, some 109 per cent. The increase in international air travel has been quite remarkable; for example, in 1951 it amounted to some 1.6 million movements. However, the total of some 59 million international passenger movements in 1978 is very modest compared with the 50 000 million or so domestic journeys being made annually at this time.

The main purposes of international travel are holidays, business, and visits to friends and relatives. Holidays account for the greatest proportion, both for visits to the United Kingdom by overseas visitors and visits abroad by UK residents. These two groups use air and sea travel in similar proportions; for example, in 1978, 60 per cent of overseas visitors left the United Kingdom by air, while 62 per cent of UK residents travelling abroad went by air. However, a very significant distinction between the two groups is the large proportion, some 58 per cent in 1978, of UK holiday makers going abroad on inclusive tours. This emphasis on holiday travel results in marked seasonality in international travel, an important reason for the growth in charter air traffic; for example, in 1978, 40 per cent of the visits abroad by UK residents were in the third quarter. Air travel is even more common for business visits.[25]

3.3.1 Air Travel

The structure of air transport in the United Kingdom has been described in section 2.6. International air travel is dominated by movements to and from the European continent and Mediterranean Sea area; for example, these areas accounted for 67 per cent of passenger movements by air in 1978. The principal countries involved in this traffic are Spain, France, Germany and Italy; for example, Spain accounted for some 14 per cent of all movements by air to and from the United Kingdom in 1978, a large part of which were on charter flights. Spain has maintained this dominance over the past decade, but air travel to more distant destinations in the European continent and the Mediterranean Sea area, such as Norway and Sweden, Portugal, Yugoslavia and Greece, Middle East countries, and the Communist Bloc, has expanded significantly.

This dominance of the European continent and the Mediterranean Sea area has been slightly eased over the past decade by faster increases in air travel between the United Kingdom and other parts of the world. Major interchange is with the United States, which accounted for some 13 per cent of all passenger movements by air to and from the United Kingdom in 1978, a comparable total to that of Spain. However, traffic to and from the United States has increased at a faster rate. Air traffic has increased at even faster rates between the United Kingdom and Australasia, South Africa, West Africa, the West Indies, the Indian sub-continent, Japan, and other parts of the Far East such as Singapore and Hong Kong.

The increasing importance of air travel to more distant countries, not only in Europe but also in the world generally, reflects two main factors: firstly, economic growth has resulted in more business travel and an increase in disposable income for expenditure on personal travel; secondly, this increased expenditure on personal travel has created suitable conditions for provision of lower-cost air travel, which has resulted in further expansion of air travel markets. Not surprisingly, travel by charter air services has expanded significantly, and conditions have been right for the introduction of unconventional scheduled services, such as the former Laker Skytrain services to the United States.

Heathrow Airport is a dominant element in the patterns of air travel. Heavy traffic growth has taken place, like that for international air travel generally: 5.6 million passengers in 1960–61, 15.7 million in 1970–71, and 27 million in 1978–9. It is interesting to compare this last figure with traffic levels at other major airports in the world in 1978 – Paris (Charles de Gaulle) 9 million, Amsterdam 9 million, Frankfurt 15 million, New York (John F. Kennedy) 25 million, Los Angeles 33 million, Atlanta 37 million, Chicago (O'Hare) 49 million. The data for these American airports understate the importance of Heathrow for international movements, because they reflect large domestic traffic movements, particularly at O'Hare. The capacity of Heathrow will be 38 million passengers per year when the fourth terminal is built. The limitation of this figure in the light of historical traffic growth, and the relatively small additional capacity that would be gained by concentrating regional international traffic at regional airports, has forced the government to seriously consider the need for additional airport capacity in the London area.[26] The geographical distribution of air travel to and from Heathrow follows that indicated for international air travel to and from the United Kingdom generally, with Europe dominant with 12.8 million terminal passengers in 1978–9, followed by North America (4.5 million), Asia (3.6 million), Africa (1.3 million) and Central and South America (0.5 million). Major traffic flows in 1978–9 were: Paris (Charles de Gaulle), 6.5 per cent of total terminal passengers; Amsterdam, 3.7 per cent; New York (John F. Kennedy), 3.6 per cent; Dublin, 3.5 per cent; and Glasgow, 2.8 per cent. These flows emphasise the European, North American and domestic connections of Heathrow. They also illustrate the potential impact of a Channel Tunnel on air traffic between the United Kingdom and nearer European centres.[27]

Even though Heathrow is the dominant airport in the United Kingdom in the pattern of air transport movements, an important trend in recent years has been for much faster expansion in traffic at Gatwick Airport. There are three main reasons for this: firstly, a deliberate policy on the part of the UK government to direct traffic to Gatwick from Heathrow – for example, charter movements, a very minor part of total movements, have declined significantly in recent years at Heathrow; secondly, expansion of the activities of the United Kingdom's second force airline, British Caledonian, at Gatwick; and thirdly, continuing expansion of charter movements. The latter make a significant distinciton between air traffic growth at Heathrow and other UK airports in general; in fact, a major role of UK regional airports is to provide for air charter operations, mainly in relation to inclusive holiday traffic.

3.3.2 Travel by Sea

International travel by sea is dominated by movements to and from the European continent and Mediterranean area, mainly on short sea crossings between England and the European mainland; for example, these movements accounted for 17.4 million (88 per cent) out of a total of 19.8 million in 1978. In comparison, movements to and from the Irish Republic at 2.3 million in 1978 are modest, while movements to the rest of the world are negligible; this last fact illustrates the supremacy of air transport in long-distance international travel.

So, international sea travel is largely by ferry on the shortest sea crossings to Western European countries and to the Irish Republic. This arrangement generates considerable inter-regional travel in the United Kingdom, particularly by road. From this viewpoint, the regions are less accessible for international travel by sea than by air, despite the shortcomings of international services at regional airports; one reason air transport is more important for business travel. Ferries carry car and coach traffic, other passenger traffic, and commercial vehicles. In some cases they are operated in conjunction with special inter-city rail services, like those between London and Dover, and London and Holyhead, and to and from Harwich. British Rail with its 'Sealink' services, together with independent companies, operate ferry services. These include hovercraft ferry services across the English Channel from Dover to Boulogne, and Ramsgate to Calais, which now account for some 10 per cent of occupied cars carried on ferry services. The most recent development in ferry services are jetfoil services between Dover and Ostend, Brighton and Dieppe, and Liverpool and Dublin. Exceptions to this general picture of ferry services are very modest movements by ocean liners on scheduled services and cruises, the former principally out of Southampton.

Dover is the busiest port with some 7.1 million passengers in 1976; it is followed by Harwich with some 1.6 million passengers, Folkestone with some 1.5 million, and Southampton with some 1 million. However, traffic growth has been uneven at ports handling European traffic; high traffic growth has taken place with Northern European traffic at Hull, at Ramsgate with its new hovercraft facilities at Ebbsfleet and at Folkestone; average growth has taken place at Dover, which also has hovercraft facilities, and at Harwich. Low traffic growth has taken place at Southampton, partly because of increasing competition from ferry services at Portsmouth, at Newhaven which has Sealink Services to Dieppe, and at Tynemouth. London has suffered a severe decline as a ferry port.

This dominance of ferry ports in South East England for travel to Europe is also reflected in the patterns of accompanied passenger vehicle traffic; this amounted to some 3.3 million vehicles in 1978, with Dover alone accounting for 1.1 million, and hovercraft services at Dover and Ramsgate some 0.3 million.

Travel by sea to and from the Irish Republic has increased over the past three years, after some years with a static market. The main port is Holyhead, followed by Liverpool, Fishguard and Pembroke Dock. A recent development has been the introduction of a jetfoil ferry service between Liverpool and Dublin. Traffic levels are being maintained at Liverpool; but significant decline has taken place at Holyhead and Fishguard, partly at the latter through diversion of traffic to new services established at Swansea and later transferred to Pembroke Dock which have enjoyed a significant growth in traffic.

As previously indicated, other international travel by sea is negligible. Southampton is the major port concerned, with other small contributions from London and Liverpool. In addition, the 1970s have witnessed some 100 000 to 200 000 passengers departing on cruises each year from these ports.

3.4 Trends in Domestic Freight Transport

As shown already in chapter 2, the main modes of domestic freight transport are road, rail, coastal shipping, inland waterways and pipelines.[28] Since the Second World War, freight transport has grown at a similar rate to the economy as a whole, a relationship observed in several countries.[29] So its growth has been significantly less than that for domestic passenger travel, but as for the latter, road transport is the dominant mode.

In terms of goods lifted, total demand for domestic freight has declined slightly; for example, some 1807 million tonnes of freight were lifted in Great Britain in 1978; the corresponding level in 1968 was some 2009 million tonnes. This decline was largely experienced by the road-haulage sector, an important explanation being the weakening industrial base of the country, particularly for heavy industry. However, road transport was still accounting for some 83 per cent of goods lifted in 1978, compared with some 85 per cent in 1968. Over this period, freight transport by pipeline showed the only significant increase in terms of goods lifted.

However, in terms of goods moved, domestic freight transport has tended to expand with the economy as a whole, as previously indicated. This implies that such growth has depended upon freight being moved over greater distances over all; for example, domestic freight transport amounted to some 142 thousand million tonne-km in Great Britain in 1976, but some 124 thousand million tonne-km in 1966. On this basis, road transport has steadily increased in dominance both absolutely and relatively, and accounted for some 67 per cent of freight transport in 1976.

3.4.1 Road Transport

The structure of the road haulage industry has been described in section 2.4. As just indicated, road transport has steadily increased its dominance of domestic freight movement.[30] However, as for the large increase in domestic passenger travel by car, this increasing dominance has been brought about mainly by serving new demands rather than gaining traffics from other modes of transport. Even so, this increase in demand for road freight has not been paralleled by increases in lorry traffic because of a trend to use of larger vehicles.

Road freight is dominant over most sectors of the economy, and there are no signs of this situation changing significantly. It is particularly dominant in the food, drink and tobacco industries where in 1978 it accounted for some 97 per cent of freight movements. It is only in the transport of heavy materials in bulk that other modes of transport make significant contributions; for example, in 1978, road transport accounted for only some 26 per cent of the movement of coal and coke, and some 28 per cent of that of crude oil and petroleum products. Even so, road transport has made inroads in recent years into rail transport markets in building materials, timber and aggregates, chemicals and fertilisers, and iron and steel.

3.4.2 Rail Freight

In terms of goods lifted, rail transport is the second most important mode of freight transport in the United Kingdom, although the overall trend is one of slowly diminishing importance; for example, it accounted for some 10.5 per cent of goods lifted in 1968 and some 9.5 per cent in 1978.

However, greater emphasis on longer hauls increases its importance on a 'goods moved' basis, on which it accounted for some 14 per cent of domestic freight movements in 1978, a contribution very similar to that of coastal shipping.

The freight operations of British Rail have previously been described in section 2.5.2. Freight traffics were at a peak just before the First World War, with some 427 million tonnes carried in 1900 and some 516 million tonnes in 1910. Thereafter they have declined, with the exception of minor temporary increases in traffics during the Second World War years and at the turn of the 1950s, the latter reflecting as increase in the carriage of coal and coke, until in 1978 some 170 million tonnes were being carried.

Coal and coke is the most important single commodity in tonnage terms carried by rail freight. It accounted for some 94 million tonnes of goods lifted in 1978, much in merry-go-round operations between coal mines and power stations. Therefore, it is not surprising that the fortunes of rail freight have been mirrored to date in those of this commodity.

Iron and steel is the next major commodity carried in tonnage terms; it accounted for some 25 million tonnes of freight lifted in 1978, with an important element being transport of iron ore between Immingham and Scunthorpe and Port Talbot and Llanwern in special trains. Thus, British Rail's revenue from freight operations is very sensitive to trends in these major industries, as present rationalisation of the British Steel Corporation illustrates. On the positive side, increasing coal-burn for electricity generation for the remainder of this century, providing coal prices remain competitive, should increase coal traffics, particularly as potential coal fields such as Belvoir are slightly more distant from existing coal-burning power stations.

British Rail has followed a policy in the 1970s of trying to reduce its dependence upon these two traffics by expansion of other trainload and wagonload traffics.[31] These accounted for some 44 million tonnes of freight carried in 1978, with important commodities being earths and stones at some 15 million tonnes, and oil and petroleum at some 17 million tonnes. However, even in this case, earnings are sensitive to wider trends in the economy as a whole, and traffics have fallen in tonnage terms with the slower economic expansion of the late 1970s; for example, other train/wagonload traffic amounted to some 42 million tonnes in 1968, reached a peak of some 53 million tonnes in 1973, but had fallen to some 44 million tonnes by 1978, as indicated.

Operations related to the activities of the National Freight Corporation are the final element of rail freight in the United Kingdom. National Carriers Limited use rail freight for trunk haul for less-than-wagonload traffic, although it has reduced its dependence on rail transport substantially in recent years. Freightliners Limited, which under the 1978 Transport Act has been returned to the full ownership of British Rail, is responsible for trainload movements of containers. These two traffics accounted for some 7 million tonnes of traffic in 1978.

Expansion of this container traffic has not developed to the potential envisaged in the mid-1960s. One important explanation is that additional traffic is more likely to amount to wagonloads rather than trainloads — this problem is discussed more fully in section 6.5. It is for such reasons that British Rail has developed its Speedlink services for less-than-trainload consignments; with ownership of Freightliners Limited restored to British Rail there is obvious potential for complementary development of these and Speedlink services.[32]

There are no significant trends in average length of haul for the major traffics carried by rail freight. Because of indirect cost and transfer cost penalties, rail freight becomes more competitive with road haulage with length of haul; it is over longer lengths of haul of unit loads that British Rail anticipates expansion of its share of the freight market. It may be that a Channel Tunnel will give rail freight a substantial advantage in this respect, particularly in connection with unit load roll-on-roll-off traffic; however, it is argued that a tunnel design capable of handling 'piggy-back' operations of road vehicles will simply result in transfer of roll-on goods traffic from ferry services, while a smaller-bore tunnel without this facility will result in minimal transfer from road to rail trunk-haul.

3.4.3 Coastal Shipping

The organisation of coastal shipping in the United Kingdom has already been described in section 2.7.3. Goods lifted by coastal shipping have not changed significantly in volume over the past decade; for example, they amounted to some 2.6 million tonnes in 1968 and some 3.0 million tonnes in 1978, some 3 per cent of all goods lifted in the United Kingdom. However, by virtue of the long hauls involved, this mode is of comparable importance with rail transport on a 'goods moved' basis as indicated.

Petroleum is the major commodity: it accounted for some 78 per cent of goods lifted in 1978. The trend is for petroleum to account for an increasing share of total traffics, and coal a decreasing proportion, even though there was a temporary decline in total traffics after the first OPEC price increases of 1974, and the onset of the related economic recession.

The major ports for inwards traffic in terms of weight of cargo handled in 1978 were London, Milford Haven and Liverpool; while Milford Haven, Forth, and Medway were the most important for outwards traffic. All these are major ports for foreign traffic, indicating its close links with coastwise shipping. So ports vary in their relative importance for inwards and outwards coastwise traffic. Milford Haven is important for both inwards and outwards movements of petroleum and petroleum products. However, in other cases, inwards coastwise traffic is dominant, as at Bristol, while in others, outwards coastwise traffic is dominant, as at Blythe, a major outlet for the Northumberland coalfield.

3.4.4 Inland Waterways

The organisation of inland waterways in the United Kingdom has been described in section 2.7.4. Its contribution to domestic freight transport is very modest. It accounted for some 0.3 per cent in 1978 of goods lifted and some 0.1 per cent of goods moved. Freight carried on British Waterways declined from some 11 million tonnes in 1955 to some 5 million tonnes in 1978, with the Aire and Calder Navigation accounting for about half of this. Other principal commercial waterways serve the Severn, Mersey, Humber, and Thames estuaries, all over relatively short lengths of haul, as suggested above by the much smaller contribution of inland waterways on a 'goods moved' than on a 'goods lifted' basis. Liquids in bulk and coal constitute a major proportion of cargoes.

The most significant expansion of the inland waterways system is taking place on the South Yorkshire Canal, This will allow craft of 700 tonnes to navigate to Mexborough, and of 400 tonnes beyond there to Rotherham. However, the British Waterways Board has a difficult task generally in persuading the Treasury that improvement schemes justify investment.

3.4.5 Pipelines

Freight moved by pipeline, already described in section 2.8, has increased very significantly: from some 32 million tonnes in 1968 to some 82 million tonnes in 1978, some 4.5 per cent of goods lifted. They carry either crude oil, such as the pipeline opened in 1977 from Anglesey to Stanlow, or petroleum products, such as those from Fawley to West London.

3.5 Trends in International Freight Transport

Freight transport makes a vital contribution to the role of the United Kingdom as a trading nation. Virtually all freight movements take place through ports in Great Britain; for example, these accounted for 97 per cent of all tonnage lifted in 1977, while ports in Northern Ireland, road transport across the boundary with the Irish Republic, and air transport accounted for 1 per cent, 1 per cent and 0.2 per cent, respectively. However, air transport is making an ever-increasing contribution in terms of value of overseas trade; for example, in 1978 it accounted for 17.6 per cent of imports by value and 19.7 per cent of exports;[33] Heathrow accounted for the largest proportion of visible trade by value in 1978 of all UK airports and seaports.

The foreign trade of the United Kingdom amounted to some 227 million tonnes in 1977; the 1721 million tonnes of freight lifted domestically that year in Great Britain provides a perspective for this.

3.5.1 International Seaborne Freight Transport

Trends in the visible trade of the United Kingdom have already been discussed in section 1.4.1, the importance of merchant shipping for invisible earnings in section 1.4.2, while the structure and organisation of UK seaports and shipping are described in sections 2.7.1 and 2.7.2, respectively.

Four important developments have taken place regarding trends in international freight transport by sea to and from the United Kingdom

    (1) changes in the relative importance of commodities carried in foreign trade;

    (2) changes in the relative importance of trading partner countries;

    (3) the increased use of containerisation and ro-ro facilities;

    (4) changes in the relative importance of different UK seaports.

There is, or course, a considerable interrelationship between these developments.

International seaborne freight has increased with the expansion of world trade. Until 1973 this was generally reflected in overall increases in tonnage handled by UK seaports. However, the beginning in 1974 or monopolistic action by the OPEC cartel in raising oil prices, slower economic growth which this action engendered, and the development of UK North Sea oil reserves, have together resulted in a significant reduction in the import of crude oil; for example, imports of tanker cargoes increased from some 100 million tonnes in 1967 to a peak of some 136 million tones in 1973; since then a steady decline has taken place, until in 1977 some 82 million tonnes were being imported. This reduction is reflected in a general decrease in the handling of petroleum at UK seaports, with the signficant exception of those directly connected with North Sea oil developments, such as Orkney, Forth, Tees and Hartlepool, and Grimsby and Immingham. This changed oil-supply situation has also resulted in a significant increase in export of tanker cargoes.

However, the general trend is still one of expansion for both exports and imports of dry cargoes, even though the economic recession of 1975–6 caused a temporary setback; for example, dry cargo exports amounted to some 24 million tonnes in 1967 and some 40 million tonnes in 1977, while imports amounted to some 67 million tonnes and some 76 million tonnes.

This increase in dry cargo imports is being accompanied by increasing dependence on transport in foreign registered vessels, while the reduced tanker imports and increased tanker exports have become more dependent on transport in UK registered ships, all with implications for invisible earnings, as previously discussed in section 1.4.2.

These increases in the tonnages of dry cargo imports and exports have been most significantly reflected in recent years in increased exports of foodstuffs, particularly to the other countries of the EEC, and in increased imports and exports of manufactured goods; the latter has already been discussed in terms of the visible trade of the United Kingdom in section 1.4.1.

These changes in the relative importance of different commodities have been accompanied by changes in the pattern of trade. This is well illustrated by reference to tanker cargo imports. Until 1974, increasing demand for petroleum made imports necessary from even more distant supplier countries; thus, between 1967 and 1974 imports of tanker cargoes to the United Kingdom increased some 36 per cent in tonnage terms, but by some 100 per cent in tonne-mileage terms. Subsequent slower expansion in the demand for oil together with exploitation of North Sea oil reserves has resulted in a very significant reduction in demand for tanker capacity, with attendant implications for shipbuilding as discussed in sections 1.1 and 1.2.2. Between 1972 and 1977, even though tanker cargo imports to the United Kingdom declined from some 128 million tonnes to some 82 million tonnes, their over all share between Near and Short Sea, and Deep Sea, origin countries did not change. However, for the former, imports of Norwegian oil increased at the expense of Libyan oil, while for Deep Sea supplier countries the proportion of oil from the Persian Gulf increased at the expense of the proportion from Nigeria and Venezuela; these last two countries, being nearer the United States than the Persian Gulf, having increasingly directed oil exports to the United States over this period.

The most significant development in patterns of trade for dry cargoes in the 1970s has been the increasing importance of trade with Near and Short Sea countries, and particularly the other countries of the EEC. The increasing importance of the latter is most makred for imports of dry cargoes, which reflects, of course, the developing imbalance on imports and exports of manufactured goods, discussed previously in section 1.4.1; for example, dry cargo exports increased from some 32 million tonnes in 1972 to some 40 million tonnes in 1977, with some 13 million tonnes (41 per cent) and some 20 million tonnes (49 per cent), respectively, destined for other EEC countries; dry cargo imports amounted to some 78 million tonnes in 1972 and some 76 million tonnes in 1977, with some 13 million tonnes (17 per cent) and some 22 million tonnes (28 per cent), respectively, originating from other EEC countries.

These trends of increases in tonnage terms in both the imports and exports of manufactured goods, of increases in the exports of foodstuffs, and of the increasing importance of Near and Short Sea countries, particularly other countries of the EEC, have all contributed to the increasing emphasis on containerisation and on ro-ro traffic in seaborne trade.[34, 35, 36, 37] ; for example, total container and roll-on-roll-off traffic increased from some 14 million tonnes in 1970 to some 34 million tonnes in 1978, with the fastest increase taking place in ro-ro services by road goods vehicles and trailers, as one would expect with the increasing importance of the Near and Short Sea trades.

The major ro-ro services are those provided by road goods vehicles and trailers, while the major special lift-on services are for containers of at least twenty feet in length. In comparison, ro-ro services in railway wagons are minor, accounting for some 902 thousand tonnes of freight in 1978, compared with the 13 249 thousand tonnes carried on road goods vehicles and trailers. Ro-ro services for railway wagons are operated at Dover and Harwich and have shown a tendency to increase in recent years.

All these developments have resulted in very significant changes in the relative importance of different seaports in the United Kingdom. The point has already been made that in 1978 Heathrow Airport handled the greatest value of visible trade of the United Kingdom. The other 'top' ports on this basis were, in descending order, Dover, London, Southampton, Liverpool, Felixstowe, Harwich, Hull, Immingham, and Milford Haven. Heathrow handled some 14.1 per cent of the visible trade of the United Kingdom, while Milford Haven handled some 1.7 per cent.

As the effects of the general decrease in the handling of petroleum since 1974 have already been discussed, further comment will be confined to dry cargoes.

Trends in the handling of dry cargoes in tonnage terms at UK seaports can be classified in several ways as follows.

(1) Dover is in a class of its own. Throughput has increased very significantly with a predominance of roll-on services by road goods vehicles/ trailers.

(2) Throughput at the traditional very large ports of London and Liverpool is in decline, more obviously so at Liverpool.

(3) Throughputs at smaller ports are tending to increase; good examples are Medway, Shoreham, Goole, Boston, King's Lynn and Great Yarmouth.

(4) Throughputs at ports on the West Coast are in general decline; the obvious exceptions are Holyhead with its traffic with the Irish Republic, and Fleetwood with its coastwise traffic with Northern Ireland.

(5) Throughputs at ports in Eastern Scotland and North-Eastern England show mixed trends: in some cases traffic is increasing, as at Grimsby and Immingham, and at Goole; in others it is fairly steady, as at Forth, and Tees and Hartlepool; while traffic is declining at Tyne and Hull.

(6) Throughputs are increasing at ports on the East and South coasts of England.

The most fundamental trend regarding UK seaports has been the increasing importance of Dover, Harwich, Felixstowe and Immingham, at the expense of the longer-established traditional ports of London, Liverpool, Southampton, Clyde, Hull, Forth, Manchester and Bristol. This change can be explained in terms of the increased importance of trading links with mainland Europe, the relative prosperity of the South and East of England, and the relative decline of the local industrial bases supporting these traditional ports. Other factors are labour relations, the importance of deep water facilities with the introduction of large specialised vessels, provision of special facilities for handling cargoes, and ease of road access.

It is sometimes argued that better labour relationships are an explanation for the increasing traffic throughputs at smaller ports. The success of Felixstowe is often ascribed to private ownership, although both Goole and Immingham, which are controlled by the British Transport Docks Board, have similar claims as ports where traffic has increased significantly. Provision of special handling facilities is increasingly a minor factor as it becomes imperative for ports to offer comprehensive facilities in order to compete for traffics.

There is little up-to-date information on mode of inland transport to and from ports. The Martech Report estimated that 56 per cent of imports were moved by road in 1964, 33 per cent by water and direct discharge, and 11 per cent by rail; while 75 per cent of exports were moved by road and 16 per cent by rail.[38] It is likely that the road mode has become even more dominant, particularly with expansion of unit load traffic.

British Rail has special freight services, connecting via Dover and Harwich to the Trans Europe Express Merchandise Network (TEEM), and via Holyhead to the Irish Republic. Obviously a key development regarding a greater role by British Rail in the handling of international freight is the Channel Tunnel project.[27] The main contribution of British Rail to international freight traffics is currently through services such as those for the British Steel Corporation in transporting iron ore between ports and steel works, as in the cases of Immingham and Scunthrope and Port Talbot and Llanwern, although the latter example is affected by the current rationalisation plans of the British Steel Corporation.

3.5.2 International Air Freight Transport

In terms of value of goods lifted, air freight has become very important in UK international freight traffic; for example, it accounted for some 6.1 per cent of exports by value in 1960 and some 4.6 per cent of imports; in 1978 the corresponding figures were 19.7 per cent and 17.6 per cent.[25]

In 1978, Heathrow accounted for 14.1 per cent of the visible trade by value of the United Kingdom, and some 76 per cent of visible trade by value through UK airports. In contrast, other airports had minor roles in the movements of air freight; for example, in 1978 Gatwick and Manchester were the next most important airports, accounting for some 4.4 and 3.1 per cent by value of visible trade through UK airports.

This concentration of air freight at Heathrow constrains expansion of air freight services at other UK airports. Therefore, trunking of freight by road to and from Heathrow over quite long distances is common; for example, even British Airways trunk haul freight by road between Manchester Airport and Heathrow.

Air freight is more sensitive to fuel costs than air travel. So, increasing fuel prices combined with slower expansion in world trade have constrained the expansion of air freight services in recent years. A further complication has been increased competition for air freight, between operators of all-freight services and operators of passenger services with freight capacity in very large aircraft. The latter have been content to see their freight revenues grow as a result of very competitive pricing, and so increase their cash flow in times of high cost inflation; one result has been declining profitability of all-freight air services.[39]

3.6 Transport Trends and Technological Change

It is fitting to conclude this chapter with a discussion of the importance of technological change for trends on transport. Technological change influences demand for physical movement in two main ways

(1) by reducing its unit costs
(2) by increasing the 'work' capacity of transport systems

Usually, but not always, these effects are interrelated.

A change in technology is a fundamental requirement for technological change. However, technological change is more likely if a change in technology is timely from the viewpoint of commercial application. Of course, it could be argued that changes in technology are likely to be timely, because there should be some relationship between research and development effort, and perception of the need for them, if the costs of research and development must be paid for by successful commercial exploitation. There are, of course, examples of changes in technology which are untimely from this viewpoint — perhaps it is no coincidence that they tend to take place outside the commercial world; for example, fuel cells were developed in university research long before they found their most important application in space exploration; national emergencies, especially war-time, have provided important impetes for significant developments in the technology of air transport and transport fuels.

The two most significant changes in technology in transport this century have been development of the internal combustion engine and the jet engine. The internal combustion engine, through the independent road vehicle, has been a major force for social change, with very significant effects on lifestyles in general and urban structure in particular. The low weight and high power/ weight ratio of the jet engine led to the very large revenue-earning capacity of aircraft now in use. Perhaps less important, but still significant, changes in technology have been the increased use of solid state electronics and computers in transport in recent years. These have made possible control of large complicated transport systems; examples are the British Rail Total Operations Processing System (TOPS) for controlling freight rolling stock, and passenger documentation systems in air transport. Further miniaturisation of electronics is obviously likely to have even further application in these areas.

The extent of technological change has varied between different transport systems. The most significant change in passenger travel has taken place in air transport. The history of civil aviation has been one of improvements in the revenue-earning capacity of successive generations of aircraft through increased speed and capacity; unit costs have fallen as a result, thereby helping to popularise air travel.[40] However, it has become more and more difficult to reduce unit costs in this way; possibly the onset of higher oil prices in 1974 was a watershed for these developments. This is a consideration which weighs quite heavily in decisions by aircraft manufacturers to build even larger sub-sonic aircraft.

Elsewhere in passenger travel technological change does not compare favourably with that which has taken place in air travel. For road transport the most significant technological development was the internal combustion engine at the beginning of this century. Thereafter, steady improvement of motor cars and buses has taken place in terms of reliability and average speed, but this improvement could not be described as significant; their passenger capacity has hardly changed.

Likewise, rail passenger transport systems have not changed significantly this century; again, development has been one of steady improvement. The Advanced Passenger Train and automatic train control on the London Underground are exceptions to this situation in the United Kingdom; however, neither is associated with increases in revenue-earning capacity like those achieved in air transport.

Technological change has been most significant over all for freight transport, with the most significant technological change having taken place in air transport and sea transport. Development of very large aircraft has provided a significant potential for air freight, not only on freight services but also on passenger services. Similarly, there has been a trend to very large merchant ships. However, specialisation has been more important in this case, with very large oil tankers, other large bulk carriers, and container ships. These developments have required complementary improvement of on-shore facilities for cargo handling.

Containerisation is a good example of timely technological change.[36] Expanding world trade in the late 1950s and 1960s, particularly in perishable agricultural produce and in manufactured goods, and increasing labour costs at ports, created suitable commercial conditions for investment in containerisation. The most significant aspect has been, of course, the increases in handling-capacity of berths.

Air transport and sea transport enjoy the advantage that their mediums have permitted the trend to very large craft, providing adequate handling facilities are available. Rail transport also offers these economies of scale, providing there is sufficient demand for rail freight; for example, merry-go-round operations between coalmines and power stations provide high capacity services in the United Kingdom, while very large capacity freight trains are used in mineral exploitation in other parts of the world.[41]

The main technological change, but not a significant one, in road haulage has been the trend to larger vehicles. However, the size of lorries is constrained by limitations on axle loading and considerations of road geometry. All road transport has enjoyed the benefit, in terms of operating speeds, of an expanded motorway and generally improved trunk road network in the United Kingdom. However, with investment in roads now being reduced, these benefits will be limited.

The most significant technological developments have taken place where transport markets have been expanding. Air and sea transport have generally satisfied this condition. Even hovercraft, and more recently jetfoils, have been introduced where demand was increasing for short sea ferry services to and from the United Kingdom, even though there are doubts about their commercial viability. In other words, market trends have warranted investment in more capacity, generally in the shape of larger craft.

By comparison, technological development in declining transport markets, such as local public passenger transport and rail transport, has not been as significant. The emphasis in these cases has been in using technological development to reduce costs of operation; examples are one-man operation on buses, automatic control and automatic signalling of rail systems, automatic track maintenance, the Total Operations Processing System for controlling rail freight rolling stock, and special high capacity trains such as those used in merry-go-round operation. Labour costs have generally been reduced by increasing overall productivity by higher capital investment.

Two interesting exceptions to these two classifications, in terms of trends in demand for different transport services, are travel by motor car and the Advanced Passenger Train.

Travel by motor car has expanded very greatly without significant technological development. The main explanation is that the motor car has apparently reached its potential in terms of passenger capacity, speed, acceleration, and range. It is only in terms of fuel consumption and emissions that it could be improved significantly; declining oil costs in real terms until 1974 was not a suitable climate for the former development. Manufacturers only now are becoming concerned with fuel consumption because it has become an important market factor; in addition, there is growing official concern from governments that motor cars should be more energy efficient. However, with oil prices barely increasing at the same rate as overall price inflation in the United Kingdom, there is still some uncertainty that demands for smaller or more fuel-efficient cars will become permanent.

Investment on the Advanced Passenger Train justifies Treasury investment criteria.[42] Demand for inter-city rail passenger travel is currently expanding, largely though as a result of concessionary-fares schemes rather than an increase in base load traffic. Even though Inter-City traffic makes a significant contribution to the indirect costs of British Rail's operations, it is reasonable to question whether it still enjoys an element of subsidy from the Public Service Obligation Grant, particularly in the pricing of these concessionary fares. In that case, perhaps the Advanced Passenger Train is an example of significant technological change taking place in an industry which is declining over all, because the intricate cost structure of rail transport makes it quite impossible to estimate with confidence the total costs of such a development.

There are many examples in transport of untimely technical innovation. Suggested solutions to the transport problems of cities include monorails, air-cushion vehicles propelled by gas turbines or linear inductance motors, magnetic-levitation vehicles, passenger capsules propelled by compressed air, and automatic taxi systems.[43] All these involve the high capital and disturbance costs of a separate way; with the exception of monorails they all represent advanced technology. They have not found general use for two main reasons: there is not in the developed world increasing demand for local public passenger transport; their capital and operating costs compare poorly with those of conventional systems.

The higher-speed performance of air-cushion and magnetic-levitation vehicles make them more suitable for application in long distance transport, but even in this case there is the very great problem of provision of a special track. The

French and the Japanese have made the greatest advances in this field. In the United Kingdom a magnetic-levitation surface access system is currently under construction at Birmingham Airport.

Finally, a comment is required about future technological change in transport. Possible future economic scenarios include slower economic growth and higher oil prices, conditions that will result in slower expansion in demand for transport, and therefore, if the previous hypothesis is true, less benign for technological change. However, against this must be balanced the eventual need of a new energy source for transport; in this context, road vehicles run on synthetic liquid hydrocarbon fuels, independent electric road vehicles, more rail electrification, trolley-buses, coal-fired and nuclear-powered merchant ships, hydrogen-fuelled aeroplanes, and even airships, are all possible developments. [44] However, these will most likely have to take place in a much more uncertain world; for that reason alone present systems will be replaced very slowly, particularly as no significant changes in technology are in sight. Substitution of physical movement by telecommunication might also play a role, although activities which could be affected are likely to be quite limited without significant changes in the social and economic structure of society. [45]

References

1. Transport Act 1947
2. National Road Traffic Forecasts, Department of Transport Memorandum (London, 1980)
3. Department of Transport, *National Travel Survey 1975/76* Report (HMSO, 1979)
4. D. Maltby, I. G. Monteath and K. A. Lawler, *Urban Transport Planning and Energy: A Quantitative Analysis of Energy Use*, University of Salford, Dept of Civil Engineering, Working Paper 3 (Salford, 1976)
5. *Long-distance Travel Survey: 1977/78* (Department of Transport, London, 1978)
6. 5p Peak Surcharge Sought by Oxford, *Motor Transport* (26 December 1975)
7. South Yorks Freeze Already Costs £1m, *Motor Transport* (14 November 1975)
8. D. Maltby, K. A. Lawler and I. G. Monteath, A Monitoring Study of Rail Commuting on Merseyside: 1974–76, *Traffic Engng Control*, **19** (1978) 278–82
9. S. R. Williams, P. R. White and P. Heels, The Exeter–Barnstaple Line: A Case for Improvement or Closure, *Modern Railways*, **33** (1976) 300–3
10. A. Godfrey, The North and West Route Today, *Modern Railways*, **35** (1978) 108–11
11. A. Eden, Metro Gets Moving, *Modern Railways*, **35** (1978) 412–16
12. P. H. Bly, The Effects of Fares on Bus Patronage. *Transport and Road Research Laboratory Report* 733 (Crowthorne, 1976)
13. W. J. Tyson, A Study of the Effects of Differential Bus Fares in Greater Manchester, *J. Chartered Inst. Transp.*, **37** (1975) 334–8

14. Half Fares for All Pensioners Plan, *Motor Transport* (7 October 1977)
15. R. A. Vincent, R. E. Layfield and M. D. Bardsley, Runcorn Busway Study, *Transport and Road Research Laboratory Report* 697 (Crowthorne, 1976)
16. J. G. Smith, Passenger Business Planning of the Inter-City Services, *Modern Railways*, **32** (1975) 440–42, 488–91
17. Dept of the Environment, *Merseyside Interchange Experiments – A Summary Report* (1975)
18. P. H. Martin, The Harlow Dial-a-Bus Experiment: Predicted and Observed Patronage, *Transport and Road Research Laboratory Report* SR 256 (Crowthorne, 1977)
19. Symposium on Unconventional Bus Services: Summaries of Papers and Discussions, *Transport and Road Research Laboratory Supplementary Report*, 336 (Crowthorne, 1977)
20. R. A. Vincent and R. E. Layfield, Nottingham Zones and Collar Study – Overall Assessment, *Transport and Road Research Laboratory Report* LR 805 (Crowthorne, 1977)
21. A. D. May, Supplementary Licensing: An Evaluation, *Traffic Engng Control*, **16** (1975) 162–7
22. Comparative Assessment of New Forms of Inter-City Transport, *Transport and Road Research Laboratory Report* SR 1 (Crowthorne, 1970)
23. A. W. Evans, Inter-City Travel and the London Midland Electrification, *J. Transp. econ. Pol.*, **3** (1969) 69–95
24. Department of Trade, *Airport Strategy for Great Britain*, Part 1: The London Area (1975), Part 2: The Regional Airports (1976) (HMSO)
25. *Trade and Industry* **37** (1979) 498–503
26. Dept of Trade, *Airports Policy*, Cmnd 7084 (HMSO, 1978)
27. Channel Tunnel Advisory Group, *Channel Tunnel and Alternative Cross-Channel Services* (HMSO, 1975)
28. P. J. Corcoran, A. J. Hitchcock and C. M. McMahon, Developments in Freight Transport, *Transport and Road Research Laboratory Supplementary Report* 580 (Crowthorne, 1980)
29. A. H. Tulpule, Trends in Transport of Freight in Great Britain, *Transport and Road Research Laboratory Report* LR 429 (Crowthorne, 1972)
30. M. A. Cundill and B. A. Shane, Trends in Road Goods Transport 1962–1977, *Transport and Road Research Laboratory Supplementary Report* 572 (Crowthorne, 1980)
31. G. F. Allen, The Rail Freight Offensive: Aggregates by Rail, *Modern Railways*, **35** (1978) 365–9
32. G. F. Allen, Rail Freight Presents Speedlink – But Still Wants Its Freightliners Back, *Modern Railways*, **34** (1977) 425–7
33. *Trade and Industry*, **36** (1979) 435
34. McKinsey & Co., *Containerisation: the Key to Low Cost Transportation*, a Report to the British Transport Docks Board (London, 1967)
35. Growth in Container Traffic at British Ports, *Commercial Motor* (29 January 1971)
36. G. van den Burg, *Containerisation* (Hutchinson, London, 1975)
37. Arthur D. Little Limited, *Transhipment in the Seventies: the Potential for the Transhipment of General Cargo Between the UK, the Continent*

and Scandinavia as Part of the Development of Container Operations, a Report to the National Ports Council (London, 1969)

38. Martech Consultants Limited, *Britain's Foreign Trade*, a Report to the Port of London Authority (London, 1966)
39. Cargo Airline Squeezed Out, *Transport* **1** (1980) 61–2
40. R. Miller and D. Sawers, *The Technical Development of Modern Aircraft*, (Routledge & Kegan Paul, London, 1968)
41. H. P. White, Transport Moves with Technology, *The Geographical Magazine*, **LI** (1979) 793–9
42. APT in Perspective, *Railway Gazette International*, **136** (1980) I–XXIV
43. A. P. Young, D. Maltby and T. Constantine, Urban Transit Systems, *Official Architecture and Planning*, **32** (1969) 1454–60
44. D. Maltby, Alternative Energy Sources for Land Transport, *Proceedings PTRC Summer Annual Meeting*, University of Warwick (1980)
45. J. M. Nilles *et al.*, *The Telecommunications–Transportation Trade-off*, (Wiley, New York, 1976)

4

Wider Relationships Between Transport and Socio-economic Activity

In the previous chapters we have examined the role of the transport industry in the national economy, the organisation of the transport system, and trends in recent years in the work done by the various transport modes. We turn now to an examination at a more local level of the reciprocal relationship between transport and social and economic activity.

4.1 The Reciprocal Relationship between Transport and Socio-economic Activity

Intuitively it is obvious there is a relationship between the level of transport provision on the one hand, and in the nature and distribution of economic and social activities on the other. But this relationship is not always direct, and there are a number of points to be taken into account.

(1) The provision of adequate transport facilities *permits* economic and social development, which would not otherwise be possible. But the provision does not *determine* that development, which depends on a combination, often complex, of favourable factors.[1]

The extensive iron ore deposits of the Hamersley Range (Western Australia) depended on the building of railways to the coast for their exploitation. But exploitation also depended on the demand for ore from the expanding Japanese steel industry. Kilembe copper mine, on the flanks of Mount Ruwenzon in Uganda, could not be brought into production until the completion of the Kampala–Kasese railway in 1956. But it was later closed because of the fall in world copper prices.

In the United Kingdom railways played a vital part in the nineteenth-century growth of successful seaside resorts such as Brighton, Blackpool and Bournemouth. But while a railway station was necessary for all resorts, there were rail-served resorts which were unsuccessful. We may cite the Kentish examples of Allhallows, Leysdown and Littlestone. Again, electrification of the Southern Railway's suburban network undoubtedly stimulated suburban growth.[2] The 1926 electrification in North West Kent led to an increase of population in Chislehurst and Sidcup UDC from 18 500 in that year to 61 700 in 1939. But over the period there were other favourable factors at work, including availability of land, falling building prices and ready availability of cheap mortgages.[3] But on the other hand, enforcement of the London Green Belt policy prevented equivalent post-war development along the electrified Swanley—Otford—Maidstone East line.

(2) Quality of service in terms of cost, time and convenience is more important than the mere provision of a line of transport. It was the very cheap excursion fares in the mid-nineteenth century that led to great increases in the numbers of factory workers and their families going on day and period trips to the seaside. It was low-cost season-ticket rates and increased train speeds and frequencies which encouraged long-distance commuting in the mid-twentieth century.

(3) The relationship between socio-economic activity and the provision of transport facilities is a reciprocal one. On the one hand the existence of such activity will generate a demand for transport; on the other hand the provision of facilities will affect the level and nature of the activity. By 1800 London and Birmingham had emerged as centres of commerce and industry, thus creating the demand to close the 179 km gap between them. By 1730 the road had been turnpiked, by 1805 there was direct canal communication, and in 1838 the London & Birmingham Railway was opened. These events further stimulated economic growth and consequently a continuing upgrading of the transport links. Thus, in 1959 the M1—M45 link was opened and improved again in 1970 with the completion of the M6, while in 1967 the railway had been electrified.

(4) The facilities offered by a line of communication are rarely static. Advances in technology lead to cost changes, and therefore to changes in activity and in the location of that activity. With the reduction in unit costs made possible by very large sea-going bulk carriers,[4] iron ore can be imported into Great Britain at lower cost than it can be obtained from the domestic fields. Thus the bulk of South Wales primary steel-making capacity is now concentrated on the two coastal plants at Port Talbot and Llanwern, both connected to the deep-water terminal at Port Talbot, although both these operations have been scaled down by the British Steel Corporation as part of its recent rationalisation measures. A century earlier there were numerous plants located near the ore in the Heads of the Valleys. In more recent times the steel plant at Corby (Northants), established in the 1930s to use nearby ore, became uncompetitive during the 1970s.

But, whatever has been said, the nature of transport provision must be one of the many factors which must be taken into account in making locational decisions. This is equally true whatever the scale of the decision, whether it is to establish a new steel plant, to enlarge or relocate an existing factory, or to purchase a new house.

4.2 Transport and Economic Development

It is possible to classify industrial/commercial activity as

(1) *Primary* — The production of food, raw materials and energy.
(2) *Secondary* — Manufacturing industry.
(3) *Tertiary* — The provision of services, including transport, wholesale
and retail distribution, banking, professional services, education, entertainment
and tourism.

4.2.1 Primary Activity

In the United Kingdom, primary industry includes the production of coal, oil
and gas (from the North Sea), and electricity. We can take as an example the
relationship between electricity production and distribution and transport.
Between 1955 and 1966 consumption of electricity more than doubled, and this
was expected to continue. The increase, however, flattened out during the
1970s.[5] It was, however, necessary to provide much additional generating
capacity. To achieve the potential economy of scale through the use of very
high capacity generating sets, much of this new capacity was in the form of
'Super Power Stations' of about 1500—2000 MW capacity. Since electricity
generation was now one of the few continuing outlets for coal, to protect the
latter industry it was decided by central government that these plants should
mainly be coal-fired. The consumption of each station would be about 5 million
tonnes annually.
Locational requirements were

(1) access to coal
(2) geographical relationship with the market
(3) access to very large quantities of water for cooling
(4) a considerable area of level, low-cost land

Many of these new stations are located along the River Trent between Rugeley
(Staffs) (1530 MW) and Cottam (Notts) (1940 MW)[6] at places where railways
from the coalfields cross the river. The stations are reasonably near the centre of
gravity of the market in the Midlands, and cooling water is readily available, as
was the land. It was in connection with these power stations that British Rail
evolved the merry-go-round (mgr) system.[7] This greatly reduced the tonne-km
costs of the line haul, and the terminal costs became the principal ones. These
are fixed irrespective of distance, and therefore, if other factors make it
worthwhile, stations could be located well away from the coalfields. Thus
mgr-fed power stations have been located at Fiddlers Ferry (Warrington) (1948
MW), supplied from Yorkshire pits, at Ironbridge (Salop) (1054 MW), supplied
from North Staffordshire, and at Didcot (1915 MW), supplied from South
Staffordshire and South Wales.
Oil-burning stations on the other hand were built near refineries, where there
was a ready local supply of fuel oil at lower cost than coal brought from a
distance. Thus, Pembroke (1960 MW) is located adjacent to the Milford Haven

group of refineries, while Littlebrook D (near Dartford) (1960 MW) is near the refineries on the Lower Thames.

Since the cost of transporting oil over long distances is lower than that of coal, not only because tonne-km costs are less, but also because a tonne of oil contains more energy than a tonne of coal, market-orientated power stations in remoter coastal locations are oil-burning: for example, at Plymouth (115 MW) and at Ballylumford (Northern Ireland) (1034 MW).

The influence of transport on agriculture has been equally profound, though often it is indirect. Two examples can be taken: (i) the production of liquid milk, and (ii) market garden crops.

Up to 1930, milk was transported to urban markets by rail, in churns. The churns were conveyed to local stations, either by the farmers themselves or by contractors. Production of liquid milk therefore tended to be confined to areas within easy reach of a railway station. With the establishment of the Milk Marketing Board in the 1930s, which was charged with the organisation of milk collection from the farms, collection was guaranteed from all farms, whatever their location. Since in the inter-war period milk was one of the few expanding sectors of the agricultural industry, it meant that even remoter upland farms now had a chance to supplement their incomes through the regular monthly milk cheque. It also meant that milking could begin later, as there was no longer the need to catch early trains. In many cases the routes of the collecting lorries are varied at intervals, so that the same farms are not always at the start of the round.

The development of bulk carriage has also reduced costs, and this enabled milk to be transported over long distances, such as from Appleby (Cumbria) to London. Transport in glass-lined tank vehicles was first introduced for trunk haulage by road or rail from factory to city bottling plants. But in the last few years collection from farms has been entirely switched to tanker lorry.

Prior to 1939, milk production in many parts of Northern Ireland could only be used in butter production. But with the establishment of roll-on-roll-off facilities on the Stranraer–Larne ferry in that year, and with the changed demand patterns of the war years, bulk transport of liquid milk began between factories at places such as Enniskillen and bottling plants in Glasgow.

The production of market-garden crops requires light soils, which warm up quickly in spring and allow an early harvest to take advantage of high prices on the early market. Because of the requirement for a minimum period between harvest and market, market gardening traditionally became market-oriented, being located on the outskirts of cities and large towns; for example, the Thanet Sands of North West Kent and the glasshouse belt of the Lea Valley (Essex). Remoter areas, such as the Vale of Evesham and North East Bedfordshire, were dependent on rail transport and therefore on proximity to stations. Ruth Gasson[8] has shown that with the development of road transport, which now conveys virtually the whole market-garden output, accessibility to market has become easy throughout lowland Britain. Market gardening has therefore tended to become more and more concentrated on the most suitable soils, irrespective of distance from markets.

On a larger historical scale, transport development broke down the need for self-sufficiency in the marginal uplands of the British Isles. Previously, the inhabitants were dependent on the crops they could raise, hence Dr Johnson's famous definition of oats as food for men in Scotland and horses in England. The uplands of much of Britain are unsuited for arable crops, but well suited to grass and the production of store cattle and sheep for fattening in the lowlands. Thus, in many of the more marginal areas no arable crops at all are now grown.

4.2.2 Secondary Activity

For an assessment of the relationship between transport and manufacturing industry we can divide the latter into heavy and light.

Heavy Industry

For a case study of transport and heavy industry, we can select *cement manufacture*. Heavy industry may be defined as manufacturing industry in which capital investment per worker is high, as is the proportion of total costs of the end product represented by the cost of raw materials. Loss in weight of raw materials during the manufacturing process is also normally high. For all these reasons transport costs tend to be a higher proportion of total costs than in light industries. Heavy industry includes primary steel production, oil refining, heavy chemicals, and brick making.

Cement is a bulky commodity with a low value/weight ratio. The raw materials, limestone and clay, with smaller quantities of gypsum, are comparatively restricted in occurrence, and large quantities of fuel (coal or oil) are needed per unit of output. On the other hand it has a nationwide market in the building, construction and civil-engineering industries. Transport costs therefore loom large in costs of manufacture and distribution.

By 1966, 65 per cent of the output was delivered in bulk to the final point of consumption. The remaining 35 per cent was delivered in bags from distribution depots, to which it was forwarded in bulk from the manufacturing plants. In that year 16.5 million tonnes were produced from forty-seven plants in the United Kingdom. Only two of these were supplied with raw materials from any long distance — by slurry pipeline (p. 75). Twenty-seven plants were located on chalk outcrops in the South East, particularly on Thamesside (both North and South banks). Much of the movement was therefore from these, where there was a surplus of production over the Greater London market demand, to distribution depots in the Midland and the North. Otherwise, movement was normally from plant to distribution depot in the nearest large city.

With the development of bulk handling, rail costs have been reduced, so this mode can compete with coastal shipping on long hauls, and with road on short. There were thus trainload movements from Cliffe (Kent) to Uddingston (Strathclyde), some 700 km, at one end of the scale, and from Pitstone (Herts) to King's Cross, 55 km, and Hope (Derbyshire) to Northenden (Manchester) , 36 km, at the other. The majority of the depots were supplied by rail, but two were wholly, and one partly, supplied by road, and two, at Leith and in the Isle of Wight, by coaster.

In the decade after 1966 there have been few major changes in this pattern of distribution. A new plant at Dunbar now supplies by rail all four distribution depots in Scotland. The regular long-distance movement from Cliffe is now therefore intermittent, being confined to times of maximum demand. As with heavy industries, such as steel-making and oil-refining, economies of scale can be obtained from larger plants, and these can be traded-off against the costs of the extra tonne-km involved in distributing the finished product. In 1970 a new cement plant with an annual capacity of 4 million tonnes went on stream at Northfleet (Kent), replacing all the pre-existing Associated Portland Cement Manufacturers plants in the area. Clay is supplied by 11.2 km of pipeline under the Thames from Ockenden (Essex) to Swanscombe, where it is mixed with locally obtained chalk and pumped a further 4.8 km to the plant. Some one million tonnes of coal is brought in annually from Welbeck and other East Midlands collieries by 14 block-mgr trains weekly, each with a 1264 tonne payload. About 240 000 tonnes of gypsum is railed from Mountfield (near Hastings) in 9 trains a week, with 660 tonne payloads. Outward, about 1.5 million tonnes of cement is railed to distribution depots, the other 2.5 million being distributed locally in South London and Kent by lorry, mainly in bulk.[9] About 53 loaded trains are therefore required weekly. Since they are of specialised wagons, an equal number of balancing empty trains are also run. These 106 freight trains a week to and from the plant must be integrated with the service, on a line with a heavy freight service to and from other industrial plants and an intensive passenger service with an off-peak frequency of six trains an hour each way. Some 350 loaded lorries also leave the plant daily onto an already congested road network.

Light Industry

One of the main features of British industry since 1920 has been the growth of light industry, especially those producing consumer durables. Light industries are characterised by smaller inputs of raw materials and energy in relation to the output of finished goods, whether measured in value or volume terms. Transport costs are thus a much smaller component of total costs than in heavy industries. In many cases these costs are less than 5 per cent of total costs, so that even dramatic change in transport costs have only minor consequences on total costs of the finished product at the point of consumption. Finally, there is normally less opportunity for scale economies, and plants therefore tend to be smaller, while power is from electricity and gas. Location in relation to supply of raw materials and energy, and of access to markets, is of much less importance to light industries, and these are termed *footloose*.[10]

Thus, the total demand for transport by each plant is less in terms of tonne-km per unit of output than that of plants engaged in heavy industry. But light industry is now such an important sector of British industry, so widespread, and plants so numerous, that the aggregate demand for transport is considerable. It is no coincidence that the period that has seen the growth of light industry also saw the establishment and expansion of the road-haulage industry. Because of the flexibility of this mode and of its economic characteristics (that is, low unit costs in small-scale operation, but lack of scale economies), it is an ideal mode for the handling of complex, but small-scale traffic-flows from a multitude of origins to an even greater multitude of destinations.

As these patterns are so complex and the data needed to simulate them so costly to obtain, analysis is much more difficult than with the simpler patterns of transport for heavy industry. Particularly lacking are details of origins and destination. It is of little use knowing how many lorries pass a check-point without knowing where they come from, where they are going to, and what commodities they are carrying.

Transport and the Motor Vehicles Industry of the West Midlands: a Case Study   The few large final assembly plants are located on the outskirts of Birmingham and Coventry. These depend on the numerous component plants scattered through the region. These in turn depend for their supplies on even more numerous, often small-scale, metal-working plants producing screws, washers, and so on.

There was only one integrated primary-steel plant in the West Midlands (at Bilston, closed in 1978) and two large producers of semi-finished steel from ingots obtained from elsewhere. There is thus a considerable deficiency in the supply of raw materials, coiled steel sheet, steel bars and billets, and non-ferrous sheets and bars. These are concentrated on the West Midlands from all parts of the country by lorry and block train. In 1965 individual wagonloads of steel were railed to 150 depots and private sidings, usually for onward delivery by road. In that year the number of public terminals was reduced to 9, directly served by 14 block trains daily from the steel plants. There are now 6 of these terminals.

Transfer between plants of the semi-finished products is by road, the movements being both very numerous and requiring careful planning. Inventory investment is reduced by the elimination of as much stock as possible held at the receiving plant, but to achieve this requires regular and punctual deliveries. Here the flexibility of road haulage can be exploited to maximum advantage. Many firms operate their own fleets or hire them exclusively on long-term contracts, so they can retain full control over scheduling. Others use instead, or additionally, British Road Services or private hauliers.

When, during the 1950s, the motor industry wished to expand, it was forced by the government to build new plants in development areas. British Leyland still operate such a plant in Central Scotland at Bathgate, while the Rootes Group plant at Linwood, now owned by Talbot, was closed in 1981. Such plants were usually connected with the parent plants by road and rail services.

Finished vehicles are distributed on their own wheels, by transporter lorry, or by rail. In general, the mode used depends on distance and volume. If the latter is sufficient, rates are low for trainload consignments. Railheads have been established at King's Norton, Dorridge, and Tyseley.

The West Midlands metal industries also produce a vast range of other products, principally distributed by road. As early as 1958 a Ministry of Transport survey[11] revealed that, even where rail rates were lower, road was preferred because of reduced transit times and greater reliability. But in addition, most of the finished products are distributed in quantities more appropriate to the lorry than the trainload. However, since 1966, the advent of containerisation, particularly in the export trade, has led to the establishment of two freightliner terminals at Dudley and at Lawley Street (Central Birmingham), the latter being associated with the adjacent Landor Street Inland Port, where containers are 'stuffed' and 'stripped' by *Groupage Agents* under customs supervision. There are similar road-orientated inland ports.

The *function* of transport in connection with manufacturing industry, whether heavy or light, as shown in the case study of the West Midlands, is threefold

(1) the concentration of raw materials and semi-finished products upon the plant when and where required
(2) the transfer of semi-finished products between linked plants in the chain of manufacturing processes
(3) the distribution of the finished products from the plant to distribution depots and onward to the point of final consumption or retail sale.

4.2.3 Tertiary Activity

The links between tertiary activity and transport are rather less obvious, but nevertheless are real and important. Location of retailing and other services, such as banking or entertainment, depends on the accessibility of the shop, office or football ground from the area it serves.[12] The more specialised the service, the larger (in terms of population and purchasing power) the area it must serve. A first-division football club must have a larger ground and therefore a larger catchment area than a fourth-division one. It is for this reason that the town centre (the Central Business District − CBD) has been attractive to departmental stores, specialised shops, and commercial and local government offices. This is because of the convergence of public transport routes on the town centre. Therefore, the better the transport links, the more tertiary activities attracted to the CBD. Thus, employment in the London CBD (the City and West End) is over one million, and in that of Manchester, some 110 000 (p. 135).

The increasing use of the car for access to services has resulted paradoxically in a reduction in the accessibility of the CBD, not only because of road congestion, but also because of the increase in parking difficulties. This has led to the development of the out-of-town shopping centres in peripheral locations, accessible from ring-roads or other main highways and with ample land for parking.[13] In Greater Manchester, 'hypermarkets' were opened in the 1970s on the outskirts of the conurbation at Irlam and Hyde. They have also been opened near smaller centres, such as at Barr Hill, three miles outside Cambridge.

Congestion costs, which include a transport element as well as high rentals and wages, have also led to the removal of many offices, commercial and government, from Central London. Though it has been government policy to encourage their relocation in development areas, many of the new office blocks have been sited in relation to suburban railway stations, among them, East Croydon, Sutton and Ealing Broadway.

But much relocation, particularly of public services, has been ill-considered from the transport viewpoint. Local government offices, schools and hospitals have been resited on the edges of towns without regard to the implications for public transport and even road access. In Greater Manchester, the Wythenshawe hospital complex has been located on a 'greenfield' site, which reduced land costs, but which is approached only by narrow and winding roads, often only country lanes, incapable of accommodating buses or any large volume of car traffic.

4.3 Transport and Social Development

Social development has been considerably influenced by the increased mobility conferred by transport development. For the average person this has increased their accessibility to place of work, suitable housing, shops, services and leisure activities. But it must be remembered that mobility and accessibility are not synonymous, and are not even necessarily directly linked. Prior to the transport revolution of the nineteenth century, the rural population was largely immobile, but had access to local shops, market, and what rudimentary services were available. In our own time, though the rural population has become highly mobile, accessibility to shops and services is being reduced through closure and concentration. The minority who are not mobile are therefore deprived of access to services.[14]

Thus, increased mobility can be considered in terms of (i) the *benefits* it brings and (ii) the *costs* incurred.

4.3.1 The Benefits

The benefits may be considered in terms of increased opportunities in selecting a place to live, in the journey to work, and for shopping and leisure activities. The journey to work has two aspects. The possibilities of increasing its length have in turn increased the choice open to a person to live in a better environment of their own choosing. On the other hand, they have also increased the choice of employment available without moving house. This has greatly extended the area within commuting range of large urban areas.(p. 126) But two specific examples may be given here: (i) the considerable growth after 1955 of North Staffordshire villages, such as Baldwin's Gate and Loggerheads, which were once very isolated, but which are now popular with commuters working in the Potteries and Stafford; (ii) similar growth in North Bedfordshire villages, such as Oakley and Harrold, once considered well out of London commuting range, but now accessible by driving to railhead at Bedford. It has also allowed people resident in at least the more accessible rural areas to widen their choice of employment by commuting to nearby towns.

Access for those mobile through car ownership to specialised shopping facilities and to services has also been increased. But this form of increased access is probably more marked in rural areas and large conurbations than in medium and small towns, where a wide variety of services always was, and still is, located within walking distance.

In the same way, access to leisure facilities, organised sport, individual sport such as sailing, or general access to country and seaside, have all greatly increased through increased car ownership.[15] Although in the early nineteenth century Wigan miners took their families to the seaside at Southport, travelling by canal to Scarisbrick Bridge and thence by road, it was railways that, from 1850 onwards, made the seaside holiday normal for middle-class families and the day trip popular among the working class. The advent of paid holidays during the inter-war years and increased car ownership spread the holiday habit. After 1960, the *inclusive tour* (pp. 65, 94) brought Continental holidays within reach of all, and are now leading to American and African holidays becoming commonplace. Once again, choice has been increased, and, as far as Great Britain is concerned, while the railways tended to foster growth of compact resort towns, the car allows static or touring caravan holidays wherever planning authorities permit.

4.3.2 The Costs

This increase of access through greatly increased mobility has, however, incurred costs, which must be weighed against the undoubted benefits conferred. These costs may be imposed on other transport users (for example, congestion and accidents) or on the community (for example, noise), though some costs (for example, pollution) are imposed on both groups. The chief costs are as follows.

Accidents

In terms of fatalities/injuries per passenger- or vehicle-km, accident rates in the United Kingdom by all forms of public transport are comparatively low. In 1976 and 1977 no passenger was killed in a train accident on British Railways. This was achieved by rigid control over the movement of the transport unit, particularly in the case of rail with its fixed track, but also in the case of air with its traffic-control system; and by very high standards of maintenance and inspection of the transport units. All this is usually enforced by legislation imposing statutory obligations on the operators.

In the same terms of passenger-km, accidents involving cars and lorries are also relatively low. In 1977, 2.5 persons were killed and 31 seriously injured per 100 million vehicle-km (motor vehicles plus pedal cycles). It must also be emphasised that since 1950, as vehicle numbers and mileage performed have both increased, the accident rate has declined. In 1977 the number of road accidents had increased over those of 1950 by 44 per cent. But in the same period the number of vehicles had increased by 325 per cent, while the index of vehicle-km (1949 = 100) had increased from 114 to 558.[16]

But because the numbers of vehicles, vehicle-users and pedestrians are so large, the absolute numbers of people killed and injured on the roads are very high, and present a serious problem. In 1977 there were 6614 fatalities, 1.0 per cent of all deaths, and in addition 81 681 persons were seriously injured and 259 766 slightly injured.

There are considerable variations in accident rates including

(1) Between rural and urban areas. Because of traffic densities, and also because of greater conflict between vehicles and pedestrians, accident rates are higher in urban areas.

(2) Between classes of roads. Urban main roads with numerous intersections and heavy flows of vehicles and pedestrians are particularly dangerous. But suburban streets with numerous parked cars and playing children have problems. On the other hand, although individual accidents may be extremely spectacular, motorways are one of the safest classes of roads in relation to traffic volumes. This is due to prohibition of many classes of traffic, and grade separation at intersections.

(3) Between age groups. Children are very vulnerable as pedestrians. While in 1977 road deaths accounted for 1.0 per cent fatalities in the population as a whole, they accounted for 23.2 per cent of deaths to children between 5 and 9 years and no less than 46.3 per cent of fatalities in young persons between 15 and 19.

(4) Between hour of the day and day of the week. Because traffic flows are heaviest then, peak hours, that is, 0800–0859 and 1600–1759, are times of increased traffic accidents. But, in addition, because of the relationship between drinking and driving, there is also a noticeable increase in accident rates between 2300 and 2359. In 1977 there were 2045 casualties on Mondays during those hours, but 5904 on Fridays.

A literature has grown up which attempts to cost accidents.[17] Medical costs and loss of earnings are relatively easy to assess. But assumptions as to the price of a life tend to be heroic.

Congestion

The congestion suffered on urban roads leads to increased costs. *Congestion costs* are defined as those imposed by an additional vehicle using a particular stretch of road. Providing the traffic is moving freely, no costs are incurred, but costs increase rapidly as average speed falls with the extra vehicles coming onto the road.[18] In the case of buses and goods vehicles, congestion costs can be easily calculated on a basis of lowered productivity over unit time. But, for private cars, estimates of monetary values of driver and passenger time is more arbitrary.

Traffic Peaks

A particular aspect of congestion costs are those incurred by the accommodation of traffic peaks. Peak costs may be defined as the costs of providing extra capacity for the sole purpose of accommodating the difference between the basic off-peak traffic and that of the peak period.[19] This extra capacity may be in the form of infrastructure, that is, the provision of extra road space or railway track which would be unnecessary were there no peak; or in the form of extra transport units, buses or trains, used only for the peak traffic; or in the form of the extra labour needed to operate those units.

To take two examples, in 1974 Tyne and Wear PTE required 791 buses to maintain the basic off-peak service, but 1100 were required for the evening peak period. Secondly, the large Southern Region terminus of Cannon Street, with eight platforms and a complex layout on the approach, which is on a bridge over the Thames, has virtually only one purpose, to accommodate City commuters. In 1978, during the annual census period, there was a daily average (Monday to Friday) of 34 262 departing passengers. But 31 690 of these left between 1600 and 1959, and 19 516 between 1700 and 1759. The peak period commuters were conveyed in 67 trains, the remaining 2572 passengers outside the peak being provided with 84 trains.

Peak problems are not confined to urban areas; they may also occur on the approaches to or within seaside resorts and popular beauty spots. Additional road space and extensive parking must be provided at resorts. At holiday times there is considerable congestion on approach roads and on roads within the Lake District and Peak District National Parks. In the popular Goyt Valley the Peak District National Park closes the narrow lanes at summer week-ends, and at one time provided peripheral car parks and a connecting minibus service. All this represents peak costs.

Peaks may be daily or seasonal. In airport planning seasonal peaks are taken into account by the application of the *Standard Busy Rate*, which is defined as the thirtieth busiest hour in the year, for calculating accommodation.[20]

Atmospheric Pollution

The Clean Air legislation has led to very significant reductions in atmospheric pollution from domestic and industrial premises over the last twenty years. But at the same time, increased motor traffic on city streets has led to increased atmospheric pollution from exhaust emissions. The British climate is not normally conducive to the 'smogs' experienced in Californian cities, where long continued periods of atmospheric conditions lead to concentrations of exhaust emissions at low levels, sometimes with fatal consequences. On the other hand, sulphur dioxide and lead pollution from heavy traffic trapped at street level can damage health. The cost of atmospheric pollution is, however, very hard to quantify.[21]

Noise

Costs incurred by transport noise may also be hard to quantify.[22] Objective measurement of noise is made more difficult, as personal reaction to a given level of noise varies greatly. A level of noise which would be acceptable for one individual would lead to loss of sleep and even health problems in another. Also, it has not been possible so far to measure the comparative effects of intermittent and continuous noise at comparable levels.

In the case of airport noise, the cost of double-glazing all homes in an area subject to noise above an agreed level can be directly calculated. But this is more difficult for loss of sleep, damage to hearing and increase in nervous disorders. The effects of aircraft noise on property values are also hard to calculate. Work in the area of Manchester Airport produced conflicting evidence.[23] Apart from aircraft noise, the environment is desirable, and proximity to the airport is a positive advantage for aircrew and airport workers, which would tend to raise home prices otherwise depressed by noise. Also to be taken into account are increased costs to operators and reduced revenue to airports incurred by reducing numbers of night take-offs.

Vibration

In old towns, where streets are narrow and lorry traffic heavy, damage may eventually be done to buildings by continual vibration. The timescale is, however, open to question.

Visual Intrusion

This is also hard to quantify directly. But some costs resulting from noise, vibration and visual intrusion may be costed directly. They all tend to loss of value of the houses affected, and this can be calculated. Prior to 1973, compensation was paid only to owners of property demolished in the course of road construction. In that year the Land Compensation Act was passed, which provides for the payment of compensation for reduced values resulting from environmental deterioration caused by new roads. The costs of by-passing and/or rebuilding of towns can also be identified.

But the consequences are much wider than the zone directly affected by a road, railway or airport. Reference has already been made (p. 120) to the fact that virtually the whole coastline, except perhaps in the north of Scotland, is now accessible to car users for holiday purposes. Long stretches have already suffered from uncontrolled housing and caravan development, and rigid control is needed to preserve the remainder. Similar controls are needed not only in the National Parks, but in those areas designated as 'areas of outstanding natural beauty'.[15]

Planning Blight[24]

This is caused by long-term uncertainty as to the exact location and time of any improvement or addition to the transport infrastructure. This may take the form of a new airport or an extended runway, a dock extension, or a new road. But blight most commonly results from the planning of urban motorways, as more property is affected per mile, though rural areas can also be affected.

The announcement that a motorway is to be built between two points is normally accompanied by the publication of a number of preferred routes. There may be long delays, often of many years, before the exact line is finally decided. This results in uncertainty as to the future of any property considered to be located on or near a possible line. The value will be adversely affected, sales will slump, and there will be a reluctance to spend money on maintenance or improvement. In towns, whole areas may become run-down, even if they may not be on the line eventually selected.

Even when a line is finally fixed, there may also be long delays before construction begins, and this will adversely affect property along the line. Planning procedures must aim to reduce blight as far as possible by reducing the periods of uncertainty.

4.4 Transport and Regional Development

Since 1930, successive British governments have almost constantly pursued a policy of redistribution of industry between regions.[25] This has implications for transport, negative as well as positive.

The depression of the 1930s was felt more severely in areas of older industries, especially the traditional heavy industries, than in the two areas where new light industries were springing up after 1920: Greater London and the West Midlands. In the years after 1945, Southern and Eastern England also shared in industrial growth. These newer industries were more 'footloose' than the traditional heavy industries, which tended to be tied to the coalfields (section 4.2), and were more market-orientated, so tended to locate in areas where population and purchasing power were greatest, and which in turn were increasing their attraction because of their industrial expansion.

In addition, the less prosperous areas have had much less than their share in the increase of tertiary activity, which has characterised the employment structure since 1945.

Measures taken to encourage relocation of industry have included the provision of transport infrastructures, mostly road schemes. The development areas have received more than their share of motorway construction, if this were based simply on population or vehicle density. The North West of England has become an exceptionally favoured region in terms of motorway provision.

Some development areas, notably West Cumbria, have, however, remained very isolated and lacking in adequate road links. Agreement by British Leyland to establish a bus-manufacturing plant at Workington was conditional on the improvement of the long A66 link to the M6 at Penrith. Although the eastern part has been completed, upgrading much of the remainder has proved difficult, because of environmental considerations in the Lake District.

Finance has also been provided for the upgrading of suburban rail networks, especially within the CBD, in Glasgow, Liverpool and Newcastle (pp. 59, 149). Stimulation of tertiary activity in these development-area cities could have been in the minds of central government, though not specifically stated.

Measures to encourage relocation of industry have, however, fallen short of offering discriminatory freight rates in favour of the development areas. Other

EEC countries have practised this in pursuit of regional policies. Thus, Italian state railways are required to offer much lower rates on traffic to and from the Mezzogiorno (the South) than between other regions.

4.5 Transport and Land-use Activity [26]

We have just seen that there is a clear connection between transport development and socio-economic development, and that this connection is reciprocal. Since the physical expression of economic and social activity is the use to which land is put for the purpose of agriculture, manufacturing industry, commerce, housing and recreation, we may expect the same reciprocal connection between transport and land-use. It is a peculiar fact, however, that this connection was not fully recognised among physical planners until the 1960s. Before the publication of the Buchanan Report (1963) much land use planning was carried out independently from any transport considerations.

4.5.1 Transport and Urban Development

The consequences of developments in transport can be traced both in the general overall growth of towns in terms of population and area, and also in their internal structure. Thus, the various sub-regions of the urban area, together with their distinctive morphology, can be traced to successive stages in transport technology.[2]

(1) Prior to the transport revolution of the nineteenth century, there was a universal dependence on walking. But even so, separation of work and residence was beginning during the eighteenth century, and the town centres were beginning to lose their residential population. In the case of London, between 1750 and 1840 (when the railway age could be said to have begun), not only did the purely residential West End grow up, but residential suburbs such as Islington for middle-class city workers. These latter, by virtue of their Georgian housing, have regained in recent years their social popularity, because of their environmental quality coupled with ease of access to Central London.

(2) The consequences of the steam railways began to be felt soon after 1840, but gained momentum after 1860. This allowed longer journeys to work, but houses tended to be clustered within walking distance of the suburban stations, producing a series of suburbs like beads on a string. This housing was of two distinct types: (i) large villas in large gardens with a housing density of 1—4 dwellings per acre, and (ii) terrace housing of about 20—30 dwellings per acre, for clerks and artisans. In London, Dulwich, Surbiton and Chislehurst can be taken as examples of the first kind, and Hornsey and Tottenham of the second.

(3) The electric tram, which became important after 1900, with its more frequent stops, tended to produce ribbon development along the main roads radiating from the central area. Where the tram routes paralleled railway lines, the ribbons linked the older steam railway suburbs.

(4) The motor bus, which became an effective influence after 1920, was

much more flexible and allowed suburban development to spread continuously outward at lower densities, filling in the interstices between the ribbons along the main roads, and extending those ribbons even further into the rural areas.

(5) If the city was large enough, the extent of this continuous sprawl was even greater if rail lines were electrified, especially in the case of London.

(6) Finally, during the 1930s and particularly after 1950, the motor car freed the commuter from dependency on access to public transport. Very low-density housing could therefore be provided anywhere up to thirty miles from the city centre. If Greater Manchester and Merseyside were decentralised on the North American model, there would be continuous housing from the Pennines to the coast and from Lancaster to Crewe.

Such uncontrolled sprawl has, however, been prevented by planning control. Legislation, including the 1938 Green Belt Act and the 1947 Town and Country Planning Act, has been aimed at preventing continuous expansion of conurbations by the creation of Green Belts, by concentrating housing development in rural areas into certain villages scheduled for expansion, and on the macro-scale by confining development into corridors, such as that along the M23 motorway and electrified railway between London and Brighton.[27]

Conversely, the different sub-regions of the city each now have specific demands on transport services. These are dealt with in section 5.2.1.

4.5.2 Urbanisation

One of the major social trends in Great Britain since 1800 has been the increasing proportion of the total population who live in towns. But areal growth of the built-up area has been even more significant than population growth. In 1841 the population of Greater London was some 2 million, living on 18 square miles, which incidentally is about the same as the built-up area of the Brighton conurbation with a present population of 230 000. By 1961 the population had expanded to 8 million, but the built-up area now occupied about 725 square miles.

This was the result of a combination of factors, but one of them, the provision of transport, was fundamental in that it permitted this growth. The main consequence was to allow ever-increasing separation of work and residence, both in terms of increasing geographical distance and of increasing downward spread through the social classes. There is a saying, attributed to the late Lady Simon, that in the old days Manchester businessmen lived over their premises in Market Street, but now they live over their income in Alderley Edge (the names can be substituted to suit any large city).

Whatever a commuter's income may be, the amount of time available to him is fixed, and time spent on the journey to work is time taken from other activities.[28] The commuter has consistently shown that, in general, he is not prepared to take more than one hour on this journey to work, whether in the 1830s or in the 1970s, whether walking, or driving a fast car and using a motorway. The geographical spread of commuting has therefore increased with increasing speed of car and rail transport. It has also increased with increase in

.able income, so that since 1945 long-distance commuting, though linked
ome, is by no means confined to those with higher incomes.
30 miles (48 km) journey to work is therefore acceptable in the case of
:ncial conurbations, and 60 miles (98 km) in the case of London. Since
Rugby, 82.5 miles (132 km), can be reached in one hour from Euston, no
: between Preston (Lancs) and Brighton (Sussex) is beyond commuting
,e of a major conurbation. Very few parts of England and Wales are without
)mmuting element in their economically active residential population. In this
,, among others, urbanisation has become virtually complete.

4.5.3 Problems of Inner-city Areas

Successive central governments as well as local authorities have been concerned
with reducing congestion in the inner areas of large cities, and nowadays much
is heard of policies towards the 'inner-city'.[29] Unfortunately a definition of
'inner-city' is difficult, and unless we are clear it may lead to misunderstanding.
Theoretically it should include all the older built-up area, the CBD, the
surrounding area of mixed industry and housing, and the inner suburbs dating
from before 1914. But inner-city has become a technical term to define a type
of land-use, rather than a geographical location. Thus, the CBD and the more
prosperous of the older suburbs are excluded, and areas of declining industry
and of local authority housing included, wherever they are. For our purposes
we will therefore use the term *inner area* to define the whole of the older parts
of the city and use *inner-city* in the sense just outlined.

Inner-area congestion takes the form of undesirably high housing densities,
the over-close intermingling of housing and industry, pressure on roads and
public transport on the approaches to and within the CBD, and high rentals in
the latter. Reduction of congestion has been achieved by the following means.

(1) Slum clearance and the provision of local authority housing, usually
in locations peripheral to the city. These estates might or might not be
associated with outward movement of industry. St Helier, Harold Wood
(initiated by the London County Council) and Chelmsley Wood (City of
Birmingham) do not include industrial areas, while Wythenshawe (City of
Manchester) has three such areas.

(2) Overspill agreements for the transfer of population and industry
from one local authority area to another. This has been aided by the 1952 Town
Development Act. Thus, Basingstoke (Hants), Ashford (Kent) and Haverhill
(Cambridgeshire) have received population and industry from London, and
Winsford (Cheshire) from Liverpool. In all, sixty-eight such schemes were
started between 1962 and 1978.

(3) The establishment of New Towns under the 1948 New Towns Act.[30]
Twenty-three of these have been designated in England and Wales, and to these
must be added Letchworth and Welwyn Garden City, established before the Act.
In addition, six have been designated in Scotland and four in Northern Ireland.

It will be seen that schemes included in the first of these three categories tend
to increase transport demand, as they increase the separation of work and

residence, and increase the average length of journey to work. Local authority estates were often associated with extensions of the municipal transport network (p. 49). The London County Council extended their trams to their Grove Park estate to connect it with inner London at cheap fares. In more recent times, in the 1960s, car traffic from the Wythenshawe estate contributed to the severe congestion on the Princess Parkway link with central Manchester.

On the other hand, New Towns were established to reduce the length of journey to work by locating industry within the comparatively small town. One indirect objective was to relieve pressure on the transport systems of the inner areas. The Expanded Town concept had the same objectives and implications as that of the New Towns.

Attempts to reduce congestion were also made by

(1) Relocation of industrial premises, small workshops, factories and warehouses from the inner areas to suburbs, and to New/Expanded towns, and development areas. Warehouse location in inner areas was because of proximity to railway freight depots. But with the transfer of general goods traffic to road haulage, sites on ring-roads, with ready access on the one hand to inter-city motorways, and on the other to the city road network, are more advantageous.

(2) The relocation of offices from the CBDs of London, Birmingham and Manchester. As already mentioned, the period between 1945 and 1970 saw a great increase in employment in the tertiary sector and therefore in the demand for office space. This forced up rentals in the main commercial centres. Many firms found it advantageous to move out from the CBD. The government also encouraged this movement by the 1965 Control of Offices and Industrial Development Act, which limited office building in CBDs, especially in Central London, and by the setting up in 1966 of the Location of Offices Bureau.[31] From an address in Chancery Lane in the City of London, the latter provided advice on how to move out of Central London!

In 1976 these decentralisation policies were abruptly reversed, even to the winding-up of some New Towns, such as Central Lancashire New Town, as central and local government became concerned by the loss of employment, population, and rate income from the inner areas and particularly the inner-city.[32] This reversal obviously has considerable implications for transport planning.

4.5.4 Transport and Civic Design

Civic design may be defined as the design, as opposed to the planning, of the overall shape of the town and of the relationship between its various parts, that is, the transport infrastructure, the residential, commercial and industrial areas, and the individual buildings. Civic design has had a long, though intermittent, history in Britain. Roman towns (for example, Verulamium, Chester), Edwardian 'Bastides' (for example, Salisbury, Conway) and Georgian foundations (for example, London's West End, Edinburgh New Town, Bath) were all planned in terms of street layouts, building plots, and the public and private buildings.

On the other hand, the 'great rebuilding' of the Elizabethan era was not accompanied by an overall design, and there was little attention paid to this during the unprecedented urban expansion of the nineteenth century. However, new main roads were often driven through crowded inner-cities to accommodate increased traffic, and these were lined with good-quality buildings. King William Street, Queen Victoria Street and Holborn Viaduct are London examples, and Corporation Street, Manchester, a provincial one. Railway building also led to the redesign of the corridors they created through the inner-cities. Often the lines were built on viaducts, such as those approaching the southern termini of London, and the Manchester, South Junction and Altrincham (MSJ & A) line in central Manchester. Under these schemes, streets were realigned, and housing provided for the inhabitants dispossessed from dwellings which were often inferior. Dobson's design for the centre of Newcastle-upon-Tyne was, however, a unique example of unified redevelopment of a city centre in the nineteenth century. There were, however, many new towns founded which owe much to civic design. Among these were company towns such as Saltaire and Port Sunlight, railway workshop towns such as Crewe, industrial towns such as Barrow-in-Furness and Middlesbrough, and resort towns such as Bournemouth.

At first, the motor car did not have much effect on urban design. But the wartime destruction of many town centres such as Coventry and Plymouth, coupled with the increasing demand for road space and parking, led to increasing interest in urban design that accommodated the car, not only in rebuilt town centres, but on the approach roads through the surrounding inner-city areas, where the bad housing was being rapidly replaced.

The field of civic design is important and extensive, and is of significance for the student of transport.[33]

4.5.5 Specific Connections between Urban Design and Transport Planning

There are a number of points in the design of towns which affect, and are affected by, transport development.

(1) First and foremost is the still unresolved question − how far should a policy of decentralisation be pursued? In the years after 1950, overcrowding and bad housing in the inner-cities, combined with increasing congestion in the CBDs led to the adoption of decentralisation policies. A proportion of the inner-area population was rehoused on suburban estates, through Overspill Agreements with other authorities and in New Towns: industry and services such as schools and hospitals were relocated in peripheral sites; out-of-town shopping centres were established and office accommodation dispersed.

The consequences for transport were to reduce the demand for public transport on the radial routes from the CBD to below capacity, thus increasing costs, and to make the use of cars generally more attractive as the proportion of circumferential journeys increased. Obviously the transport system of a decentralised city will be quite different from that of a centralised one. Decentralisation policies were to some extent reversed in 1977, but so far there has been little recognition of the fundamental consequences on urban transport this change might have.

(2) During the 1950s, policies of unrestricted provision of road space were pursued in urban design. In this, North American practice was followed, and this continued even after the United States had come to realise that the fully motorised city was an impossibility. It was not until the publication of that extremely important contribution to the literature of urban design, the Buchanan Report (1963), that it came to be accepted in the United Kingdom that there must be some restriction on road space, and that this must be taken into account in civic design.

(3) Civic design must take into account the relief of traffic problems in central areas by the diversion of through-traffic. This can be achieved by the provision of ring-roads (p. 146). These roads also serve to generate inter-suburban travel, hitherto inhibited by the older main roads being almost incariably radial. This greater ease of circumferential movement aids decentralisation.

(4) Radial main roads (p. 43) have come to fulfil a number of conflicting functions. Civic design must be aimed at separating these functions, and leaving main radials with the single function of acting as arteries for large volumes of through-traffic between suburbs and outer ring-roads and the city centre.[34]

(5) Town centres are now being designed for limited access by motor vehicles, and for the separation of traffic and pedestrians. This depends on the provision of an inner ring-road around the CBD with access to multi-storey off-street parking. Within the ring-road, restriction on car entry may be through a combination of the following measures

  (i) pedestrianisation of streets
  (ii) limitation of parking
  (iii) prevention of through-traffic by the arrangement of one-way streets
  (iv) priorities for public transport by the closing of roads to traffic other than buses and taxis; the provision of bus lanes; the inclusion of bus and railway stations in shopping precincts

(6) Residential areas have been designed to provide small 'neighbourhoods', within which pedestrian and vehicular traffic is separated and through-traffic excluded. The concept originated in Radburn, New Jersey, and aims to provide pedestrian paths between houses, and between them and shops, primary school and play areas. Garages are grouped peripherally and approached by cul-de-sacs from a local ring-road.

(7) The United Kingdom has been rather slower than other countries to design towns and suburbs around the transport system, especially public transport. In recent years the growth of Copenhagen has been controlled by the 'Finger Plan'. This confines development to five 'fingers' or corridors, each representing a line of electric railway with a sixth corridor, the line northward along the coast to Helsingør, not being scheduled for further development. The design of the Stockholm suburb of Vällingby has been centred on the metro station.

But some progress has been made in the design of New Towns. Milton Keynes and Telford have been designed around road networks with limited-access roads and feeders to widely separated neighbourhood units. In contrast, Runcorn has been designed around segregated busways, basically in a figure-of-eight, with the

CBD at the intersection. The network of public roads is more peripheral, and designed to have a secondary role in local circulation. Mention has already been made of the corridor concept in the outer metropolitan area of South East England.

4.6 Transport and Communications[35]

Transport is only one aspect of *Communications*. It involves physical transfer over space, not only of people and things, but of information in the form of mail, newspapers, and word-of-mouth by people transported. But information may also be communicated over space by telecommunications. These include telephone, teleprinter, radio and television. It is not generally realised that telecommunications are not only complementary, they may also be in competition (pp. 7, 108).

Thus, telephone conversations are a substitute for letter-writing. An increase in telephone traffic may lead to a decline in mail traffic, and consequently in a loss of revenue for a railway administration. Increased use of telecommunications is one of the factors enabling office decentralisation from CBDs, where formerly it was necessary to locate them for easy intercommunication. In future there could also be a decline in business traffic, both by car and public transport, as the need for face-to-face contacts is reduced. It is now technologically possible to arrange conferences by two-way closed-circuit television, enabling the participants to remain in their own offices. This may also lead to business and professional people working more from their own homes. The demand for evening leisure journeys has been reduced by the spread of television and the consequential decline of the cinema.

The reciprocal relationship between the transport system on the one hand, and socio-economic activity and its physical expression in the landuse on the other, has been outlined in this chapter. This relationship must be taken into account not only by students of transport, but by physical and economic planners as well.

References

1. B. S. Hoyle (ed.), *Transport and Development* (Macmillan, London, 1973), introduction
2. H. P. White, Greater London, Vol. 3 in *A Regional Railway History of Great Britain* (David & Charles, Newton Abbot, 1971)
3. A. A. Jackson, *Semi-detached London* (Allen & Unwin, London, 1973)
4. A. D. Couper, *The Geography of Sea Transport* (Hutchinson, London, 1972)
5. Central Electricity Generating Board, *Annual Reports, Statistical Year Book*
6. *Electricity Supply Handbook* (Electrical Times, latest edition—1980); Electricity Council, *Handbook of Electricity Supply Statistics* (annual)
7. H. P. White, Unit Trains: Technology and Changing Accessibility, *Geography*, **64** (1979) 46–50

8. R. Gasson, *The Changing Location of Intensive Crops: an Analysis of their Spatial Distribution in Kent, Studies in Rural Land Use, Report no. 6.* (Wye College, Dept. of Agric. Econ., 1966); R. Gasson, The Changing Location of Intensive Crops in England and Wales, *Geography*, **51** (1966) 16—28

9. Merry-go-round Supply and Despatch for World's Largest Cement Works, *Modern Railways* (Sept., 1970) 398—9

10. R. B. Boyce and A. F. Williams, *The Bases of Economic Geography* (Holt, Rinehart, London, 1979) p. 182

11. Ministry of Transport, *The Transport of Goods by Road* (HMSO, 1958); see also B. T. Baylis & S. L. Edwards, *Industrial Demand for Transport* (HMSO, 1968)

12. NEDO, Distributive Trades Economic Development Council, *The Future Pattern of Shopping* (HMSO, 1971); J. P. Rigby, Access to Hospitals, a Literature Review, *TRRL Laboratory Report* 853 (1978); J. P. Rigby, A Review of Research on School Travel Patterns and Problems, *TRRL Supplementary Report* 460 (1979); C. S. Jones, *Regional Shopping Centres: their Location, Planning and Design* (Business Books, London, 1969)

13. Dept of the Environment, *The Eastleigh Carrefour: a Hypermarket and its Effects*, Research Report 16 (1978)

14. M. J. Moseley, *Accessibility and the Rural Challenge* (Methuen, London, 1979); C. G. B. Mitchell and S. W. Town (eds), Access to Recreational Activity: a Summary, *TRRL Supplementary Report* 468 (1979), K. H. Schaeffer and E. Sclar, *Access for All: Transportation and Urban Growth* (Penguin, Harmondsworth, 1975)

15. J. A. Patmore, *Land and Leisure in England and Wales* (David & Charles, Newton Abbot, 1970)

16. Dept of Transport, *Transport Statistics* (HMSO, annual)

17. R. F. F. Dawson, Current Costs of Road Accidents in Great Britain, *TRRL Report* LR396 (1971)

18. R. Thomas, *The Economics of Traffic Congestion* (Open University, Milton Keynes, 1974); A. Tzedakis, Different Vehicles Speeds and Congestion Costs, *J. Transp. econ. Pol.* **14** (1980) 81—103; M. Martin and R. Evans, Urban Congestion Survey 1976: Traffic Flows and Speeds in Eight Towns and Five Conurbations, *TRRL Supplementary Report* 438 (1978)

19. A. M. Milne and J. C. Laight, *The Economics of Inland Transport*, 2nd ed. (Pitman, London, 1963) pp. 123—6; P. R. White, *Planning for Public Transport* (Hutchinson, London, 1976) pp. 121—5

20. K. R. Sealey, *Airport Strategy and Planning* (Oxford University Press, 1976). I. G. Heggie, *Transportation Engineering Economics* (McGraw Hill, London, 1972)

21. A. Aird, *The Automotive Nightmare* (Hutchinson, London, 1972). Deals also with noise, accidents, etc.

22. Dept of the Environment, Committee on Noise (the Wilson Committee), *Calculation of Road Traffic Noise* (HMSO, 1975)

23. F. G. Martin, The Social and Economic Consequentials of Manchester Airport (unpublished MSc Thesis, University of Salford, 1972)

24. N. Dennis, *Public Participation and Planning Blight* (Faber, London, 1972)

25. C. M. Law, *British Regional Development Since the First World War* (David & Charles, Newton Abbot, 1980)
26. R. B. Mitchell and C. Rapkin, *Urban Traffic: a Function of Land Use* (Colombia University Press, 1954); W. R. Blunden, *The Land Use/Transport System* (Pergamon, Oxford, 1971)
27. D. Thomas, *London's Green Belt* (Faber, London, 1970); South East Joint Planning Team, *Strategic Plan for the South East* (HMSO, 1971)
28. M. E. Beesley, *The Value of Time Spent Travelling: some New Evidence in Urban Transport* (Butterworth, London, 1973); J. C. Tanner, Expenditure of Time and Money and Travel, *TRRL Supplementary Report* 466 (1979); M. G. Langdon and C. G. B. Mitchell, Personal Travel in Towns: the Development of Models that Reflect the Real World, *TRRL Supplementary Report* 369 (1978); Dept of Transport, *Value of Time and Vehicle Operating Costs for 1976*, Highway Economic Note 2 (Sept. 1977)
29. D. Everseley, *The Inner City* (Heinemann, London, 1979)
30. J. B. Cullingworth, New Towns Policy, Vol. 3 in *Environmental Planning 1939–1969* (HMSO, 1979); H. E. Evans (ed.) *New Towns, the British Experience* (Charles Knight, London, 1972); F. Schaffer, *The New Town Story* (Paladin, London, 1972)
31. P. W. Daniels, *Office Location: an Urban and Regional Study* (Bell, London, 1975)
32. Dept of the Environment, *Policy for the Inner Cities*, Cmnd 6845 (HMSO, 1977); Inner Urban Areas Act 1978
33. J. B. Cullingworth, *Town and Country Planning in England and Wales*, 7th edn (Allen & Unwin, London, 1979)
34. Dept of the Environment, Roads and the Environment (HMSO, 1976)
35. J. M. Nilles, *The Telecommunication–Transportation Trade-off* (Wiley, Chichester, 1976)

5

Local Transport Problems and Policies

5.1 Introduction

In the previous chapters we have examined the place of the transport industry in the economy of the country as a whole, the way in which the transport system is organised, trends in traffic carried and changes in the roles of the various transport modes. In the course of this examination, passing reference has been made to the various problems encountered and to the policies which have been developed to deal with these problems.

It is now proposed to deal in greater detail with these problems and policies, first on a local scale and then, in the next chapter, on a national one. It must, however, be remembered that in many cases, the problems, financial, social and organisational, are basically the same ones, the local differing from the national in scale rather than degree.

It is proposed for convenience to examine separately the problems and policies encountered in

    (1) large cities
    (2) other urban areas
    (3) rural areas

though again many of the problems encountered are common to all.

Great Britain is one of the most highly urbanised countries in the world. In 1971, 33.0 per cent of the population of England and Wales lived in the six conurbations, and a further 33.6 per cent in other urbanised and industrial areas.[1] In addition, 10.8 per cent lived in the Outer Metropolitan Area (OMA) around Greater London, which is also highly urbanised. But even the population of the true rural areas can be regarded as being to some extent urbanised, in that many of the economically active residents work in towns, while most rural dwellers look to towns for education, shopping and many of their leisure activities, demanding access to facilitaties similar to those enjoyed by their urban counterparts. Urban and rural ways of life have been converging over the last fifty years.

5.2 Large Cities

It is proposed, somewhat arbitrarily, to select a figure of 250 000 inhabitants
as the lower limit of 'large'. This follows one division of urban size in the
National Travel Survey (1972/73). In addition, most large cities, such as Leeds,
are part of larger conurbations or urban areas, and there are only two cities
of over 200 000, Hull and Plymouth, which are really 'free-standing', in the
sense that they are at least thirty miles from a centre of comparable size and
functions.

5.2.1 Urban Structure

As mentioned in chapter 4, the design and layout of towns has important
implications for transport. The structure of the major cities in Great Britain
tends to have the following components, each of which generates a different
structure of demands for transport.

The Central Business District (CBD)

This is characterised by a concentration of employment in commerce, retailing,
warehousing, administration, entertainment and professional services. This
results in very high land-values and rentals. Consequently, buildings are
becoming higher to increase the ratio of floor-space to ground-space, and
functions are becoming more specialised. Previously, small-scale workshop
industries, such as clothing, jewellery, and furniture, were important. But
these have largely died out from the CBD in the face of high rents. Warehousing
is also rapidly declining, seeking more accessible sites near ring-roads and
radial motorways. In addition, a resident population is almost absent. In
1971 there were 1.24 million jobs in the 'conurbation centre' of Greater
London, but a resident population of only 173 500. The figures for the
conurbation centre of Birmingham were 103 910 and 3790 respectively.

Employment in the CBDs is declining[2] because of a loss of industrial
employment, mechanisation of office jobs, and decentralisation forced on
firms by high rentals and wages. In 1966 there were 140 000 jobs in the
Manchester CBD; by 1971 this figure had fallen to 122 000 and by 1977 to
109 000. At least until 1976, when it was abruptly reversed (see section 4.5.3)
the policy of both central government and many local authorities was to
encourage decentralisation of the CBD by such measures as the 1965 Control
of Offices and Industrial Development Act.[3]

The CBD generates the largest single traffic flow in any large city, a flow
subject to severe peaking in the morning and evening of working days. But
street congestion within the CBD is severe throughout the working day. For
the transport planner and operator the journey to work to the CBD remains
the biggest single problem in the large city. But in devising policies to deal with
this problem, and in making long-term investment decisions, there are a number
of factors, imponderable rather than quantifiable, which must be taken into

account. These include an estimate of likely trends in government policies towards decentralisation or centralisation; the extent to which economic forces will continue to encourage decentralisation independently of government policy; and how far the current microprocessing revolution will affect office employment.

The 'Decayed Collar'

The area surrounding the CBD was formerly characterised by industry closely intermingled with bad housing and intersected by main roads and railways converging on the CBD. Of all types of area this one has received most attention from planners since 1945. The principal objective, now largely accomplished, has been the separation of housing and industry and the renewal of the housing stock. But not all the problems have been solved, and new ones have been created. The new housing is occupied by an increasingly homogenous population, semi-skilled and unskilled workers and their families. Because there has been no statutory obligation to relocate displaced firms, industry is in severe decline, though since 1977 government policy is aimed at arresting and reversing this decline. The area is still badly cut up by lines of transport, which now include environmentally intrusive urban motorways. Car ownership is low and the area is particularly dependent on public transport. Provision of the latter is made more difficult because buses suffer from street congestion, and in the morning peak are often full by the time they reach the inner areas.

Industrial nodes

These are formed by concentrations of manufacturing industry along lines of transport, port areas and industrial estates. These areas attract a circulation pattern of their own in terms both of journey to work and the collection and delivery of freight.

The Inner Suburbs

Those areas built up prior to 1914 include

  (1) small working-class terrace houses
  (2) large houses, formerly middle class, but now badly decayed
  (3) more rarely, areas of good-quality housing and of high and rising land-values (for example, St John's Wood, London, and Edgbaston, Birmingham)
  (4) areas of renewal by local authorities
  (5) more infrequently, renewal by private enterprise, especially in the form of flats and maisonettes
  (6) in a few cases, areas of decayed, but of architecturally or historically interesting housing, have since 1950 or 1960 seen a reversal of fortune. They have become fashionable, being taken over by professional people employed in

the CBD, and with suddenly rising land-values, the environment was improved. This process, dubbed 'gentrification', has occurred in Barnsbury and Islington,[4] areas of Georgian houses in inner London, and along the historic Royal Mile of Edinburgh.

Car ownership varies greatly, and the demand for public transport, especially for journey to work, remains high.

The Outer Suburbs

These were built up generally between 1920 and 1940, but with post-war extensions. They consist mainly of private housing of a moderately low density, interspersed with large local authority estates, which were part of their slum-clearance schemes and which, unlike the private housing, were often associated with extensions of the municipal transport system. Car ownership is high and the demand for public transport is declining. If the city is a large one, and especially if there are rail services, because of traffic congestion at peak periods, journey to work to the CBD by public transport may be holding its own or declining more slowly.

Subsidiary Nodes

In the form of subsidiary CBDs, these are found within conurbations. They attract circulation patterns of their own, which may reach large proportions (for example, Croydon, Wolverhampton, Bolton).

The Urban Fringe

Finally, there is an area of discontinuous, car-based, urban sprawl, which characterises the period since 1950. This would be even more extensive but for planning policies aimed at limiting urban sprawl. These have been strongly enforced, resulting in very high prices for any houses and building land available.

5.2.2 Congestion

Urban areas are areas of population concentration, and congestion in city streets is no recent phenomenon. London's Metropolitan Railway was opened in 1863 with one of its objectives to reduce street congestion.[5] Provision of infrastructure has always tended to lag behind demand. Congestion is therefore experienced not only on the roads, which affects bus traffic as well as private cars, but also on fixed-track rail systems. This is because of investment in track and signalling being insufficient to handle peak traffic. Congestion costs form a significant addition to urban costs.

5.2.3 The Private Car

One of the prime causes of congestion, and one of the fundamental problems of transport in large cities, has been the growth of car ownership and consequently that of car usage and demand for road space (see sections 2.2.1 and 3.2.1). But though car ownership generally has increased, it has done so over the various areas of the city at irregular rates, and disaggregation of the figures is necessary in order to appreciate the situation for the purpose of transport planning. For example, the former County Borough of Salford has often been quoted as an area of low car ownership. But as shown on p. 45, the aggregated 1971 figure of 97 cars per 1000 people conceals wide variations.

Table 2.1 shows car ownership in representative wards in one sector of the Manchester conurbation from inner-city to outer-urban sprawl. It will be seen that car ownership levels tend to increase with distance from the city centre and to vary with the social composition of the ward. Again, as pointed out on p. 45, the proportion of households without cars is important for the transport planner.

The purposes for which the cars are used are also of importance. The demand for journey to work by car is very high, and increasing. The 1971 Sample Census[6] revealed that in Greater London 25.6 per cent of the work journeys were by car (table 5.1), while in the other conurbations it varied from 23.55 per cent in Central Clydeside (Greater Glasgow) to 34.03 per cent in the West Midlands. In other large cities, outside the designated conurbations, the proportion is similar. For example, in the case of Sheffield it was 31.72 per cent.

The proportion of work journeys by car to the conurbation centres (table 5.2) closely reflected that of the particular conurbation as a whole. There were however two exceptions, Greater London and Clydeside, where the figures were only 12.37 and 17.63 per cent. In other cities the CBD is not differentiated.

It is difficult to extract comparable figures for more recent years, but it is reasonable to suppose that the proportion of journeys to work by car has continued to increase. For example, the 1975/76 National Travel Survey gives the proportion by 'car/van/lorry' as 39 per cent in the 'London Built-Up Area'.[7]

In single-car households the car is usually used for the journey to work by the principal male breadwinner, which leaves a considerable residual demand for public transport by other members, which must be added to that from non-car-owning households. In addition, though no quantitative work has been published, it is reasonable to suppose that many fewer working-class wives drive than do middle-class ones, though this may be regarded as a temporary phenomenon.

The use of the car for purposes other than for the journey to work and for business is also growing (see section 3.2.1). The 1975/76 National Travel Survey recorded 35 per cent of shopping trips as being by car (46 per cent walking), 57.5 per cent of 'social' journeys (26.4 per cent walking), and 50.5 per cent of 'entertainment' journeys (28.9 per cent walking). The effect of increased use of cars for shopping has had several consequences. Shopping trips by individual households have probably become less frequent; the use of the neighbourhood shop has declined; there has been decentralisation of retailing from the

TABLE 5.1 *Modal Split of Journey to Work, 1971*
Major Conurbations

	Train	Bus	Car	Foot	Motorcycle	Cycle	Other (not specified)
Conurbations							
Greater London	24.30	22.90	25.60	17.16	1.11	2.21	6.69
West Midlands	1.16	34.89	34.03	20.33	Ø	2.64	6.95
Greater Manchester	2.77	36.42	29.92	21.44	Ø	2.09	7.35
Merseyside	4.93	39.16	27.88	18.29	Ø	2.62	7.12
West Yorkshire	Ø	41.04	29.28	21.09	Ø	Ø	8.59
Tyneside	4.06	42.70	24.53	22.25	Ø	1.47	4.98
Central Clydeside	6.79	46.47	23.55	18.49	Ø	Ø	4.70

Based on 10 per cent sample, 1971 Census of England and Wales, Scotland
Ø: less than 1.0 per cent

TABLE 5.2(a) *Conurbation Centres*

	Resident Population	Employment
Greater London	173 505	1 241 000
West Midlands	3 790	103 910
Greater Manchester	665	122 690
Merseyside	4 550	91 540
Tyneside	1 370	66 710

Source: 1971 Census of England and Wales, Scotland

TABLE 5.2(b) *Modal Split of Journey to Work, 1971 Conurbation Centres*

	Train	Bus	Car	Foot	Other (not specified)
Greater London (Central London)	67.18	14.71	12.37	2.14	3.60
West Midlands (Central Birmingham)	8.11	51.20	32.89	3.67	4.13
Greater Manchester (Central Manchester)	14.29	49.56	29.53	3.05	3.12
Merseyside (Central Liverpool)	16.73	47.45	26.76	4.56	4.50
Tyneside (Central Newcastle)	8.40	52.91	28.45	6.85	3.46
Central Clydeside (Central Glasgow)	21.60	54.28	17.63	3.64	2.83

Based on 10 per cent sample, 1971 Census England and Wales, Scotland traditional 'High Street' to peripheral 'hypermarkets' and 'out of town' shopping centres where parking is convenient and one-stop shopping more possible.[8] Week-end leisure trips to country or seaside tend to be *en famille* and by car.

Increased car use has meant a very great increase in personal mobility, both from the viewpoint of leisure and of journey to work, the latter leading to increased choice in place of residence (see section 4.3.1). But there are also negative consequences, which include the following.

(1) A great increase in the demand for road space. Policies aimed at meeting this demand must take into account the extent to which this can and should be met. There is evidence that the provision of road space to satisfy existing demand also generates new demand. The effort to provide fully for demand can become self-defeating by curtailing the amenities and reducing the environmental quality of the city by the over-provision of road and parking space.

(2) A decline in the demand for public transport. This decline, however, is very patchy and therefore it has not been possible to reduce costs commensurately. For the journey to work in large cities, especially to the centres, there is still a heavy reliance on public transport. But there have been considerable reductions in the demand for evening and week-end trips.[9] For example, the number of passenger journeys by bus in 1977 were some 78 per cent of those of 1966 in the case of London Transport, and 67 per cent in that of the PTEs.[10]

(3) An increase in road congestion, particularly at journey to work peaks. The average car-load at commuter peaks is of the order of 1.5 persons, and therefore the space occupied per commuter is very much greater by car than by other modes (figure 5.1). This has led to increasing peak and congestion costs.

(4) With decentralisation, congestion has spread to the outer urban areas and to circumferential movement. Delays at junctions between radial and circumferential roads are now as serious as those experienced in the 1950s and

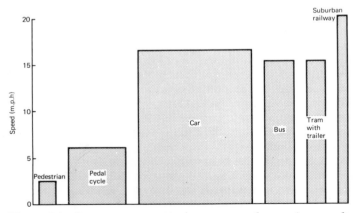

Figure 5.1   *Space per commuter/average speeds − various modes*

1960s at the inner ends of radial roads. They may even be worse now than in the inner areas. On the main southern radials from the Manchester CBD, congestion is now worse at distances beyond four miles from the centre than within that distance.

5.2.4 Walking and Cycling

Although quantitative studies are lacking, the transport planner should take into account the large number of pedestrian trips. Even in Greater London these reached some 17 per cent of journeys to work in 1971, and in the other conurbations up to 22 per cent in the case of Tyneside (table 5.1). Naturally, the significance of this mode is much less for work journeys to conurbation centres. Where these are distinguished, only in the case of Tyneside did it exceed 5 per cent in 1971. But walking will be of great significance in inner-city areas and in the suburbs if distances are less than one mile. Pedestrian flows are also large in volume during the working day, both within the CBD and in Subsidiary Nodes. The numbers walking, if the journeys are short (less than one mile generally), will increase as a result of any large increase in bus fares. The experience is normally to lose considerable numbers of short-distance passengers immediately, and for them to drift back to some extent as they become used to the higher fares.

Journeys by cycle and motorcycle, as can be seen from the tables, are of much less significance, even though there may be a tendency since about 1977 for a reversal of declining trends, as fares and motoring costs increase.

5.2.5 Buses

Overall carrying by municipal operators declined from a peak in 1950–51 of 7000 million passengers to 4200 million in 1968–9. The decline has continued, though at a slower rate, and in 1977 the figure was 3168 million (PTE and Municipals). Between 1970 and 1977 London Transport bus passengers declined from 1502 million to 1374 million. Similar figures for Greater Manchester PTE were 623.2 million and 442.5 million respectively. It has been suggested that several hundred bus trips per annum are lost per car purchase.[11]

But though declining, the proportion of journeys to work by bus is still high. In 1971 it was 36.3 per cent in Greater Manchester. In conurbations other than London, generally the proportion of commuters travelling by bus to work in the CBD is higher, varying from 47.45 per cent in Merseyside to 54.28 per cent in Greater Glasgow. But in London, buses only accounted for 14.71 per cent of central-area commuters, the result of longer distances, greater congestion, and the provision of rail services.

The decline in ridership has been particularly significant for weekday evenings and at weekends. For example, in 1959, between 0900 and 1600 the percentage of the total passengers in Manchester was 32.5, and between 1800 and 2300, 25.5 per cent. By 1969, carryings between 0900 and 1600 were 40.5 per cent of the total, but those between 1800 and 2300 had fallen to 19.5 per cent.[12]

Operators' problems are therefore increasingly financial. In the first place, vehicle mileage has not declined to the same extent as have passengers. The average load has therefore fallen, so that revenue is a declining proportion of costs. In the second place, the proportion of the fleet maintained for peak services has increased, thus increasing peak costs. In 1975 the number of buses required by Tyne and Wear PTE to maintain the evening peak hour services (1600–1700) was 1100 against the 791 needed at midday. Thirdly, wages, which account for over 60 per cent of operating costs, have risen at a faster rate than fare increases. Fourthly, congestion costs, imposed by increased car use, have increased. Lower average speeds mean lower vehicle and crew productivity, as well as leading to further passenger loss.

Until the mid-1950s municipal bus operation was broadly profitable. Thereafter the problem has been to find the necessary funds for capital replacement and service improvement. In recent years, too, there has been an increasing gap between receipts and operating costs. In 1978 the direct operating costs of London Transport buses were £156.8 m., against fares revenue of £134.0 m. In the same year, revenue from Greater Manchester PTE bus operation amounted to only 74 per cent of direct operating costs.

5.2.6 Fixed Track Systems

By 1960 the tram had finally disappeared in Great Britain, with the sole exception of Blackpool. There was thus no attempt to upgrade street tramway networks into Light Rail (or Light Rapid Transit) systems common in large Continental cities with high-speed, high-capacity vehicles running on track, which is largely reserved and which has been put underground within the CBD. Nor, with the possible exception of the Tyne and Wear Metro (p. 149) have there been plans for reintroduction.

Railways (many lines cannot with any justification be termed Heavy Rapid Transit) are thus the only fixed-track system in British cities. With the exception of London, and possibly Glasgow, investment in urban rail systems has tended to lag behind that in other parts of the world. Greater Manchester, with a population of 2.6 million and a large CBD, is still without even plans for a metro system. It must be one of the largest cities in the developed world in this situation.

Because of its size, Greater London is heavily dependent on rail; in 1971, 24.3 per cent of journeys to work, and 67.18 per cent of those to the central area, were by this mode. There are a number of subsidiary flows which are of sufficient volume to justify rail transport. During 1978, its first full year of operation, Heathrow Central station at London Airport was used by 6 million passengers. Shopping–commercial centres such as East Croydon are also becoming more dependent on this mode.

London's rail network can be divided into the 'Underground' system of 383 route-km (1977) and the suburban services of British Rail. The former is wholly electrified, and in 1978 carried 546 million passengers, the revenue of £177.6 m. exceeding direct operating costs by £15.4 m. Its principal functions are to provide a connection between suburbs and central area, and to act as a local distributor within the central area, though it also serves numerous local centres. In 1977, some 428 000 passengers reached destinations in the central area by London Transport trains between 0700 and 1000 each working day (table 5.3), 320 000 travelling by this mode the whole way, while a further 108 000 transferred to these trains to complete journeys begun on British Rail.

British Rail's system is, in effect, an integral part of its whole system, and in many ways it is difficult to separate London suburban operations and traffic from its other functions. Suburban trains share tracks and terminals

TABLE 5.3 *Passenger Traffic Entering Central London During the Morning Peak Period* (07.00–10.00)

Mode of Transport	1966	1977
British Rail:		
Southern Region	297 500	258 016
Eastern Region	121 100	99 767
London Midland Region	26 500	30 515
Western Region	10 700	12 027
Total British Rail	455 900	400 325
L.T.E. Rail Total	538 700	428 299
Less Overlap with British Rail Services	122 500	108 316
L.T.E. Rail Total (Less Double Counting)	416 100	319 983
Total Rail (Excluding Double Counting)	872 000	720 308
L.T.E. Bus	174 900	139 412
Total Public Transport	1 046 900	859 720
Private: Cars	142 100	169 989
Motorcycles	16 700	15 420
Pedal cycles	7 000	6 412
Total Private Transport	165 800	191 821
Total Passengers Entering Central London	1 212 700	1 051 541
Passenger Vehicles:		
Cars	100 200	124 006
Motorcycles	15 400	14 670
Pedalcycles	7 000	6 412
L.T. Buses	4 600	2 948
Total Passenger Vehicles	127 200	148 036

Source: London Transport Executive

with Inter-City trains, while semi-fast services to destinations as distant as Ramsgate, Bournemouth and Birmingham call at numerous suburban stations.

Because the London Transport system is much less extensive south of the Thames, the Southern Region carries by far the largest suburban traffic. There are significant flows from the inner suburbs as well as from the middle and outer, which the Southern Railway did much to create by its inter-war electrification policy.[13] In terms of commuter-flow to the central area, 258 000 passengers were carried daily in 1977, some 64 per cent of the total passengers carried by British Rail into Central London.

The principal operating problem lies in making optimum use of limited line capacity and rolling stock in the running of peak services. The financial problem is the very heavy peak costs. For example, the large, eight-platform terminus of Cannon Street and its approach lines are retained almost solely for the commuter peaks, and therefore all the associated costs can be allocated to those peaks. In 1978, 156 trains arrived daily, 66 of them in the morning peak, and these brought in 93 per cent of the total daily passenger arrivals. A further problem is the decline in traffic from inner suburban stations, which cannot be matched by an equivalent reduction in train mileage.

Outside London, the proportion of total journeys-to-work made by rail is much less significant. In 1971, in the seven conurbations, only Central Clydeside exceeded 5 per cent, and in the West Midlands it was only some 1 per cent. The flows to the CBDs are more significant, varying from 8.11 per cent in the West Midlands to 21.6 per cent in Central Clydeside. At least until the mid-1960s, rail was considered to have a declining role, even in this traffic (p. 87, 149).

With the exception of the Glasgow Underground, provincial conurbation rail services were the responsibility of British Rail before the 1968 Transport Act (see section 5.2.10); they received no special financial provision before that Act and had no coherent policy towards them until the mid-1960s. Although grants were received to electrify some of the Glasgow suburban lines in the early 1960s, other improvements were usually by-products of main-line investment.

The only urban areas with reasonably developed systems, as opposed to individual services, were Birmingham, Manchester, Liverpool, Newcastle upon Tyne, West Riding, Glasgow and Cardiff. But development, investment and commercial policies varied, owing to a combination of historical accident, attitude of local management and geographical circumstances. Thus, the Mersey crossing led to a heavy dependence on rail for commuting from the Wirral suburbs to the Liverpool CBD, in spite of a very run-down system. The very peripheral location of Temple Meads station to the Bristol CBD was the main cause of the virtual extinction of the Bristol suburban services by 1960. Conversely, though the Cardiff CBD is smaller, the two stations, Central and Queen Street, are in much better locations. This is the principal factor in the continuing importance of the Cardiff suburban services.

5.2.7 Circulation Patterns

These are extremely complex in the large city, but may be divided into three

(1) *radial* — movement to and from the CBD
(2) *circumferential* — movement to and from subsidiary centres and nodes: industrial, shopping and transport (airports, etc.)
(3) *counterflow* — movement along the radial lines, but outward against the main inward flow

It is also important to distinguish between traffic *terminating* in the central area, and *through*-traffic. Further complexity is provided in conurbations by major subsidiary nodes (p. 137), which create their own radial and circumferential patterns.

Policies aimed at optimising transport facilities to accommodate all these patterns have varied, both over time and between the various planning authorities.

5.2.8 Road Policies

Before the introduction of the TPP system (p. 149) in 1974, grants from central government were available to local authorities for major road schemes in large cities. With their aid, considerable improvements have been made to urban road networks since 1960, though in many cases these have not fully matched traffic increase.

We can distinguish between improvement of existing roads and new construction. In the first category most attention has been paid to radial roads. The aim has been to increase capacity by widening, grade separation at major intersections, and elimination of kerbside parking. Policy is also aimed at reducing the access function of these roads by removing shops and concentrating them in precincts; by reducing the number of houses along them; and by blocking up minor side turnings.

New construction to motorway standards of radials has been somewhat patchy. With the realisation that large commuter flows cannot be wholly provided for by motorisation, there has been a trend towards reducing investment in radial motorways in the inner areas.

To reduce pressure on roads in the central area, inner ring-roads have been provided. Much new investment was needed as these roads were lacking in the pre-motor-age city. Because British cities lacked any sort of fortification built after the introduction of artillery, they contrast with many Continental ones, where the opportunity was taken with the removal of these fortifications to provide an inner ring-road around the city centre — the *ringstrasse* or *boulevard*.

Most city plans envisage *inner* and *outer ring-roads*. The former surrounds the CBD and serves as a major distributor. A good example of a complete inner ring is that of Birmingham, though because of the long period taken to build it,[14] it varies greatly in design, and one section dating from the 1950s is lined with shops. The outer ring-road is normally designed to relieve the central area of through-traffic. In large cities this may be a minority of traffic entering the central area. For example, in 1962 a traffic survey conducted in Greater Manchester[15] revealed that only 12 per cent of vehicles entering the central area started their journeys more than six miles from it, and were for destinations other than within it. But even so, in absolute terms, through-traffic may be large in volume and will have significant consequences on the inner areas. However, outer ring-road construction has also generated much new circumferential traffic. There has also been a considerable outward movement of industry and warehousing from the inner-city area, as sites near outer ring-roads have much easier access.

Major road schemes have, however, led to increased environmental intrusion. For example, there is evidence that the Birmingham inner ring-road circles the CBD too closely, preventing expansion, and reducing the value of property bordering it. Because of the need for grade separation at intersections, urban motorways must either be built below or above the level of the ordinary road network. If the road is depressed the cost is greatly increased, but elevated motorways are visually intrusive and noise pollution is high. Because of these problems of cost and environmental intrusion, major urban road developments have been more readily accepted in the inner city. Here they are associated with redevelopment programmes, which also include slum-clearance and rehousing. Conversely, in the outer suburbs they are considered by residents to cause severe environmental problems.

Previously it was the practice to compensate only for residential property actually demolished. But vigorous protest, coupled with the demonstrations at the opening of Westway, the M4 extension into inner London, led to the 1973 Land Compensation Act, which provides for loss of amenity. This has led to a significant increase in the already very high cost of urban road construction.

This, together with the great diurnal variation in demand for road space, has meant that policy has been moving towards limitation on private cars entering the CBD, especially those of commuters. This can be achieved either by not providing the road space needed to meet maximum demand, or by limiting demand, possibly by charging for road use.[16] The latter is technically possible, but it is both operationally and financially difficult to implement. It is for this reason that road policy must be linked with parking policy.

5.2.9 Parking Policy [17]

Provision must be made for parking at the destination of each trip from the driver's home. This is easier in the outer sectors of the city, where there is a greater supply of land and land-values are lower. Within the CBD the problem is at its most acute. There is insufficient space to meet demand without, as has happened in North America, the virtual destruction of many other CBD functions. An associated problem is to distinguish between demand from commuters and from those using the shopping and other services.

On-street opportunities are limited by the need for prohibition on all major roads, at least between 0800 and 1800, in order to maximise traffic flow. Many side roads are too narrow, or are lined with premises needing access for loading and unloading goods. A time limit is often used for the limited number of on-street parking places during working hours. This is referred to as *cut-off* parking. In large cities parking meters are provided, which normally allow a maximum period of two hours, but which may be less.

Off-street parking in the CBD is extremely costly to provide, land values are high, and parking must normally be in multi-storey parks or underground car-parks. Lower-cost areas can sometimes be found on sites awaiting development in the 'decayed collar'. Sometimes *'park-and-ride'* facilities, that is, peripheral car-parks with bus connections, the price included in the parking fee, are provided. This is particularly useful at times of peak demand, notably for Christmas shopping. The provision of parking at suburban railway stations, in effect large scale park-and-ride, is also desirable.

A coherent charging policy is also desirable, and to implement this, unified control is necessary. In the 1960s, at the height of the office-building boom, Manchester City Council gave planning permission for office blocks only if parking was provided in the basement. This is now regretted, as these spaces are outside local authority control. About 70 per cent of parking spaces in Bristol CBD are under private control. There can also be conflict between authorities on charging policy, as has arisen in Greater Manchester between the county and the district councils.

There are two aspects of charging-policy. The first is the charging-scale at city-centre parks. If all-day parking is to be discouraged, the rate per hour should rise rapidly for periods in excess of about four hours. A variant can be to charge cars driven out of the park during the evening peak at a higher rate than those removed before or after. This has been adopted in Cambridge multi-storey car parks. The second is the zoning of charges, making those in the central area high, those on the periphery slightly lower, and those at suburban stations very low or free.

5.2.10 Public Transport Policy

In the years after 1945, full motorisation for large cities was regarded in North America as a practical goal. Unfortunately, as the impracticability of this policy was being realised there, it was being adopted in Great Britain and, at least outside London, investment in public transport was stagnating. The basic problem was that while funds for road improvements were available from government *grants*, investment in public transport had to come from interest-bearing *loans*. This latter source was becoming more difficult with revenue falling in relation to costs.

The 1968 Transport Act, however, gave legislative support to the growing realisation that public transport had a continuing role in the large city, and powers were given to the Minister of Transport to provide grants for rail infrastructure projects on the same terms as for roads. Grants could also be given for replacement of bus fleets. In addition, *Passenger Transport Authorities* (PTAs) were set up, establishing the principle that policy making and investment for both roads and public transport should ultimately come under a single authority. This principle was taken further by the 1969 Transport (London) and the 1972 Local Government (England and Wales) Acts, which respectively transferred London Transport to the control of the GLC and established the metropolitan counties (p. 47).

These policies were also implemented in 1974 by the introduction of the *Transport Policy and Programme* (TPP) system. Each metropolitan county must produce annually for the Department of Transport a five-year rolling programme for road improvement and maintenance, and for investment and operating subsidies for public transport, both road and rail. The non-metropolitan ('shire') counties, except that their financial responsibilities towards public transport are less, must do the same.

The TPP forms the basis for payment of annual grant, the *Transport Supplementary Grant* (TSG). This is paid on that part of the TPP considered to be above the 'threshold', and is usually between 60 and 70 per cent of the expenditure above the threshold. Expenditure below, such as that on minor roads, will to some extent be covered by the *Rate Support Grant* (RSG), the rest coming from the local rates. Since 1978 there has been for the shire counties an important, but separate element within the TPP in the form of the Public Transport Policy and Programme (PTPP).

Under the 1968 Act and subsequent legislation there has been considerable investment in rail facilities in London and other conurbations – considerable by pre-1968 standards rather than world standards.[18] In London, the Victoria–Brixton extension of the London Transport Victoria Line and the Baker Street–Charing Cross section of the Jubilee Line were financed in this way. 'Infrastructure' was interpreted generously, and electrification of suburban services from Moorgate and King's Cross to Royston via Welwyn Garden City and via Hertford, as well as from Moorgate and St Pancras to Bedford, have also been financed.

Tyne and Wear PTE received grants for the *Metro* system (p. 143), which introduced two new principles into the British transport scene, the introduction of so-called Light Rapid Transit, and the taking over of British Rail services and infrastructure, the latter resulting in a long rearguard action by both the British Railways Board and the rail Unions. Suburban lines, de-electrified by British Rail, have been re-converted under a new system, and the light-rail vehicles projected over new lines tunnelled under the CBD. In Liverpool, British Rail, acting as agents for Merseyside PTE, received grants for constructing the Loop and Link tunnels to bring their electric suburban trains under the CBD. But the similar plans for Greater Manchester were not approved.

In all the PTE areas agreements were negotiated with British Rail, the latter providing services within the area at levels and fares prescribed by the PTE and subsidised by it. Through the 1970s the PTEs showed increasing interest in the part rail services could play in conurbation transport. A good example of this rail-biased policy for major traffic flows has been the up-grading of the Four Oaks–New Street–Longbridge service across Birmingham. Although the New Street–Longbridge section formed part of the busy Bristol Road corridor, British Rail had run only two or three trains in the peak periods. The PTE built new stations, rehabilitated many of the others, and in May 1978 a basic 15-minute service with extras at peak periods was inaugurated. Marketed as the 'Cross-City Line' it was an immediate success in terms of passengers carried, and by August 1979 these had reached 30 000 per day.

In their earlier days the PTEs were faced with the need to integrate the bus fleets they had taken over, with great diversity of vehicles, commercial policies and conditions of service for employees. Unification policies were therefore an important priority.

Bus priorities were also introduced to protect buses from the consequences of road congestion. These include the provision of bus lanes, which are both 'with-flow' on wider streets, and 'contra-flow' in connection with gyratory traffic-management schemes. The west-bound lane in Piccadilly (London) is a good example of the latter. In some cases, as in that of Oxford Street (London), streets have been closed to all traffic except buses and taxis. One-man-operation (OMO) (pp. 51, 90) has been widely introduced on city services, as well as those in suburbs, though the inevitable increase in passenger boarding time has brought problems. In 1978, 60.2 per cent of the vehicle mileage operated by Greater Manchester PTE was by OMO.

The 1980 Transport Act greatly eased entry into stage carriage work but so far with little effect.

Fares Policies

These can be aimed at maximising revenue and/or maximising traffic. These goals are not necessarily compatible and the policies of most operators represent a compromise. Policies must now take into account the impossibility of covering costs, and subsidies are received by all operators in large cities through the TSG and the rates. Operators also provide concessionary fares to senior citizens and school-children, the loss in revenue being offset by grants from the local authorities. In 1978 these support grants provided some 15 per cent of revenue for the West Yorkshire PTE and 40 per cent for those of Merseyside and Tyne and Wear. In the case of South Yorkshire, with its low-fares policy, the support grants account for some 64 per cent of revenue.

In general, the aim has been to keep operating subsidies as low as possible, but at the same time to maximise traffic. The Metropolitan County of South Yorkshire was the first to accept the principle that public transport should be provided on the same basis as municipal services such as education and refuse collection. By maintaining fare levels since 1974, despite strong opposition from central government during a period of high inflation, they have moved a long way to implementation (pp. 36, 89). Traffic increases have resulted, especially for off-peak services, and sometimes to an embarrassing extent. However, the Law Lords' decision in December, 1981, that the reduced fares policy introduced by the GLC in October, 1981, was illegal under the terms of the Transport (London) (1969) Act has obvious implications for reduced fares policies generally. In so far as subsidy has become an element of increasing importance in local public passenger transport in the 1970s, even accepted as such by central government through the TPP system, it is clear that clarification of this issue is called for, possibly through new legislation.

Marketing Policies

The formulation of a fares policy is only a part of an overall marketing policy.

The basis of this should be the identification of the nature of the demand for the product (in this case, urban public passenger transport) and the formation of policies to shape the product to the demand and to sell it.

It was not until the falling traffics of the 1960s and the creation of the PTEs that much attention was paid to marketing. Services tended to be based on subjective estimates of demand, though these tended to be closer to reality in the case of municipal operators than in the case of London Transport, who were slow to provide bus services to new suburban areas, or to recognise the demand for circumferential, as opposed to radial, limited-stop 'Green Line' services. The 1970s, however, saw increasing use by operators and planners of more sophisticated marketing tools, such as on-vehicle and home surveys.

In the 1930s, under the direction of Frank Pick, London Transport developed a house style based on a very high standard of design, which was generally applied, whether to stations or to posters. Though the impetus has since faltered, this tradition has continued. The PTEs have also done much to promote a house style as part of their marketing policy; from the viewpoint of design, that of Greater Manchester must be singled out among the more successful. Large cities whose bus services are provided by the municipality or a National Bus Company subsidiary appear to have much less coherent marketing policies.

Co-ordination Policies

Until 1968 the co-ordination of bus and rail services was largely conspicuous by its absence. It was by no means highly developed even between the bus and rail operations of London Transport. However, this has largely been rectified in the provincial conurbations by the PTEs. A good example is provided by the opening in 1976 of Greater Manchester Transport's Altrincham Interchange. Altrincham is the terminus of an intensive electric train service from Central Manchester. The station itself was modernised and, since its location is very convenient, a bus station was provided in the forecourt. The bus services were remodelled to provide connections with the train service, and there is ample car-parking, which at the time of writing was free. Its success in terms of increased passenger use led to the opening in 1980 of a similar interchange at Bury in the northern part of the county, though here a new site was chosen which involved the diversion of the railway.

Most PTEs have also introduced some form of inter-modal season tickets. The main objective is to divert commuters from both buses and cars to rail for the 'trunk' section of the journey from suburbs to city centre, where there are convenient bus services for suburban collection and downtown distribution, so permitting rationalisation of parallel bus services and possibly easing traffic congestion.

Unfortunately, co-ordination is much less well developed in Greater London where there is no single transport authority. The GLC has no statutory planning or co-ordinating powers over the BR network, while relationships between the GLC and its London Transport Executive have sometimes been poor. There is, however, an advisory committee for medium- and long-term planning representing the GLC, London Transport and British Rail.

5.2.11 Land-use Planning Policies

By the mid-1960s, planners had accepted that land-use and transport are part of a single system. Failure to recognise this fact had led to some serious errors in planning decisions. The rebuilding of Euston Station (London) can be taken as an example. The 7.5 hectare site was completely rebuilt between 1962 and 1968. But British Rail were refused planning permission to erect office blocks on the roof, although permission was given to redevelop neighbouring areas for this purpose. Subsequently, powers were obtained to build blocks in front of the station, but meanwhile the roof of the latter had been built incapable of supporting buildings, so this large central site has been completely wasted. This may be contrasted with the intensive development over New Street Station (Birmingham) and the adjoining bus station, which provides a central site for shops and offices, with ready access by public transport, completely clear of streets. It is to be hoped that major land-use planning decisions will be taken with due consideration for the transport implications.

5.3 Medium and Smaller Towns

In many ways the transport problems of medium and smaller towns are those of large cities, differing only in scale, while the policies which have evolved as a result have also been similar. Thus, most towns between 50 000 and 250 000 have the same problems of road congestion in the centre, peaking of traffic, demand for parking and declining bus-patronage. The review will therefore concentrate on those areas where the problems differ.

5.3.1 Structure and Circulation

The structure of these towns is very much simpler than that of large cities. The CBD, which they have in common with large cities, is not only by far the largest centre in the circulation pattern, but is sometimes the only large one. Though small, the CBD still suffers congestion, and in towns of over 100 000 there is a diurnal peak problem. But, in addition, smaller towns may suffer weekly peaks of market traffic, while resort towns, both coastal and inland, will have seasonal holiday peaks.

5.3.2 Modal Split

Table 5.4 gives details of modal split in work journeys, based on the 1971 Census. The selection of towns has been purely subjective, the intention being to include examples of as wide a variety as possible of function and social composition.

As might be expected, the importance of pedestrian journeys generally increases with decreasing size of town, so that in the examples of smaller towns this mode accounts for between 35 and 40 per cent of all commuting journeys and is the dominant mode. There is not the same relationship in cycle journeys, because of the influence of local topography. Thus, Market Harborough, on a gently undulating area, has some 13 per cent work journeys by cycles, while

TABLE 5.4 *Modal Split of Journey to Work, 1971 – Selected Towns*

	Persons Employed	Train	Bus	Car	Foot	Motorcycle	Cycle	Other (not specified)
Sheffield CB	266 180	φ	47.52	31.72	14.35	φ	φ	6.41
Bristol CB	215 420	1.09	26.93	45.76	16.49	2.34	2.39	5.00
Leicester CB	177 390	φ	34.56	37.60	16.53	1.40	4.17	5.74
Brighton Conurbation†	113 470	3.87	31.51	34.81	19.68	1.30	1.62	7.21
Southampton CB	111 570	1.80	27.30	43.36	13.91	3.12	5.12	5.39
Plymouth CB	106 980	φ	29.20	40.49	19.31	2.25	1.05	7.70
Norwich CB	84 443	1.28	20.02	46.25	15.26	3.53	10.40	3.26
Oxford CB	81 120	φ	20.47	43.42	13.31	5.80	11.77	5.23
Northampton CB	68 870	φ	23.33	41.9	20.50	1.84	5.55	6.89
Blackpool CB	58 350	φ	28.69	32.89	19.95	1.13	3.39	13.95
Blackburn CB	54 630	φ	34.21	33.52	24.29	φ	φ	7.98
Exeter CB	49 960	1.40	20.59	47.17	17.87	3.32	4.39	5.26
Burnley CB	39 680	φ	31.30	32.26	28.26	φ	φ	8.19
Chester CB	36 990	1.16	27.33	40.50	19.41	1.16	5.38	5.06
Maidstone CB	35 080	2.77	26.00	40.99	21.15	1.82	2.10	5.17
Shrewsbury MB	30 300	φ	17.85	42.97	22.21	1.39	8.41	7.17
Loughborough MB	26 530	φ	17.98	41.50	24.20	1.62	10.05	4.64
Nelson MB	12 760	φ	21.47	28.29	40.75	φ	1.10	8.39
Newbury UD	12 420	1.53	12.48	47.75	23.51	2.50	7.49	4.74
Market Harborough UD	7 620	φ	5.28	37.27	36.35	1.97	12.73	6.40
Colne MB	7 310	φ	22.57	31.46	37.20	φ	1.64	7.93

Source: 10 per cent sample, 1971 Census of England and Wales, Scotland
φ Less than 1 per cent
† Brighton CB, Hove MB, Portslade UD, Shoreham UD

Colne, of similar size but located in a hilly area, has only some 2 per cent. Journeys to work by motorcycle remain consistently unimportant, for the most part accounting for between 1.5 and 4.0 per cent of commuting journeys.

There is no obvious relationship between the importance of commuting by car, and town size. It depends more on the function and social composition of the town. Thus, in the sample, Newbury, with 47.75 per cent of work journeys by car, and Nelson (Lancs) with 28.29 per cent represent the extremes, though they are of similar size. Equally, Brighton and Southampton are similar in size, but car journeys account for 34.81 per cent of commuting in the former case and 43.36 per cent in the latter.

On the other hand, bus journeys tend to be more closely related to size, though there are other factors to be taken into account. In general, the smaller the town, the less significant the bus mode, presumably because distances become less and walking more important.

5.3.3 Road Policies

The provision of road space to satisfy demand will present similar difficulties, with only scale differences from the problems experienced by large cities. But in one respect the smaller town differs. With decreasing size, through-traffic becomes of greater importance compared with terminating-traffic. The provision of an outer ring-road, or by-pass if the flow of through-traffic is linear in form, can therefore be very effective in reducing congestion, and improving the environment in the town centre and its approach roads.

Unfortunately, planning policy has allowed house-building along earlier ring-roads and at too many intersections, thus reducing average speeds and consequently capacity. A good example of this is the south-western section of the Derby ring-road. The economics of ring-road/by-pass construction should also be taken into account. The small Border town of Welshpool (Powys) does not normally suffer unduly from through-traffic. However, it lies on holiday routes to the Welsh Coast and this causes very severe congestion, but only on twelve to fifteen weekends in the year. The cost of the proposed by-pass should therefore be debited to these few days.

The scale of road improvements should also be carefully designed so as not to overshadow the scale of the town. It may, however, be possible to provide an inner ring-road, which can facilitate the making of the town centre into a traffic-free precinct. This has been successfully achieved in the case of Chester. But the inner ring-road at Huntingdon has had an adverse effect on the townscape.

5.3.4 Public Transport Policy

As we have already seen, the smaller the town, the more important walking becomes and the easier the use of private transport. But the Buchanan Report of 1963,[19] which had such a profound effect on planning policies, emphasised that there was a continuing residual demand for public transport even in the case of Newbury (Berks), with a population of 15 000. Certainly towns of over

50 000 do require local bus services, though the level and quality of the services provided varies very greatly.

Traditionally, bus services were provided either by the municipality or by Territorial companies (p. 49). Municipal operators were prevented from working across the boundary of the local authority, although during the inter-war years many suburbs grew up beyond them. These were served by the local Territorial company, and working arrangements between the Corporation and Territorial operators was often a problem.

After the 1974 local government reorganisation the district councils became responsible for any municipally owned services within their areas, though the shire counties were given the transport-planning powers. The Districts also lack powers to extend their existing services, other than by purchase from the NCB or Independent operator, if they agree. There are a number of indications that relationships between NBC subsidiary companies and District operators are too frequently poor.

As in larger cities, bus priorities are often provided. In recent years too there has been a tendency to allow buses and pedestrians to mix in otherwise traffic-free areas. Queen Street and Cornmarket (Oxford) provide a good example. In this way buses are enabled to reach the most central points in the CBD.

Operation of small municipal bus fleets differs in some respects from that of larger fleets. There is better communication between management and crews, and labour relations are much better. There is a greater flexibility of approach to day-to-day problems, and it is not unusual for a bus to be taken out by an Inspector or member of the management staff if there is a shortage of drivers.

Financial results of the smaller fleets also tend to be better than those of larger ones. So far, municipal operators have either covered costs or the district councils have been prepared to provide the necessary operating subsidies; for example, City of Chester Transport serves a town of 63 000 with a fleet of fifty buses. In the period 1970–78 passengers carried have remained stable, fluctuating between 10.2 million in 1970 and 9.45 million in 1978. Gross revenue consistently exceeded working expenses.

5.3.5 Parking Policies

Parking policies must be similar to those in large cities. If the CBD is of any size, that is, in towns of over 100 000 and in many smaller ones, some limitation on all-day parking is necessary, but adequate parking for short-stay shoppers and business callers must be provided, as much of the town's trade depends on them. But there is an additional constraint. Charging policies must take into account those of the neighbouring towns with which the town is in competition for the provision of shopping and other services.

5.3.6 Historic Towns

A number of towns with populations of about 100 000 have particularly historic centres in terms of layout, surviving buildings and environment. Examples are

Oxford, Cambridge, Bath, York, Norwich and Chester. These towns pose
particular problems. On the one hand the environment and character of the
town must be preserved, but on the other hand the town must be allowed to
develop the normal functions of a town of comparable size.

Road layout can rarely be altered, or existing roads and intersections
improved, because of disturbance to the historic buildings lining them. The
provision of an inner ring-road or of distributor roads around the central area
may be equally difficult. The only reasonable line for an Oxford inner ring-road
was through Christ Church Meadows. Proposals to use this line aroused so much
opposition that the scheme has never been implemented. The site of Bath, in the
deep and steep-sided valley of the Avon has also hitherto prevented the
construction of an inner ring.

Chester can be cited as an example of successful adaptation to the motor age.
Here the completion of an outer ring-road to divert the heavy flows of through-
traffic was a necessary preliminary to adaptation of the town centre. But
terminating-traffic is also very heavy, as Chester has a very extensive shopping
hinterland. An inner ring-road was also necessary. Except in the southern sector,
where existing roads could be used, new construction was involved. To the east
and north this could be sited outside the mediaeval wall, but in the west it
severs part of the historic centre from the rest.

Fortunately, there were areas of sub-standard housing within the walls, and
this allowed the siting of a number of multi-storey car parks accessible from
the inner ring-road. In the centre, a combination of elimination of on-street
parking, and the closure of two lengths of 50 yards of road to all traffic except
buses, retained limited access to shops, while greatly reducing the numbers of
vehicles in the streets within the ring-road.

5.4 Rural Areas

Problems of transport in rural areas has received a great deal of attention in the
literature[20] and in recent years from planners and legislators.

The basic problem is that car ownership, both in terms of cars per head and
of the proportion of households with cars, has increased even more in rural
than in urban areas (p. 44). In general too, the more remote the rural areas,
the higher the level of car ownership. Thus, in 1971, the counties of
Montgomeryshire and Radnorshire had the highest levels in England and Wales.
This has resulted in a marked decline in the demand for public transport and
therefore in its provision. At the same time, other services, shops, sub-post
offices and surgeries, have tended to disappear from the smaller and remoter
villages. For those without the use of cars there has therefore been a decline
in both mobility and access.[21] Since the mid-1960s, it has come to be
realised there will always be a minority of the rural population with either no
acess at all to cars or no access during the working day, as in one-car households
the car is used for the journey to work. There is thus a continuing need for a
minimum level of public transport. But as yet there is no agreement as to what
constitutes a minimum level of service, or how this can be provided.

The scale of the problem differs from area to area. In rural areas around the major conurbations, the Home Counties, North East Cheshire, and Warwickshire, for example, population densities are relatively high and towns closely spaced. There is therefore still a sufficient traffic potential, and the public transport services, bus and rail, have not experienced any severe reductions. Other rural areas benefit from a location on an inter-urban route. But the problem of public transport provision becomes more acute in the remoter areas, whether these be East Anglia or Mid-Wales.

The growth of tourism by private car, which has fundamentally increased the area accessible for day trips as well as period holidays, poses a further problem. Severe seasonal pressure is placed on the network of minor roads within areas of particular beauty, inland and coastal, and of historic interest. The National Parks, the Lake District, Snowdonia, and the Derbyshire Peak District among them, have particularly severe local problems. But difficulties are also experienced in coastal areas, such as St Ives (Cornwall) and Lulworth Cove (Dorset), as well as in rural beauty spots such as Kinver Edge and Cannock Chase in the West Midlands.[22]

5.4.1 Rail Transport

During the nineteenth century a network of rural branch lines grew up. But there is good evidence many of them were never economic and were only maintained by cross-subsidisation. With the general decline in railway profitability, and with increasing bus and lorry competition for the small traffic flows basically unsuited to rail, closures began on a wide scale in the 1930s. But it was the implementation of the Beeching policies[23] between 1963 and 1968 that finally led the railways to cease any significant role in general freight carrying in rural areas and, with certain exceptions, passenger carrying as well. The exceptions are mainly in the area served by Southern Region, which still maintains an intensive inter-urban service stopping at rural stations; outer suburban lines from major provincial centres, such as that from Manchester to Chester via Northwich; and lines retained because of political pressure, such as the Central Wales and the lines north of Inverness. It should also be remembered that closure of wayside stations on main lines has been just as extensive as that associated with complete closure of branch lines.

However, technological and operational innovations since 1968 have undoubtedly reduced running costs significantly. Under the 1968 Transport, and 1972 Local Government Acts, shire counties have been given powers to subsidise services, though a loophole in the 1974 Railways Act has prevented much use being made of these. If a passenger service is in operation over a particular line, it is part of the Public Service Obligation Network (p. 64). Freight traffic pays only its direct operating costs plus a notional 'rental' for the use of tracks. The passenger service can be increased in agreement with the county, the latter paying only the marginal costs. But if the county wishes to restore a service on a freight-only line, the county becomes liable not only to the direct costs, but to virtually all the track costs as well.[24]

However, some stations, among them the legendary Llanfair PG (Anglesey), have been reopened under guarantee from the particular county, while Clwyd

County supports the opening of the Conway Valley line on summer Sundays. The Yorkshire Dales National Park Authority have paid for the reopening of stations on the Settle–Carlisle line, and hire trains to run from stations in West Yorkshire on summer week-ends. An agreement with Cornwall County led to British Rail opening a station at Lelant Saltings in 1978, and providing an intensive park-and-ride service at holiday peaks to St Ives, allowing tourist cars to be prohibited in the resort.

The proliferation of steam-operated preserved lines[25] has led to a widespread recognition of their tourist potential (thus confounding the generalisation that demand for transport is derived), and many are supported by Tourist Boards. In conjunction with British Rail, 'Great Little Railways of Wales' conduct a sophisticated marketing exercise.

5.4.2 Bus Transport

During the inter-war period a very complete network of rural bus services developed, and by 1939 very few villages were without a daily bus service. This was aided after 1930 by the policy of the Traffic Commissioners, who protected the lucrative inter-urban operations of the Territorial companies on the tacit assumption they built up a cross-subsidised rural network. Not only were rail passengers diverted, but much new traffic was created. In the years immediately after 1945, disposable incomes rose in rural areas, but petrol was rationed and car sales limited, so new peaks in bus patronage were achieved.

But after 1955, traffic began to decline, and during the 1960s this reached catastrophic proportions. Carryings on rural services frequently declined faster than on inter-urban ones (p. 86), though disaggregation of figures is difficult. Revenue declined much faster than costs, in spite of the nearly universal adoption of OMO. In attempts to maintain revenue, fare increases led to further traffic loss. Services were reduced by opening out headways, and after its formation in 1968 the NBC, pursuing its financial objectives, began to withdraw services wholesale.

At the same time, however, the 1968 Act also empowered shire counties to provide operating subsidies for those services they wished retained, the Minister of Transport being obliged to match the local authority contribution. In this way many rural services were reprieved, though willingness to support services varied greatly between counties. Many were willing to support Independent operators where they offered to provide the service at less cost than the NBC. Some entrepreneurs, one could call them enthusiasts, such as North Downs Transport in the Orpington (Kent) area and the Mountain Goat services in Cumbria, were prepared to move into areas abandoned by London Transport and the NBC, though with mixed success. But in spite of all this, the decline both in the network and in service intervals has continued. By 1978 many rural areas were without buses, or at best have a trip on market day or Saturday.

5.4.3 Unorthodox Solutions

With this decline, and with widespread acceptance of the continuing need
for a basic socially necessary service, the search for alternative solutions
intensified. By no means all were at all successful. The use of minibuses was
widely advocated and occasionally tried. But this was no real solution as it
did nothing to reduce wage costs, which account for over 60 per cent of
operating costs.

In 1967 the Post Office introduced a minibus service centred on the
market town of Lanidloes (Powys).[26] A minibus was used to collect and
deliver mail at outlying post offices to enable fare-paying passengers to be
carried. Wage costs could thus be shared between the two functions performed,
while the cost of the vehicle would come under the bus-grant system.
Obviously routes were indirect and schedules leisurely, but the project met
with some success. But its spread has apparently been dependent on the
initiative of local management. Thus, one area where they are highly developed
is Canterbury, perhaps an area least needing this type of service.

The 1977 Minibus Act gave legislative approval to the Community Bus
concept.[27] This was first introduced in Norfolk by the Eastern Counties
subsidiary of NBC. The bus company provides and maintains a minibus to
operate a feeder service from villages without a regular bus service. This is
driven by trained volunteers, thus eliminating the principal cost. It may be
early days, but at the time of writing there is no evidence of rapid introduction
of the scheme.

Community Car services are also now legally possible. Volunteers offer to
transport people without cars on trips for shopping, surgery visits, etc., being
reimbursed with their out-of-pocket expenses from Social Service funds.

Most county councils operate regular scheduled school transport with
hired vehicles. It has been suggested that these could be used at very low
marginal costs to carry ordinary fare-paying passengers (the authors are of the
opinion such passengers would have to be desperate to make use of such a
facility!).[28]

It is the intention of the 1980 Transport Act to reduce drastically the scope
of service licensing while Trial Areas and Experimental Areas are introduced
in the 1981 Public Passenger Vehicle Act. But in conditions of declining demand
and almost universal subsidy it is hard to see how increasing freedom of entry
can have any beneficial effect. Whatever the legal position, in practice the
county councils are the effective arbiters of who shall operate what routes.

Some solutions are aimed at reducing congestion at beauty spots. As parking
is so limited at famous viewpoints, Gwynnedd County Council have introduced
the 'Snowdon Sherpa' service operated by Crosville, from Caernarvon around
Snowdonia. The Peak Park authority sponsored services operated by Potteries
Motor Traction between Stoke-on-Trent and Dovedale.

5.4.4 Co-ordination and Planning

The involvement of the shire counties in rural transport planning, other than in the provision and maintenance of roads, began with the 1968 Act, when they were given powers to subsidise public transport. The 1972 Local Government (England and Wales) Act required them to produce a co-ordinated transport plan, and from 1974 they were required to submit annually a TPP, which like those of the metropolitan counties, formed the basis of their Transport Supplementary Grant. Under the 1978 Transport Act they were required to consult with all passenger transport operators within their area, and produce a PTPP before producing their TPP. Transport planning has therefore become an integral function of planning departments, and the appointment of Transport Co-ordinators has become necessary.

The possibility, though not the guarantee, of the emergence and implementation of fully co-ordinated local transport plans therefore exists. But an intractable problem remains, in that operating subsidies take up an increasing proportion of public funds available for public transport, and perhaps at the increasing expense of capital investment. The concept of local authority involvement in rural public transport, though common in areas of low population density in many countries such as Norway and Switzerland, is only very slowly winning acceptance. There is still a widespread impression that a normal market exists and that restoration of freedom of entry, increased efficiency on the part of existing operators, or the adoption of unorthodox solutions will in some way reduce costs to existing revenue levels and still give an adequate service. However, there is evidence of increasing flexibility of attitudes coupled with increasing realisation of need. It is to be hoped good intentions will be translated into practice, as this is necessary to maintain even the most basic levels of rural services.

5.5 General Conclusions

(1) The universal increase in car ownership and wage levels has brought many benefits to users of local transport in terms of mobility and access. But it has also brought problems of congestion, environmental intrusion and road safety in urban areas, and even to rural beauty spots, and declining standards of public transport provision everywhere.

(2) Satisfying the demand for road space, particularly in urban areas, brings problems of land-use conflict, environmental deterioration, and the creation of new demand. Problems may be divided into those connected with the provision of roads and those connected with provision of parking.

(3) A residual, but widespread and continuing need for public transport, which in some cases may be indispensable.

(4) A need for co-ordination between the various modes and between public transport, road provision and car-parking policies.

(5) The consequent need for transport planning on a local scale and consequently the continuing involvement of local authorities.

(6) A continuing need not only for support from public funds for investment, but also for part of the operating costs.

(7) While the involvement of central government is necessary for the formulation of overall policies to provide a framework within which local

authorities can work, there is a problem of over-dependence on central government for the funding of solutions to local problems.

(8) The need for flexibility of approach and a full understanding of the consequences of their attitudes and decisions by legislators, planners, operators and trade unions.

(9) It will have been noted that on the local scale, problems of freight transport and the formulation of policies to deal with them do not loom nearly as large as they do on the national scale. The main exceptions are the problems of environmental intrusion by heavy goods vehicles, and problems of loading and unloading in congested urban areas.

(10) The connection between urban design and underlying policies on the one hand, and transport provision on the other, is close. Policies, official and unofficial, aimed at centralisation or at decentralisation or urban functions will obviously affect transport planning policies. Conversely, transport policies will affect the form and function of urban areas.

References

1. Office of Population Censuses and Survey, *Census, 1971, Great Britain Advance Analysis* (HMSO, 1972)
2. For studies of the Manchester CBD see H. P. White (ed.) *The Continuing Conurbation* (Gower, London, 1980) especially chs 3, 5, 15
3. P. W. Daniels, *Office Location: an Urban and Regional Study* (Bell, London, 1975); P. W. Daniels (ed.) *Spatial Patterns of Office Growth and Location* (Wiley, Chichester, 1979)
4. K. Pring, An Examination of the Problems Characteristic of the Inner Urban Ring of London, and some Possible Ways of Solving Them, with Particular Reference to Barnsbury (unpublished MSc Thesis, University of Salford, 1972)
5. T. C. Barker and M. Robbins, *A History of London Transport*, Vol. 1, The Nineteenth Century, Vol. 2, the Twentieth Century to 1970 (Allen & Unwin, London, 1962 and 1974)
6. Office of Population Census and Survey, *Census 1971, Workplace and Transport to Work* (HMSO, 1975)
7. Department of the Environment, *National Travel Survey 1975/76 Report* (HMSO, 1979)
8. R. L. Davies, *Marketing Geography with Special Reference to Retailing* (Corbridge Retailing and Planning Associates, 1977) (Methuen, London, 1977)
9. London Transport Executive, *Annual Reports*
10. Government Statistical Service, *Passenger Transport in Great Britain* (HMSO, annual)
11. S. Wabe and O. B. Coles, The Short and Long-run Cost of Bus Transport in Urban Areas, *J. Transp. econ. Pol.*, 9 (1975) 127—40
12. P. R. White, *Planning for Public Transport* (Hutchinson, London, 1976) p. 43

13. H. P. White, Greater London, Vol. 3 in *A Regional History of Great Britain* (David & Charles, Newton Abbot, 1971)
14. J. Holliday, *City Centre Redevelopment* (Knight, London, 1973)
15. South East Lancashire and North East Cheshire Area Highway Engineering Committee (SELNEC), *A Highway Plan* (William Morris Press, 1962)
16. G. Roth, *Paying for Roads* (Penguin, Harmondsworth, 1967); Ministry of Transport, *Road Pricing: the Economic and Technical Possibilities* (the Smeed Report) (HMSO, 1964)
17. S. Brierley, *Parking and Motor Vehicles* (Applied Science Publishers, London, 1972)
18. For a world review: J. M. Thomson, *Great Cities and their Traffic* (Gollancz, 1977). For detailed studies of London: M. F. Collins and T. M. Pharoah, *Transport Organisation in a Great City: the Case of London* (Allen & Unwin, London, 1974)
19. C. D. (Sir Colin) Buchanan/Ministry of Transport, *Traffic in Towns* (the Buchanan Report) (HMSO, 1963)
20. See among others: H. D. Clout, *Rural Geography: an Introductory Survey* (Pergamon, Oxford, 1972); R. Cresswell (ed.), *Rural Transport and Country Planning* (Leonard Hill, London, 1978); The Independent Commission on Transport, *Changing Directions* (Coronet, London, 1974)
21. M. J. Moseley, *Accessibility: the Rural Challenge* (Methuen, London, 1979); P. W. Daniels and A. M. Warnes, *Movement in Cities* (Methuen, London, 1980)
22. H. B. Rodgers, *Cannock Chase Study* (3 vols) (Countryside Commission/Staffs County Council, 1979)
23. British Railways Board, *The Reshaping of British Railways* (Beeching Report) (British Railways Board, 1963)
24. H. Conway and H. P. White, *Fixed Track Costs and Shifting Subsidies*, Discussion Papers in Geography 10 (University of Salford, Dept of Geography, 1979)
25. P. N. Grimshaw, Steam Railways: Growth of Points for Leisure and Recreation, *Geography*, **61** (1976) 83–8
26. D. Turnock, The Postbus: a New Element in Britains Rural Transport, *Geography*, **62** (1977) 112–18
27. Dept of Transport, *A Guide to Community Transport* (HMSO, 1978)
28. Public Passenger Vehicle Act 1981

6

National Transport Problems and Policies

This chapter considers national, or non-local, transport problems and policies; chapter 5 has already dealt with the local ones. We will confine our consideration of the development of policy in the United Kingdom mainly to the period since the 1968 Transport Act.

There are two main types of national transport problems. Firstly, there are problem areas which affect the transport sector indirectly; examples are economic growth, regional development, and energy. Secondly, there are problems directly affecting particular transport sub-sectors. Examples are

(1) Transport manufacturing – problems of employment, output, productivity, and visible trade balance.

(2) Road transport – problems of the extent of the trunk-road network, maximum size of lorries, and environmental costs.

(3) Rail transport – problems of network size, subsidy, further electrification, and worsening economic trends for freight operations.

(4) Air transport – problems of traffic growth and increasing fuel costs.

(5) Ports – problems of decline of long-established large ports and estimating future provision for conventional and unconventional berths.

(6) Shipping – the problem of decline in the role of the UK merchant fleet in the world's liner trades.

6.1 Economic Growth and Regional Development

Low economic growth, and even recession, in the United Kingdom in the late 1970s have caused three main problems for the transport sector.

(1) Central government has reduced overall public expenditure on transport. New road construction is the main area to suffer from reduced capital expenditure. The use of cash limits for current expenditure has resulted in a reduction in road maintenance and in real increases in bus and rail fares, because costs have increased at a faster rate than the levels of support.

(2) Poorer market conditions have resulted in lower levels of demand for transport manufactures and transport services. Operators of transport services

have sought revenue from spare capacity to cover increasing costs by offering selective reductions in fares or rates; for example, price competition has increased in air travel on the North Atlantic route, between scheduled air passenger operators and air freight operators in air freight, between British Rail and express coach operators, and between cross-Channel ferry operators. Rail freight operations, with their dependence on carriage of coal and coke, and iron and steel, have been severely affected by the lower levels of economic activity that have prevailed.

(3) Lower rates of economic growth have been accompanied by higher unemployment, with regional and sub-regional emphases, which have contributed to lower demand for local public passenger transport and made real increases in fares more inevitable under a cash-limits system for fare support.

However, higher rates of economic growth would not entirely solve the above problems. It is only under strict monetarist management of an economy that economic growth is a fundamental requirement for increased public expenditure. Furthermore, public expenditure is being more severely constrained by the Thatcher administration than justified by rates of economic growth, in order to reduce direct taxation significantly. Higher economic growth would result in increased demand for transport manufactures but, on present evidence, this would be accompanied by higher import penetration because of the combined effects of the poor internal cost base of UK transport manufacturing and a 'strong pound'.

There are even benefits for the transport sector of low economic growth. As indicated above, spare capacity in transport systems has resulted in cheaper fares and lower freight rates, even though at the expense of orders for transport manufactures and profitability of transport operations. Other benefits include the following.

(1) Lower consumption of scarce commodities — oil is the most topical example. However, the classical economist would argue that, while oil is finite, energy is not, and that substitution is the general solution to problems of resource depletion.

(2) More time to prepare for the significant changes in the social and economic structure of society that will be required to accommodate resource depletion problems.

(3) Some transport facilities, particularly the infrastructure, will last longer because traffics will increase more slowly.

(4) Patronage of public passenger transport systems, which has historically declined with economic growth, might decrease more slowly, and so result in better conditions for reinvestment in the event of their being needed in the future.

So, even though higher rates of economic growth are desirable to satisfy general objectives of higher public expenditure and full employment, they are not wholly desirable from the viewpoint of the transport sector in the United Kingdom.

Implicit in the discussion so far is the assumption that the transport sector merely responds to changes in the economy as a whole. Another view is that government can take action in the transport sector to stimulate economic growth, the usual practice, or to reduce it. Unfortunately, there is no definitive evidence that national economic growth is sensitive to government intervention in the transport secor.[1] There are two main explanations for this: firstly, any improvement in economic growth normally results from the indirect, rather than the direct, effects of such intervention; secondly, at the same time that such intervention may be stimulating economic growth, other factors may be having the opposite effect.

The main form of government intervention in the transport sector to stimulate economic growth has been investment in infrastructure, particularly in roads. Such intervention normally has had regional development implications; for example, this has been considered an important contribution to solution of problems of higher-than-national unemployment rates or lower-than-national economic growth rates. The road-building programmes in Northern Ireland and North Eastern England, as well as concentration of the motorway programme outside the South East of England until recently, all bear witness to this; yet unemployment rates remain much higher than average in areas which have benefited in this way from substantial improvements in infrastructure. The main explanation is that in a developed economy like that of the United Kingdom, investment in transport infrastructure only results in second- if not third-order improvements in economic growth at the national level.

Perhaps the most significant effects of investment in roads are on economic activity rather than economic growth; for example, better road access to tourist areas has encouraged the development of tourist industries. However, it should not be overlooked that this is not just a one-way process. These same areas might become at the same time more dependent upon fuel, food, and other services from adjacent regions. So the important point to make is that investment in roads might result in imbalances in the flows of goods and services between regional economies, and contribute to regional growth in some cases and regional decline in others. So it might be easier to identify investment in transport infrastructure with sub-regional or regional economic growth rather with economic growth at the national level.[2]

In view of this lack of clear evidence of the benefits for national economic growth of investment in transport infrastructure, perhaps the main justification for such investment is that the United Kingdom must have as efficient a transport system as its trading competitor countries.

Financial support for transport manufacturing industries has become another form of government investment in the transport sector since the 1960s. First the shipbuilding industry, then the aerospace industry, then, unsuccessfully, the motorcycle industry, and most recently the motor-car manufacturing industry, have had such financial support. In as much as this action has made these industries more competitive in domestic and international markets, it has contributed to economic growth, even though in principle the financial support involved might have been put to better use. But such action would ignore the local employment objectives of intervention. With important shipbuilding activity concentrated in the economically depressed areas of Clydeside, Tyneside, Merseyside, and Belfast, and British motor-car manufacturing in the West Midlands, decline of these industries has very serious implications for regional economies. So again government intervention can be more readily identified with regional rather than national economic growth.

The third important form of government intervention in the transport sector is subsidy of transport operations. As inter-city passenger operations and freight operations are required to operate without subsidy in principle in the United Kingdom, the main transport operations benefiting from subsidy are local rail and local bus operations. However, London and South East rail services cover their direct costs and make a significant contribution to indirect costs, while the subsidy element in fares in urban areas outside London is generally modest. So, attention should first be directed at the possible effects on economic growth of significant subsidy of fares on London Transport, rail operation in local services for smaller urban areas and rural areas.
local services for smaller urban areas and rural areas.

It is impossible to say that these subsidies have a significant effect on national or even regional economic growth. In principle, as with financial support of transport manufacturing, the expenditure might be put to better effect from the viewpoint of national economic growth. The main effects of fare subsidies for London Transport are to slow down decentralisation of activities from Central London and relieve road traffic congestion while the former is the main effect for Passenger Transport Executive rail services. The main effect of subsidy of local bus services and rail services in small urban areas and rural areas is probably in the distribution rather than the level of unemployment; for example, if fares were higher or no public transport was available then unemployment might be an option to commuting from a village to a nearby town but it is likely that the job so released would be taken by a more local employee.[3]

So again government intervention in the transport sector has its main effects on regional economies. This is perhaps the main conclusion to be drawn from addressing this question of the sensitivity of economic growth to government intervention in the transport sector. 'Government' has been used in the generic term in the discussion; most funds come from central government so far as transport infrastructure, support for transport manufacturing, and subsidies are concerned, but local government also provides them.

6.2 Energy

Energy affects the transport sector directly and indirectly. Higher oil prices will affect transport directly by increasing costs of operation, particularly where these form a significant part of total costs, as in air transport. It will affect transport indirectly by causing lower rates of economic growth.

The basic long-term problem may be summarised in this way: transport is virtually dependent on oil; oil prices are likely to increase with increasing depletion of oil resources; demand for oil on the transport sector is fairly insensitive to price in the short and possibly medium runs, partly because society had grown used to life styles based on cheap oil; long time-lags will be involved in the development of less energy-intensive life styles, and alternative transport systems and fuels; and government cannot be sure that the necessary adjustment in demand for oil in the transport sector will take place without a need for its intervention.

A further complication is that temporary short-term constraints on the supply of oil and oil products will become more probable as oil prices increase, as happened in the United Kingdom in 1979 over the supply of derv to bus operators.

There are some general problems of a technical nature in formulating a suitable basis for government intervention over the long-term supply of energy. Firstly, government cannot be confident about the effects of intervention because the issue of energy supply is complex and understanding of it imperfect. Secondly, selection of a suitable form of intervention is difficult because it will depend upon the nature of the economic future, which in turn is subject to great uncertainty because of the oil-supply situation.

These problems of complexity of relationships and uncertainty indicate that government intervention regarding energy supply ideally should be robust, that is, appropriate over as diverse a range of economic futures as possible, and reversible in the event of its being inappropriate.[4] The cynic might argue that these are essential conditions for no intervention by government. It should perhaps be noted that a government that is securing alternative energy supplies by large capital investments in coal, nuclear power, tidal power and wave energy, is following policies which do not necessarily satisfy these criteria of robustness and reversibility.

An alternative approach to the general problem of future energy supply would be to attempt to reduce demand for energy by significant conservation measures. Unfortunately, the evidence to date suggests that government cannot rely upon such measures to make a significant contribution to the problem.[5]

A third technical problem is that pricing of alternative energy sources in the short run might be inconsistent with less reliance on oil in the long run. This has been the case in the United Kingdom, where the prices of coal and electricity have been allowed to increase at a faster rate than the prices of oil and gas in recent years, despite the very large increases in oil prices which have taken place since 1974.

There are also technical problems particular to intervention in the transport sector. Firstly, the impact of an increase in the price of oil on demand for transport fuels is reduced further because, with the exception of transport substantial flat-rate fuel-duty element; additionally, while the latter remains unchanged it falls in value in real terms with inflation, and so counterbalances the effects of any increases in fuel price caused by higher oil prices.

Secondly, the impact of an increase in the price of oil on demand for transport fuels is reduced additionally because, with the exception of transport fuels purchased for personal private travel, increased costs are simply passed on as additional costs of production to final consumers. This can have a significant effect on demand for transport fuels where they account for a considerable proportion of total production costs, as in air transport, but the general effect is to mollify the impact of increases in oil prices on demand for transport fuels. This is particularly evident regarding petrol used in company cars; so far as the latter are concerned, of course, many motorists are insulated against the effects of more expensive oil because they do not even have to purchase petrol for their private motoring.

Thirdly, the conventional bases for investment in transport infrastructure of social-cost-benefit analysis and financial analysis are inadequate for investments that reduce energy costs or reduce dependence on oil in the long run, because they do not give particular treatment to energy costs and suffer from problems of timescale.[6] Energy costs are simply treated as one of several factors in the appraisal; the investment may proceed providing the test discount rate is satisfied and funds are available, without any explicit consideration of its possible effects on the overall level of demand for energy. There are two facets to the timescale problem: firstly, current test discount rates in the public sector imply negligible present-day values on benefits and costs at least thirty years ahead, the very time horizon when the benefits of transport investment that reduces energy costs or dependence on oil are likely to be becoming increasingly valuable; secondly, it is fairly obvious that traffic predictions used in investment appraisal will become increasingly untenable as the energy problem develops, because they reflect current relationships in transport energy use.

There has been very little intervention as yet by the UK central government regarding energy consumption in the transport sector. The main steps have been related to raising the perception of the of the cost of transport fuels; for example, petrol consumption for the urban, 56 mph and 75 mph driving cycles must now be specified for new motor cars on sale in the United Kingdom under the 1976 Energy Act.[7]

The Callaghan administration wished to transfer the main burden of duties on motor-car use to fuel tax, partly on the considerable evidence that annual mileage, and thereby fuel consumption, is most sensitive to increases in the variable costs of motoring. However, this proposal was not put into practice because of opposition on the grounds of the additional cost burden likely to be imposed by such a measure on motorists with above-average annual mileage, such as people living in rural areas and business motorists.

The present administration favours the view that long-term solution to the energy problem lies in the market mechanism rather than in intervention, and that it is therefore important to have the right pricing policies in the public sector and appropriate taxation policies. Regarding the latter, they have removed taxation anomalies between motor spirit and Derv, as well as increasing duties on transport fuels, in order to make good reductions in their real value with inflation.[8] However, there is an obvious dichotomy between this confidence in the market mechanism and the large taxation component of transport fuel prices (see section 1.5.2).

6.3 Transport Manufacturing

The worsening trading situation in transport manufacturing, and particularly the growing imbalance of visible trade in motor manufacturing, has been described in section 1.4.1. The response of successive governments has been public ownership of a major part of the industry concerned, with consequent restructuring, rationalisation and modernisation; thus, British Shipbuilders, British Aerospace, and Rolls-Royce Ltd were created. These companies are all dependent on defence contracts. In addition, Rolls-Royce depend on the success of ventures using their RB211 jet engines.

Major recent developments in government intervention have included the following: transfer of Rolls-Royce and British Leyland from the responsibility of the National Enterprise Board (NEB) to that of the Department of Trade and Industry, partly reflecting the aims of the Thatcher administration to reduce the role of the NEB; proposals to 'privatise' the more profitable yards of British Shipbuilders, although these have been limited already by the planned reduction in the surface fleet of the Royal Navy announced in the 1981 Defence Review; and the actual 'privatisation' of British Aerospace in 1981.

Future cash help for British Leyland is dependent on restructuring of the company and on productivity levels as envisaged in the Edwardes Plan.[9] The future of British Leyland itself, and British motor-car manufacture generally, depend upon the success of British Leyland's models policy. Unfortunately, the portents of increasing penetration of the home market by imports, particularly for privately purchased vehicles, are not encouraging. There is very little more help that the government can now usefully give other than the introduction of import controls. It is difficult to see how this measure, which would be politically unattractive for a Conservative administration, would help improve the efficiency of indigenous motor-car manufacture.

However, there are five main reasons for maintaining British manufacture of motor cars

(1) The visible trade balance in motor cars.

(2) The interests of car-accessory manufacture, as discussed in section 1.4.1.

(3) The interests of the West Midlands regional economy, as discussed in section 6.1.

(4) The labour skills of the industry provide general support for the engineering manufacturing industries.

(5) The increase in Public Sector Borrowing Requirement that would result from large increases in unemployment.

6.4 Road Transport

This section considers first of all problems and policies in relation to the national trunk road network. It then considers non-local bus services and road freight.

6.4.1 The National Trunk road Network

The main features of the national trunk road network are that it is financed directly by central government and includes the major proportion of roads built to motorway standards. Contemporary policy for the trunk road network was laid down by the Heath administration in 1970.[10] Its major objectives include the following.

(1) To divert long-distance traffic from towns and villages.

(2) To complete a comprehensive network of strategic trunk routes to promote economic growth.

(3) To link the more remote and less prosperous regions with this national network.

(4) To ensure that all urban areas of reasonable size are directly connected or within close proximity to this national network.

(5) To link all major ports and airports.

(6) To relieve as many historic towns as possible of through trunk-traffic.

Succeeding administrations have continued this policy in broad outline. However, the problems of economic recession in the 1970s, a related desire on the part of central government to restrain public expenditure, and the relative attractiveness of reductions in the roads programme as part of such measures, resulted first in Labour and then Conservative administrations reducing annual expenditure on the national trunk road network; use of the national roads programme in this way by central government as an economic regulator has been previously discussed in section 1.5.3.

This reduced provision for the roads programme has been accompanied by some reassessment of objectives. There has been a new emphasis on what is called 'a more selective approach'. This means that standards of provision will not be as generous, in terms of capacity standards and demand projections on one hand, and some priority in selection of schemes on the other.[11, 12] So, priority would be given to those routes which carry a high proportion of industrial traffic, those which serve the South East of England, particularly London, on the grounds that this region has had to wait while the claims of less prosperous parts of the country were met, and to routes of environmental importance.

Resource commitment to the trunk road network is determined in the United Kingdom by the priority placed by central government on this element of public expenditure in particular, and on public expenditure generally. So, the need for more road space, as indicated by increasing road congestion, just like the need for more hospital beds as indicated by increasing waiting lists, only affects the overall size of the programme if it can influence the political priorities of an administration; as just pointed out, this is less likely in relatively uncontentious areas of public expenditure like the trunk road network. So the technical task collapses to one of selection of individual schemes of improvements to the trunk road network within a fixed annual resource commitment. This is normally done on the basis of social-cost-benefit analyses for which traffic predictions are a fundamental requirement.

It is normal procedure for a scheme to be entered into a 'preparation pool' if it satisfies certain criteria; there it is ranked with other schemes according to priority, and awaits funding. The general situation from year to year is that there is a greater value of schemes in the preparation pool than there are available funds; so cuts in public expenditure simply result in even longer delays in implementation of schemes.

The major criterion for selection of a trunk road scheme into the preparation pool is that accumulated benefits should at least equal accumulated costs over the design life of the project, usually thirty years, on the basis of the Treasury test discount rate for capital investment in the public sector.[13] The ranking of projects in the preparation pool normally reflects their expected return in social-cost-benefit terms. For small road schemes, prediction of future traffic can be done on the basis of traffic growth factors recommended by central government, while social-cost-benefit analyses are normally conducted on a standard basis, usually referred to as COBA.[14] However, for larger schemes, which are more likely to influence traffic levels beyond the geographical extent of the scheme, it is customary to conduct traffic predictions on a regional, inter-regional and even national network basis. This calls for the development of traffic prediction models. As some 22 per cent of traffic on the trunk-road network is commercial vehicles, while the remainder is largely car traffic, these classes of traffic feature predominantly in the traffic prediction process.

Commercial vehicles range up in gross laden weight to the maximum of 32 tons currently permitted. The trend over the years has been for the largest vehicles to account for an increasing proportion of commercial vehicles and of freight carried by road. The thickness of the road pavement depends upon an estimate of the use of a road scheme in the course of its design life by commercial vehicles running at the maximum permitted axle load of 10 tons.[15] Therefore, estimation of these commercial-vehicle movements can be critical for pavement design considerations, as the large maintenance programmes on the M6 illustrate.

The main types of car traffic are those associated with business and leisure journeys. In addition, commuting and shopping journeys are important where the trunk road network is used for local journeys, and this can be an important capacity consideration in or near large urban areas. In some areas of the country, principally in the the South East of England, and to a lesser extent in the provincial conurbations, commuting on the trunk road network has reached regional and inter-regional proportions. In general, improvements in the trunk-road network have encouraged the spatial dispersion of home and workplace — one reason for the argument that local authorities should have some control over the planning of trunk roads.

Prediction of traffic for major trunk-road schemes is normally done on the basis of an average traffic period during the year, usually taken as a Monday to Friday 24-hour period not likely to be affected by winter weather conditions or summer holiday traffic. The selection of 15 years ahead after the opening of a new road as the design year means that the initial stages of planning are based on traffic forecasts some 20–25 years ahead, while forecasts for some 30 years ahead are used in the final design. These practices are based on considerations that beyond these timescales forecasts are subject to great uncertainty, while present-day values of benefits and disbenefits are negligible at prevailing discount rates. One complication in basing traffic prediction on Monday to Friday 24-hour periods for average seasonal traffic conditions is that future weekend traffic during the summer holiday periods can be an additional consideration for capacity and economic assessment.

The traffic prediction has two main phases: the first involves prediction of traffic interchange between different origins and destinations; the second involves assignment of these interchanges to the future road network.[16] As a first step it is customary to divide the country into traffic zones, so that traffic can be thought of in terms of either originating from, or being destined for, a traffic zone. Inevitably some of these zones are large, because it is desirable to place a limit for computational reasons on the total number of zones that can be handled in the analysis; one result is some loss of geographical precision in loading and unloading traffic on and off the proposed network. The second step is to define the future network for use in the traffic prediction. Normally this consists of the trunk road network and any other roads which are considered important. Selection of the latter involves considerable judgement as, once again, only a limited network may be used for computational reasons; for example, selection of all roads in the country which act as primary distributors of traffic would obviously result in a very complicated network.

The first phase involves predicting the total number of traffic movements to and from individual traffic zones, and the origins and destinations of these movements; for example, it is necessary to predict the total number of commuting journeys, shopping journeys, leisure journeys, business journeys and commercial-vehicle movements arriving at a traffic zone, and the origins of these journeys, for a 24-hour Monday to Friday period in the design year. There are many technical problems in this phase of the traffic prediction.

(1) The prediction process is unable to take into account the influence of additional trunk road provision on future patterns of economic development, and thereby on related patterns of traffic interchange. This is likely to be a more significant factor for prediction of traffic on trunk roads than in prediction of local traffic, because much longer savings in travel time and travel cost tend to be involved; for example, the effect of trunk-road improvement on dispersion of home and work in or near urban areas has just been mentioned, while it may affect business traffic and commercial-vehicle movements as a result of influencing regionalism and industrial location.

(2) There is great difficulty in establishing a causal basis for prediction of the types of traffic that predominate on trunk roads. By way of comparison, the major traffic 'type' with regard to the capacity of local road networks is usually 'commuting'. In this case, population and workplace distributions act as aids to prediction in three ways: by providing a causal basis; by acting as a constraint on the overall level of journeys; and by changing fairly slowly. Such advantages are absent in prediction of trunk road traffic.

(3) Longer journeys, which are a more important component of traffic on the trunk road network, are a small proportion of all journeys made by road, as discussed in section 3.2.2. In principle, this means that very large samples must be surveyed to establish the current pattern of travel on the trunk-road network; in practice, it means that very little data may be available for some interzonal traffic movements, which is hardly a sound basis for prediction.

(4) Certain types of travel on the trunk road network are unevenly distributed between different sections of the population; for example, in the course of a year, a small proportion of people making business trips may account for a much larger proportion of total business trips, while a small proportion of commercial vehicles may account for a much larger proportion of total commercial-vehicle movements. So, prediction of these traffic movements can be very sensitive to the way in which activities associated with a high propensity for use of the trunk road network develop.

(5) With increasing transport costs, particularly as a result of higher fuel costs, significant changes, such as substitution by other forms of transport, suppression of travel, and a trend to shorter journeys, might be more likely to develop for journeys on the trunk road network, simply because they tend to

be longer and therefore more expensive. However, we still have a very imperfect understanding of the relationships between physical movement and its costs.

(6) Single value prediction is now generally eschewed in recognition of the considerable level of uncertainty attached to the future. The UK Treasury recognises this fact in operation of economic models of the economy. It is given recognition in the transport sector by prediction of car ownership for a range of future economic scenarios. However, it is more difficult to implement this philosophy with traffic prediction models because they are more complicated.

(7) We have noted that changes in the stock of commercial vehicles and the way they are used are important considerations in pavement design. However, these factors are not properly accommodated into prediction of commercial-vehicle movements.

(8) Traffic interchange between zones is predicted on the basis of estimates of the total amount of traffic expected to arrive and leave every individual traffic zone in the design year, and of the deterrence to movement caused by the physical separation between traffic zones. Generalised cost is normally taken as the measure for the latter in calibrating the distribution models used to predict traffic interchange. Unfortunately, this procedure is open to criticism on at least three counts: use of generalised cost as a measure of physical separation; the sensitivity of calibration parameters to the methods of calibration; and the stability of calibrations over time.

By comparison there are not so many problems in the second phase of the traffic prediction process, the assignment stage. Provided the network is adequately described, the critical problem is determining the traffic loading on alternative routes between pairs of traffic zones. It is customary to do this also on the basis of generalised cost. Off-peak travel times are normally used in estimating generalised cost, although this practice is questionable when commuting traffic is an important component of Monday to Friday traffic movements. Capacity constraint assignment procedures might be required where alternative routes are available; for example, in and near large urban areas.

There are, then, many problems in traffic prediction of trunk road traffic. The Leitch Committee identified them.[1] It is questionable whether a more valid prediction process can be developed; certainly it is naïve to think in terms of accurate prediction.[17, 18]

Traffic prediction has become a subject of controversy at public inquiries into trunk road schemes.[19] There are three main reasons for this.

(1) Traffic estimates supporting a scheme may not be made a subject of cross-examination, although two dissenting legal judgments have recently been made on this point.

(2) The general air of mysticism surrounding traffic prediction work tends to encourage a negative response.

(3) Scepticism about the accuracy of traffic prediction has increased in the 1970s with a growing awareness developed from experience of higher oil prices and related economic recession of the uncertainty of the future.

A suitable official response to these criticisms would be to demonstrate that traffic prediction methods are valid and robust, and then there would be no sufficient reason for according them special treatment at public inquiries. This dissatisfaction about traffic prediction is part of the general disquiet about trunk road schemes that has been demonstrated at public inquiries into trunk road schemes in recent years. This situation has developed as the trunk road programme has impinged on the more populous parts of the country, and increasing numbers of people have been faced with its disbenefits. In some cases their opposition has found expression in the views of environmental groups, who argue that extension of the trunk road network is not in the general interests of providing for a future in which all resources, but particularly oil resources in the context of road transport, are near depletion. Unfortunately, as discussed in section 6.2, choice of appropriate measures of intervention by central government is difficult, because multiple objectives are involved, interrelationships are complex, and future outcomes are the subject of great uncertainty.

6.4.2 Public Road Passenger Transport

The trunk road network is used for long-distance express bus services between the main urban areas. The National Bus Company (NBC) accounted for 12 million of the 50 million journeys on express bus services in Great Britain in 1977, and some £26.3 m. of the £46.9 m. revenue; corresponding figures for private operators were 36 million journeys and £17 m. in revenue. The National Bus Company operates the main national network of services under their National Travel 'label', while the private operators have a more regional emphasis; this is reflected in the higher revenue per journey on NBC services. Patronage of long-distance express bus services has fallen significantly — in 1967 some 77 million passengers were carried — but there has been evidence of a halt in this decline since the mid-1970s. However, these services are still commerically viable, the main reason for private operators being so well represented. Under the 1968 Transport Act the National Bus Company and the Scottish Bus Group are required to cover their costs from year to year. They have done this with some success, particularly NBC; however, subsidies have become an increasingly important revenue element for their stage carriage services. It is central government policy that inter-city passenger transport should not receive subsidies. But there is some evidence that in fact National Travel is cross-subsidised from subsidised stage carriage services.[20]

Long-distance express bus services face three problems. The first is competition with rail services, which has increased in recent years as British Rail has marketed spare off-peak capacity, particularly through special ticket arrangements for families, old-age pensioners, and students, groups who were likely to travel by long-distance express bus services in the past. Central government is concerned about such competition from the viewpoint of efficient use of resources in the public sector; for example, there is some evidence that this type of traffic is now acting as a constraint on expansion of British Rail's more traditional business traffic market.

The two other problems are related to measures introduced in the 1980 Transport Act.[21] The first concerns deregulation of bus services over distances in excess of thirty miles. It might be the case that there is demand for travel by express bus services not satisfied by the present level of services; for example, we have already noted how higher levels of service can generate more patronage of rail and air services, and that modal competition appears only a minor feature of this process. In principle, this 'untapped' demand could be provided by an expansion of services by current operators, or by the entry into the market of new operators. The fact that current operators have not taken this initiative previously, perhaps for sound reasons, favours the second option; in addition, this has the advantage of increasing competition, thereby making it more likely that fares will reflect reasonable cost levels. Thus, the consumer benefits in two ways in principle: from higher levels of service, and possibly from lower fares.

It might also be the case that current operators are charging fares that are unreasonably high, because for all practical purposes they occupy a monopolistic position. However, in this case, central government is already in a good regulating position on the basis of cost information it receives on long-distance express bus services by both public and private sector operators. It is not necessary, then, to solve this particular problem, if it exists, by de-regulation.

So the case for deregulation of long-distance express bus services rests on the argument of market potential. In the event of this argument proving false, then the public sector operators, principally NBC, will be faced with problems of worsening commercial viability as they compete with new entrants, such as British Coachways, for a limited market; and travellers will face more limited services and higher fare levels, while central government will be presented with demands for subsidy as services at the margin of commercial viability become non-viable.

The second problem relating to measures in the 1980 Transport Act concerns legalisation of charges for car passengers. This measure could have an impact on demand for public transport for local journeys, particularly in rural areas, although its potential is probably already highly developed. It has been put forward, of course, as a possible solution to the difficulties of passenger transport provision in rural areas. It might have even less impact on demand for travel by long-distance express bus services for two reasons: firstly, travellers in this market tend to belong to the lower-income groups, and therefore are less likely to either own a car or know somebody with whom they could travel as a paying passenger on an inter-city journey; secondly, as discussed in section 3.2.2, the irregularity of much inter-city travel will make more difficult the arranging of shared journeys. It will possibly have the most impact where long-distance express bus services are currently used by groups of people travelling over shorter distances at frequent intervals: for example, travel into larger urban areas at weekends for recreational purposes.

6.4.3 Road Freight

Public haulage in articulated vehicles over 28 tonnes gross weight dominates road freight movements in excess of 100 km, and is, therefore, an important component of traffic on the trunk road network. Three important developments concern

(1) the EEC proposal for a 40 tonnes gross weight
(2) implementation of EEC regulations on drivers' hours

(3) changing the basis of the vehicle excise duty system so that it is more fairly related to the costs imposed on the road system by different types of vehicles

The major differences between the 32 ton/4 axle vehicle under present United Kingdom Construction and Use Regulations, and the EEC Proposal for a 40 tonne/5 axle vehicle, is that the length of an articulated vehicle will be 0.5 m greater, which will ease the technical problems of designing an articulated vehicle to carry an ISO standard 40 ft container, and the gross weight will increase by 7.49 tonnes. Axle loading will be somewhat lower by virtue of the additional axle than the current maxima of 7 tons on steered wheels and 10 tons on other wheels, and therefore, strengthening of roads or bridges should not be required. However, there are some fears about the possible deleterious effects of increasing numbers of multi-axle vehicles on deformation of road pavements supported on weaker sub-grades. The Thatcher administration has recently formally opposed the Armitage recommendation for 44 tonne lorries.[22]

So far as the industry itself is concerned, an increase in gross weight would permit economies of scale, which could be used to counterbalance increases in costs. These have occurred with implementation of EEC regulations on drivers' hours, which took final effect on 1 January 1981; the most significant change is a reduction in the time that a driver may drive daily, while some vehicles may also be subject to a daily distance limit. Costs will be increased in two ways: firstly, vehicle productivity will be reduced unless larger loads, more powerful traction units, and improvements in the road network are introduced; secondly, it is unlikely that trade unions will accept a reduction in drivers' pay consequent upon a reduction in daily driving hours. The tacheograph, standard equipment on lorries on the Continent in compliance with EEC regulations, will also have to be in use in the United Kingdom from 1 January 1982. It has been much criticised by drivers for its regulatory role, but its positive virtues lie in helping to explain the causes of accidents, and significant changes in maintenance and fuel costs.

The third development concerns the basis of vehicle excise duties. It is general government policy that freight transport should not be subsidised, one reason for comparison of tax revenue for different types of vehicles with the road expenditure that can be attributed to them. On this basis, it has been shown that, even though there is an overall balance for road freight, the largest road haulage vehicles are undertaxed.[23] So it is possible that central government might adjust vehicle excise duties to obtain a better balance between tax revenue and attributable road expenditure for different types of commercial vehicles. However, in order to do this even more fairly, it would be necessary to attribute road expenditure according to laden weight only.

Unfortunately, these comparisons of road tax revenue and attributable road expenditure are open to criticism on at least three grounds.

(1) They make the unwarranted assumption that taxation in a particular sector should bear some relationship to public expenditure in that sector.

(2) The fact that taxation of cars is not reduced in accordance with this approach illustrates its inconsistency.

(3) In as much as the depth of road pavements is determined in accordance

with predictions of commercial vehicle movements, methods of allocation of road expenditure to lighter vehicles, particularly cars, are open to question.

This problem of establishing whether road freight is subsidised or not would not exist if there were direct charging for road use. In that case, the price mechanism would relate demand for road transport with justification of capital and current expenditure in the road system. The road network could be run on a toll basis, as found on motorways in France, but, of course, it would not be practicable to apply tolls to the entire network.

This solution has been rejected for motorways in the United Kingdom for four reasons.

(1) As access points to the motorway network are relatively closely spaced, the cost of installation of toll facilities would be substantial.

(2) The cost of operation of toll facilities.

(3) The very high traffic flows likely on some motorways would lead to severe queueing problems.

(4) Traffic deterred from using the motorway system would aggravate environmental and safety problems on the remainder of the road network. (p. 44).

However, direct charging would remove arguments about allocation of expenditure to different types of user, because the facility would only be used if the value placed on use were at least equal to the charge, assuming the usual consumer surplus arguments.

In recent years, the argument has developed that taxation for road freight should also reflect the social costs caused by commercial vehicles, such as noise, vibration, and pollution. Official measures taken to deal with this problem have three main thrusts.

(1) The introduction of more rigorous roadside testing of lorries.

(2) Use of the construction and use regulations to ensure that manufacturers comply with engine noise and engine emissions standards.

(3) The passing of the Heavy Commercial Vehicles (Controls and Regulations) Act 1973, also known as the 'Dykes' Act.

An important feature of this Act was permission for local authorities to specify through-routes for heavy commercial vehicles on one hand, and to prohibit such vehicles using other routes on the other. The aim was development of a network of strategic trunk-routes for heavy commercial vehicles, in order to limit their social costs as much as possbile.

Continuing reductions in capital expenditure on the trunk-road programme have been the main reason for limited progress with this network; a less important reason has been reluctance on the part of local authorities to direct traffic to particular routes, because of a possibility of their thus being associated with problems concerning heavy commercial vehicles on those routes.

As another solution to this problem of social costs there has been consideration of break-bulk depots for road freight; consignments would be carried in large loads in large lorries between urban areas on the trunk-road network, and loads would be broken up for distribution by smaller lorries within urban areas.[24] However, the additional costs and delivery times involved make this development unlikely; furthermore, there is the problem of generation of more movements of commercial vehicles within urban areas, albeit of smaller lorries. The concept of break-bulk is used, of course, for particular traffics when volumes justify it — an example is the parcels and small freight traffic carried by the NFC subsidiaries, Roadline and National Carriers. However, the poor financial performance of these companies in recent years perhaps points to financial failings in the break-bulk concept.

6.5 Rail Transport

The British Railways Board face the following major problems.

(1) For railway operations as a whole, traffic revenue does not cover costs.

(2) A shortage of investment. This is reflected in acute needs for renewal of rolling stock and for freight terminals while profitable areas of operation are starved of investment, partly through overall shortage of investment funds and partly through competition for these funds with other operational areas.

(3) Labour shortages might justify wage increases above cash-limit target levels set by the government for the public sector. This creates problems over cash flow and creates poor conditions for negotiating more efficient working methods. Regarding the latter, the rail unions have been very reluctant to link wage increases to higher productivity.

(4) Freight traffics are particularly sensitive to the overall direction of the economy. At the same time, British Rail has put less investment and managerial effort into freight operations than it has put into inter-city passenger operations.

These problem areas are, of course, interrelated — let us consider them in more detail.

6.5.1 Financing Railway Operations

The broad financial objectives for railway operations laid down by central government are as follows

(1) to contain and reduce subsidy to the revenue account of passenger services.

(2) to eliminate any continuing requirement of subsidy to other railway business.

As in any other business, a sound knowledge of revenue and costs for individual activities is essential to satisfy such objectives. Unfortunately, indivisibility of rail operations does not permit such an ideal state of knowledge for financial control.

On the revenue side, overall demand for passenger travel by rail is sensitive to the overall supply of rail services. It is therefore necessary to be cautious in ascribing revenue simply to individual services or service sectors: for example, it is quite a simple matter to allocate the fare revenue, for a journey between a suburban station in a provincial conurbation to a London suburban station, between local Passenger Transport Executive Services, Inter-City Services, and London and South East Area Services; it is much more difficult to allow for the effect of the supply situation for local rail services on the overall level of demand for inter-city services, and vice versa.

Cost allocation is very difficult for two reasons: firstly, the indirect costs of track and signalling, and administration, form a very high proportion of the total costs of railway operation; secondly, a major proportion of track and signalling costs is insensitive to variations in traffic levels within the capacity provided. In recent years, because of the difficulties in cost allocation, the British Railways Board have followed a practice of 'Contribution Accounting' as opposed to 'Full Cost Allocation'. In contribution accounting, the surplus of revenue over direct expenses for sub-sectors of activity is presented as a contribution to joint indirect costs, and forms the basic machinery by which the Public Service Obligation Grant is calculated. However, the problem remains that there is no definitive way of allocating joint indirect costs to specific services, and so the targets set for individual service sectors for contributions to joint indirect costs are open to question.[25]

Thus, Inter-City Passenger Services and South East and London Area Services cover their direct costs and make contributions to indirect costs, while Other Provincial Services do not even cover their direct costs and are, therefore, a major beneficiary of the Public Service Obligation Grant. Regarding Passenger Transport Executives' Rail Services, British Rail receives an agreed sum annually from the various Metropolitan Counties to cover the difference between costs and the fare revenue they receive under the terms of Section 20 of the 1968 Transport Act.

It is central government policy that inter-city rail passenger services and rail freight operations should not be subsidised. It is likely that inter-city rail passenger services do receive aid from the Public Service Obligation Grant although, in view of the technical difficulties in allocating their share of indirect costs, it is impossible to define the precise extent of this support. However, in recent years, British Rail have been under pressure from central government to increase revenue from their inter-city passenger revenues so that they make a larger contribution to overall costs. A major way in which they have done this is by selling spare off-peak capacity at low prices; thus, marketing campaigns aimed at old-age pensioners, students and family groups, and even campaigns in co-operation with Kelloggs and Uniliver in the marketing of cornflakes and soap-powder, have developed.

These marketing efforts have been successful in increasing revenue, but have attracted criticism on two grounds: firstly, on some services there is evidence that they have prevented development of the full potential of 'normal fare' traffic; secondly, these low fares have been charged by coach operators with being below cost, and therefore constituting unfair competition. One answer to this second criticism is that British Rail is simply applying marginal cost pricing to the sale of surplus capacity; however, the fact that, unlike their competitors, they are in receipt of a very large subsidy from public funds, is probably the real issue underlying this criticism.

For freight operations British Rail use the principle of avoidable costs to allocate costs of joint facilities. This approach attempts to determine what costs would be avoided if an activity, say a freight operation, were to cease, while all other activities continued. This approach also identifies the avoidable cost of retaining the infrastructure, that is, the track bed, cuttings and bridges, when there is no traffic, referred to as 'basic facility cost'. Thus, 'basic facility cost' plus the sum of other avoidable costs, is equal to total costs. Unfortunately, this approach, like full cost accounting and contribution accounting, does not overcome the problems of shared indirect costs, and so, freight operations, like Inter-City Passenger Services, are open to the suspicion that they enjoy an element of subsidy from the Public Service Obligation Grant; grants for private sidings under Section 8 of the 1974 Railways Act are certainly a form of subsidy.

Over the past fifteen years, this suspicion has given rise to the 'Track Costs Argument', that rail freight is subsidised through its indirect costs, whereas road freight is in receipt of no such subsidy; as discussed in section 6.4.3, specious comparisons of road freight taxation with its share of road expenditure have been made to justify the latter. However, the whole argument is sterile, because conceptual difficulties make it quite impossible to estimate with confidence either rail freights' share of indirect costs or road freights' share of road expenditure. This need for comparison only exists because rail operations are so heavily subsidised over all, although not as heavily as in other EEC countries; if they were profitable, central government would only be concerned with this problem of shared indirect costs in rail operation if there were evidence of abuses of monopolistic power in fixing fares and freight rates.

However, it is difficult to suggest a more rational basis for allocation of 'track costs'; for example, even if central government were to finance railway track costs directly in the way that it finances the trunk road network, there would still be anomalies over user charging and investment criteria.

6.5.2 Shortage of Investment Capital

The second major problem for the British Railways Board is a shortage of investment capital. This is reflected in rail operation in an ageing rolling stock and a scarcity of investment in new projects, and generally in inadequate direction of investment to the most profitable areas of operation. The main reason for inadequate investment in rail operations is poor financial performance; for example, even after the more beneficial restructuring of finances of the 1974 Railways Act, the proportion of finances for investment generated by the business is very low, particularly considering that so much investment is required for renewal.

Major renewal needs are rolling stock for Diesel Multiple Unit (DMU), Electric Multiple Unit (EMU), and Inter-City Passenger Services. Most DMUs were introduced with the Dieselisation Programme in the mid-1950s, and are therefore approaching thirty years in age. As they are mainly used on 'loss-making' Other Provincial Services, their renewal will most likely depend upon social cost arguments and grants from central government. This dilemma has encouraged current development by British Rail of a 'low cost' rail-car based on the Leyland National coach for use on some of these services.[26] EMUs are in use mainly in the London and South East areas, but also in the Clydeside, Greater Manchester, Merseyside and West Midlands conurbations. In the case of the last three areas, renewal of rolling stock is the subject of negotiation with the Passenger Transport Executives. There is currently a major programme of renewal of Southern Region rolling stock for Inner Suburban Services in the London and South East area. The third major renewal area is rolling stock for Inter-City passenger services; for example, Mark 1, pre-1964, coaches, accounted for some 53 per cent of inter-city coaching stock in 1979.

This problem in financing renewal out of revenue from rail operations is worsened by the accounting practice of basing depreciation on historic cost. If a current cost basis were used instead, then at least the Public Service Obligation Grant would carry an increased provision for depreciation, even though it is questionable whether all traffic could bear tariffs based on current cost accounting practices.

There is also a potential problem for renewal of track and signalling in that it is charged to the revenue account of rail operations. So, once the cash limits for the Public Service Obligation Grant are fixed, expenditure of this nature can be in competition with other current expenditure needs for the limited cash flow available. In practice, of course, safety considerations prevail, but there does appear to be a strong case for special provision for expenditure of this nature within the cash-limits system.

There is also a shortage of finance for investment in new projects like the Advanced Passenger Train, further electrification, and the Channel Tunnel. All these projects satisfy rate-of-return criteria in financial appraisal, but suffer from their large demands for finance in general, and from constraints on public expenditure in particular. Because of these last two factors, central government is insisting, while the British Railways Board is exploring the possibilities, that private capital be used.

It has been argued that, because of this shortage of capital for finance, the British Railways Board has directed investment into rail operations at the expense of investment in more profitable areas, such as their hotels. This, presumably, is one reason for the recent suggestion by the Minister of Transport that the British Railways Board set up a holding company for their successful subsidiaries, to ensure that they are not starved of finance for further expansion. However, such a development would worsen the problem of generating finance for rail operation internally.

These problems in raising investment capital have turned the attention of the British Railways Board to other methods of capital financing. They include

(1) companies who provide and lease wagons using British Railways Board and private capital, for example, PROCOR;
(2) EEC funds: for example, (a) £25 m. from European Investment Bank in 1979 for 12 years at 12.25 per cent towards 18 HST sets for North East–South West services; (b) £36.9 m. from same source in 1972 for 32 East Coast Route HST sets; (c) EEC funds are also available for improvement of international routes;
(3) investment by shippers in wagons and terminal facilities;
(4) local authorities have also invested in new or reopened stations.

6.5.3 Productivity

As a public corporation dependent on substantial revenue support from central government, the British Railways Board is in a serious dilemma: on the one hand it must operate in the market; on the other its cash-flow is dependent upon the cash limits imposed by central government. Thus, even though such factors as unsocial hours result in labour shortages in parts of the country where unemployment is traditionally above average, the cash-limits system can act as a constraint on wage negotiations that might remove such shortages. This obviously creates a poor climate for negotiating more efficient working methods; for example, British Rail is a low-wage railway by comparison not only with other industries in the United Kingdom but also with other European railways; yet its staff work on average significantly more hours per year than is the general case for the latter.[27] The main explanations for these longer hours of working lie in treatment of Sunday-working outside the standard working week, and in less flexible rostering.

Two specific areas for negotiating more efficient working methods are in manning of freight trains and at terminals on London inner suburban services. So, perhaps the lesson for the rail unions is that higher wages can be gained by more efficient working practices. However, it is a conundrum that, despite such examples of inefficient working practices, it has been shown that labour productivity over all is above average among European railway systems, which possibly indicates the care with which productivity comparisons have to be treated. Also, the very significant reductions in manpower since the 1960s, consequent upon dieselisation and electrification of traction, and automation of signalling and track maintenance, should not be overlooked.

6.5.4 Freight Traffics

The main elements of central government policy for rail freight at present include the following.

(1) It should not be subsidised.

(2) Under the 1978 Transport Act, Freightliners Ltd was taken out of the 51/49 per cent joint ownership of the National Freight Corporation and the British Railways Board, respectively, created by the 1968 Transport Act, and placed under the complete control of the British Railways Board.

(3) Grants for private sidings are payable under the 1974 Railways Act, and for private rolling stock in addition under the 1978 Transport Act, where there are clear environmental benefits for transfer of traffic from road to rail.

Rail freight is most suited for bulk traffic not involving transfer with other modes, for two reasons: the very large capital costs involved in rail operations; the cost penalties of transfer between modes. It is not surprising, then, that the policy of the British Railways Board has been to concentrate on trainload traffic between private sidings and/or terminals; currently, some 80 per cent of freight lifted is conveyed in this manner. Details of this type of traffic are provided in section 2.5.2. For other than trainload traffic the basic consignment is a wagonload or container, while less-than-wagonload traffic, except for parcels, is handled exclusively by National Carriers Ltd, whose use of rail wagonload services has declined in recent years.

Development of the Freightliner container services followed this trainload concept even though it involved inter-model transfer in order to cater for conveyance of traffic 'door-to-door' (also see section 2.5.2 for details). Carryings by Freightliners Ltd has not, however, achieved the potential originally envisaged. There are a number of explanations for this.

(1) The minimum economic length of haul needed to justify the costs of transfer between road and rail turned out to be much greater than anticipated.

(2) Few areas in the United Kingdom can support the high desire lines of movement of general merchandise needed to justify expansion of the Freightliner network.

(3) Opposition within the Transport and General Workers Union to rail trunk-haul.

(4) Very large increases by the British Railways Board in the rates for trunk-haul in the mid-1970s made the Freightliner service less competitive.

Immediately post-Beeching, then, the freight policy of the British Railways Board favoured the trainload concept and the elimination of wagonload traffic. The large potential for economies in rationalising marshalling yards and rolling stock was seized upon, and it was not until the end of the 1960s that the potential of wagonload traffic was seen in a more positive light. A number of factors contributed to this development.

(1) Trainload customers wished to send consignments in wagonloads.

(2) The air-braked wagon service had been expanded to cater for 'less than wagonload' traffic carried by National Carriers Ltd — it is ironic that in later years NCL reverted more and more to road trunk-haul.

(3) Freightliners Limited was competing for potential wagonload traffic.

(4) The Freightliner network could only justify expansion in the event of very large increases in demand.

(5) The British Railways Board was under financial pressure to increase the contribution of freight operations to indirect costs.

(6) Acquisition of the TOPS system for controlling rolling stock.

The outcome was the launching of 'Speedlink' in September 1977, which by January 1980 was operating forty wagonload services and carrying 2.5 million tonnes of traffic per year, with an expected potential of 6.5 million tonnes. Now that Freightliners Ltd are under the complete control of the British Railways Board, there is obvious potential for rationalisation of the Freightliner network with Speedlink; for example, Speedlink services are already equipped with container wagon sets for handling limited container traffic.

The major problem for rail freight lies in the overall course of the UK economy. All traffics are obviously sensitive to recession. Bulk trainload traffics are particularly sensitive to a long-term trend to a service-sector orientated economy; the recent crisis in the British Steel Corporation has illustrated this point. Market potential for Freightliner and Speedlink traffic depends upon competitiveness with road transport; factors likely to be in their favour include trends in fuel and labour costs in road transport, possible better accessibility of the rail network to Europe as a consequence of a Channel Tunnel, although problems of loading gauge will remain, and possible improvements in labour productivity as a result of reductions in manning of freight trains. The trend to concentration in manufacturing industry is also likely to help rail freight operations, particularly for trainload traffic between private terminals and sidings. However, to date, road freight has dominated the carriage of general merchandise even over the hauls, and particularly for international traffic. The main reasons for this are

(1) the limited accessibility of the rail network
(2) competitiveness of road freight in terms of price and service level
(3) the better facilities of many East Coast ports for roll-on-roll-off road traffic than for rail freight.

Surplus capacity in recent years and the dominance of the small operator have contributed to low rates being maintained for road freight. The two are, of course, not unrelated. The small operator tends to have lower indirect costs, and may even be tempted to cut direct costs by not complying strictly with regulations and by reducing maintenance — for example, some 5 per cent of heavy goods vehicles examined at spot checks in 1976—7 were found to be unsafe for use on the road. It is possible that he may even underestimate costs — one reason for the high rates of bankruptcies — but, of course, despite this cost on society, the essential effect is severe competition with rail freight. It may be that the combined effects of higher fuel costs, and EEC regulatons on drivers' hours, which, it has been estimated, will generate a demand for some 5—7 per cent more lorry drivers to cater for present levels of road freight, will result in a shortage of capacity in road freight, with attendant worsening of service levels. In that case, rationalised Speedlink and Freightliner services might expect to make important advances in the general merchandise market, particularly with an improved Continental connection provided by a Channel Tunnel. Such expansion might reduce the need to re-form trains along route on certain Speedlink services. In view of such possible unfavourable trends for road freight, the lobbying of the industry for the 40 tonne lorry is not surprising.

As previously indicated, less-than-wagonload traffic is the responsibility of National Carriers Limited (NCL). In recent years, partly as a result of economic recession, this National Freight Corporation (NFC) company has suffered severe cash-flow problems in dealing with this traffic. Cost-reducing measures have included a greater reliance on road trunk-haul. Parcels freight is also a severe problem area. Currently, services are provided in the public sector by British Rail, NFC (NCL and Roadline) and the Post Office. They are a frequent subject of dispute between British Rail and the Post Office, and it is generally agreed that this is an area in need of rationalisation. However, it should not be forgotten that parcels traffic contributes the same order of revenue to rail operations as all other freight traffic, with the exclusion of coal and coke and iron and steel, and with significantly lower avoidable costs in that such a large proportion is carried on passenger services. However, costs are likely to increase as it becomes necessary to carry parcels on separate trains, as reduced schedules for passenger trains involve shorter station stops, and increasing numbers of fixed formation trains with limited accommodation for parcels, mails and newspapers, such as the HSTs and APTs, are introduced.

6.6 Air Transport

Increases in personal income, coupled with decreases in unit operating costs of aircraft as a result of technological development, have been the main factors contributing to the considerable increases in air travel. However, world economic recession is currently slowing the rate of growth, while the related factor of increasing oil prices perhaps heralds the onset of a more austere era for air transport. Important general problems in international air transport concern fare levels, energy costs, noise, and aircraft replacement. For air services provided by UK operators particular problem areas are domestic scheduled air services, airport capacity in the London area, and the structure of civil aviation.

6.6.1 Problems in International Air Transport

Fare Levels

Two factors provide broad support for the strong feeling that fares on international scheduled services are too high: the first is that such fares are fixed by general agreement of the membership of the International Air Transport Association (IATA); the second is that charter operators can offer significantly lower fares by virtue of higher load factors and lower indirect costs. Membership of IATA confers equal voting rights irrespective of financial performance; a result, not surprisingly, is that fares for the different international markets are fixed at levels acceptable to the majority of airlines operating on them, a process likely to favour the 'high cost', rather than 'low cost' operator. There are several reasons for this method of regulation of air fares on international scheduled services.

(1) All international air services are the subject of agreement between, and regulation by, at least two governments, who have a general interest in how fare regulation affects their national operators, and will have a particular interest in the case of a state airline.

(2) In the many cases of an air service between two countries being served by an airline from each country, it is unlikely that both airlines will have similar cost structures.

(3) In general, it is unlikely that airlines will have similar cost structures on particular routes, for reasons of economies of scale, cross-subsidisation from other services or activities, and subsidy from government.

(4) For particular markets, high fares might be used to protect carriers who operate at a disadvantage from a viewpoint of economic geography; for example, low fares in Europe might encourage de-trunking to and from the United Kingdom on the North Atlantic market, to the benefit of UK operators and disadvantage of other European operators, and possibly even American operators.

The hypothetical case of deregulation of international scheduled air services would benefit the most highly efficient (largely American) airlines and the most highly subsidised ones (mainly those of Communist countries). Fares might fall, provided remaining airlines did not abuse any monopolistic power, but services below the margin of commerical viability would cease. The latter development would be contrary to one of the main objectives of governments of developing countries in establishing a state airline, albeit a highly subsidised one in some cases: namely, to have some control over accessibility to the international community. In practice, of course, deregulation could not happen, because international air transport takes place by agreement between governments, which, in the general case, would be subject to the protection of the interests of national airlines. This short discussion clearly emphasises the important role of regulation in international air transport.[28]

Nor is substitution of international scheduled air services by charter operation practical in the general case, because all markets do not have a potential for increasing load factors while retaining present service levels. However, the Laker Skytrain services between the United Kingdom and the United States illustrate the latent demand for cheaper air travel, albeit at lower service levels.

Regulation of air fares on international air services, increasing costs, and potential competition with innovative operations like Skytrain in particular and charter operation in general, have had two main effects. Firstly, scheduled operators compete amongst themselves on the basis of quality of service, as measured by ease of reservation, quality of in-flight service, and modernity of aeroplane. Higher average load factors can lead to higher operating margins, but they also have the negative effect of making reservation more difficult. Aircraft have to be replaced well in advance of technical obsolescence in order for an airline to remain competitive; usually they find service in non-scheduled operations for the remainder of their useful lives. This makes aircraft replacement a very significant financial requirement in international scheduled operations.

Secondly, scheduled operators market spare capacity at discount prices in order to benefit from the very large demand for cheaper air travel — and in so doing compete with charter operators — and also to increase their cash flow at a time of financial pressure from the general problem of cost inflation. It is sensible for them to expand their activities in this way in view of the very large potential demand for cheaper air travel. It is possible to draw a parallel here with the way British Rail market spare capacity on their Inter-City Passenger Services. However, the general results are a proliferation of fares on scheduled services, which has the effect of increasing scepticism about fare regulation, and a risk of losing Economy Fare passengers who object not only to paying more for the same 'in-flight' services as passengers with discount tickets of one type or another, but also to the overall lower levels of service related to higher load factors. Once again a parallel may be drawn with British Rail's Inter-City Passenger Services.

British Airways have introduced 'Club' fares on a limited number of European services, partly in response to this problem: these replace first-class fares but are priced at the economy-fare level plus a small surcharge; Club passengers will be seated in the front of aircraft, quite separate from other passengers, and receive better service. In this way economy-fare travellers, who are more likely to be business travellers can receive preferential treatment for a small surcharge, compared with travellers, on cheaper tickets. However, this proposal has the obvious risk of offending first-class passengers, who may prefer development has the obvious risk of offending first-class passengers, who may prefer to travel with airlines offering first-class facilities, and the more subtle but equally serious one of British Airways being generally identified with not providing for first-class passengers, as well as the risk of offending economy-fare inclusive.

Latest developments in marketing spare capacity came, perhaps ironically, from an innovative scheduled operator, Laker Airways, and from a charter operator, Britannia Airways; Laker provided for economy-fare passengers on its Skytrain services, while Britannia Airways has recently proposed to the Civil Aviation Authority a plan to sell cheap seats on its packaged-tour flights.

In summary, then, deregulation of fares on international scheduled services is unlikely, although pressure from Laker resulted in a marked lowering of transatlantic fares; the effects on fare levels of Laker's demise remain to be seen. Perhaps the greatest potential for deregulation is in Western Europe, within the framework of a common transport policy for the European Economic Community; but the problem of de-trunking will have to be solved in this case. Even though the case for deregulation of international services might not be generally accepted, the proliferation of fares and spare capacity which have resulted from regulation is unsatisfactory, and it is difficult to envisage that this situation will be consistent with an era of high energy costs, and possibly physical energy shortages.

Energy Costs

Fuel costs form a much higher proportion of total operating costs in air transport than in water- or land-based transport. Therefore, air transport costs are more sensitive to the problem of increasing oil prices; for example, profit forecasts for British Airways in 1979 severely underestimated fuel price increases. The problem, then, is not only one of higher fuel costs, but also a question of their magnitude and timing from year to year. The latter uncertainty makes much more difficult the financial management of air transport, particularly of scheduled services with their higher indirect costs, which are more difficult to reduce in the short run, and makes especially difficult the financing of capital investment out of revenue.

Possible responses to this problem vary with timescale: in the short run, fuel can be conserved by reducing to a minimum transport of excess fuel and ground-running of engines, and by more use of more energy-efficient ground power supplies for apron servicing; in the medium term there can be investment in more energy-efficient aircraft and, subject to the constraints of timetabling and air traffic control, operation at slower cruising speeds and more fuel-efficient flight profiles; in the longer run, there could be development of a more energy-efficient variable-pitch bladed turbine, and alternative transport fuels, with the most likely candidate being synthetic kerosene, although there is currently considerable interest in hydrogen fuel systems.[29]

It is inevitable that overall demand and supply of air transport services will respond to this changing fuel situation. Shorter sector services are most sensitive to higher fuel costs because such a high proportion of fuel is consumed in take-off. It is because of this factor that there is now very considerable worldwide demand for replacement of short/medium-haul narrow-bodied jets, with the two rival replacement candidates being the proposed Boeing 767 and the A300 aircraft of Airbus Industries, both wide-bodied, more fuel-efficient, aircraft. With increasing costs of fuel, and even temporary disruptions in supply, scheduled services at and below the margin of commercial viability, mainly on light-density routes, are likely to be curtailed. On the demand side there is also likely to be increased competition over shorter sector routes from faster surface transport services, which will also offer the advantage of being more energy-efficient. One final factor that could contribute to fuel savings is higher average load factors.

Thus the fuel problem may, as it develops, force more rational use of air transport capacity, particularly, of course, in scheduled operations. This will be partly achieved by technical 'fixes', such as 'stretching' wide-bodied jets and introducing 'double-decker' seating arrangements in 'jumbo-jets', but sooner or later capacity must be brought into a closer relationship with patronage. Hopefully, this will be accompanied by more consistent fare structures and fewer anomalies between scheduled and charter operations, as already indicated.

Noise

Aircraft noise became a serious problem in the vicinity of airports with the introduction of second generation long-distance jet aircraft, like the Boeing 707 and the Douglas DC8 in the late 1950s. The problem arose on two main counts: these aircraft were larger and required more powerful engines: the latter were based on military versions, which had high jet velocities and therefore bad noise characteristics. The major problem with noise was at take-off, when engines were providing maximum thrust. However, complaints about landing noise increased with traffic growth, with particular annoyance at the high-pitched whine made by engine compressors and the use of reverse thrust in landing. In addition, there were complaints about ground-running of engines in connection with maintenance procedures.[30]

The problem became more serious with traffic growth, more use of night operations, and residential development near airports. Regarding the latter, there are three main considerations: airports and the more-expensive housing areas both tend to be on the windward side of urban areas; house purchasers tend to balance the advantages of being close to an airport in terms of travel accessibility and job opportunities, against the disadvantages in terms of noise, air pollution and traffic congestion; an airport attracts industrial development in its vicinity because of the accessibility to markets that it offers.

Governments took the general view that noise from jet aircraft should not exceed noise levels made by larger piston-engined aircraft. The figure adopted at

Heathrow for the maximum permissible noise level at the first built-up area after take-off is 96 dBA during the day. The measures introduced by the authorities to deal with the problem include special take-off procedures, monitoring of take-off noise, banning or restricting night operations, noise-insulation grants, rating reductions on grounds of noise nuisance, and incorporation of new requirements for noise insulation into building regulations for new development.

The normal procedure used by pilots on take-off to satisfy noise level standards is to use full thrust to climb as steeply as possible, and then to throttle back by the time the first built-up area is reached. Unfortunately, even though noise is a less serious problem on landing, the constraints of the glide path mean that noise reduction depends on engine development. Noise screens and mufflers are used in ground maintenance.

Airlines have also had to invest in fitting noise suppressors, or 'hush-kits', to first-generation civil jet engines. These reduce the fuel efficiency of the engine, and also, by virtue of extra weight and increased drag, increase the overall fuel consumption of the aircraft. Second-generation civil jet engines are either bypass or ducted fan type, with the result that jet velocities, noise, and fuel consumption are lower. However, to date, it is the long-range large jet aircraft, like the Boeing 747, the Douglas DC10 and the Lockheed Tristar, which in the main have this type of engine, because aircraft development has advanced more quickly to third-generation jet aircraft in this part of the market. Concorde, however, is not part of this pattern — its development, with Bristol Olympus engines based on the ill-fated TSR2 project, proceeded despite these noise problems, although its high rate of climb at take-off mitigates the problem to an extent. By contrast, it is in the short/medium-range market where investment in quieter jet aircraft is now required. So, noise reduction, like fuel economy, makes aircraft replacement an important consideration in this part of the market.

Aircraft Replacement

There are two main grounds currently, then, for aircraft replacement: noise reduction and fuel consumption, with an emphasis on the short/medium-range market. A third consideration is air freight.[31] Transport of freight by air is even more sensitive to increases in fuel cost than air travel. This factor, and low freight rates offered by passenger carriers in order to increase their cash flow, raise a serious query over the future development of freight-only operations, with obvious implications for aircraft and airport design. In the short/medium-range market an example of the next generation of aircraft has appeared in the shape of the A300 of Airbus Industries, with its wide-bodied fuselage and twin high bypass ratio engines. Developments in the long-range market are likely to include higher-passenger-capacity subsonic aircraft.

Technical specifications are now a relatively minor factor in aircraft-investment decisions by operators. A factor of increasing importance in recent years is financing arrangements; for example, Airbus Industries is facing stiffer competition from Boeing in the short/medium-range market, now that the latter is quoted on European stock markets and can benefit from lower interest-rate finance available in Europe. Sale of Rolls-Royce RB211-engined Lockheed Tristars to

Pan-American possibly would not have been successful without the backing of the Rolls-Royce engines by the U K Export Credit Guarantee Department. Other factors affecting investment decisions are fleet commonality, and the prospects of earnings through maintenance work. Commonality in parts is obviously one area of potential economies at a time of cost inflation; it is for this reason that British Airways are standardising on Boeing aircraft, as illustrated by the very large recent purchase of 737s.

6.6.2 Problems in UK Civil Aviation

The main problem areas in civil aviation in the United Kingdom concern domestic air services, airport capacity in the London area, and the structure of civil aviation.

Domestic Air Services

Demand for travel by domestic scheduled air services is relatively low, with no significant growth taking place in the 1970s. It is sensitive to trunking to and from London because of the limited international services operated from regional airports and, in view of the short sector distances involved, to increasing fuel costs. In recent years, increasing competition from faster rail services has been countered by the introduction of air shuttle services between London and the main regional centres. This could also be a major consideration in the important London—Paris/London—Brussels market with the completion of a Channel Tunnel. With shuttle services, travel by air is made as readily available as travel by train, although the marginal costs, in terms of having an additional aircraft always available, can be much greater. Despite such innovations there is still the problem of airport accessibility for such short in-flight journey times, particularly in the London area, although this problem is partly alleviated by industrial and commercial development within access of airports in recent years.
   The problem of trunking is a complex one: obviously it is necessary when demand for international services at regional airports is low; on the other hand, the two major UK international scheduled operators, British Airways and British Caledonian, have an interest in maintaining trunking at its present level, from the viewpoints of using their domestic networks based on London to market international services, of cash flow, and of centralising maintenance operations. One development that could lead to better international services outside London would be for Continental operators to use regional airports as 'air-bridges' to North America, as in the case of KLM services at Manchester. However, this would not be in the short-term interests of UK operators, even though it might be useful in negotiating lower air fares in Europe, which could result in more de-trunking between mainland Europe and the United Kingdom, with benefits for UK operators of international scheduled services.
   Central government policy for domestic inter-city passenger travel has three main objectives, as previously indicated: it should not be subsidised; there should not be unfair price competition; and resources should be used efficiently. In

practice, of course, it is impossible to judge whether these objectives are being met, because of the very complicated cost structures involved, particularly for railway operation, as just discussed in section 6.5, and the general procedure in inter-city travel of appraising investment policies within, rather than between, potential competitor modes. It is likely that there is an element of subsidy in all three modes: in air travel from international services and possibly from landing charges at less busy airports; in inter-city rail travel from the Public Service Obligation Grant; and in coach travel through maintenance arrangements with local stage carriage services. In the nature of scheduled services all three modes carry surplus capacity, but none excessively; so it cannot be readily argued that there is wasteful use of resources. Scheduled air services in Scotland, serving the Western Isles, certainly do not cover their costs, but these receive fare support from central government on the same principle of social necessity applied to subsidy of some rail services.

Airport Capacity in the London Area

Passenger movements at Heathrow Airport are now approaching its capacity of 30 million, with three terminals; when the fourth terminal is completed, for which approval was obtained in 1979, its capacity will be increased to some 38 million passengers per year. So, with annual growth in international air transport movements still in excess of ten percent per year despite increasing oil prices and world economic recession, it is likely that additional capacity will have to be provided in the London area in the 1980s. This can be done by development of facilities and encouraging traffic growth at airports other than Heathrow; Gatwick, Luton and Stansted are the possible candidates.

Luton is ruled out by problems of restriction by urban development and air traffic control compatibility, while Stansted, as yet, fulfils only a minor role in providing for London's air traffic. In the immediate future, then, expansion at Gatwick is the only reasonable development; a second terminal is planned, but proposals for a second runway have been discounted by opposition on environmental grounds. So, in the late 1980s—early 1990s there is likely to be a need for even more additional airport capacity, the reason for the resurrection of proposals for a 'Third London Airport', with Stansted currently the most likely location. These developments at Heathrow and Gatwick illustrate the development of airport capacity problems in the 1970s at terminals, with the introduction of very large aircraft, even though the ultimate limit on capacity is the number of runways.[32, 33]

It is the policy of central government to encourage traffic growth at Gatwick as the medium-run solution to this problem of airport capacity in the London area. Its main instrument is negotiation of new scheduled services on condition that Gatwick is used. It is helped in this respect by the use of Gatwick by the United Kingdom's second-force airline, British Caledonian, as its base of operations, a factor not unrelated to the recent approval by the Civil Aviation Authority of new services by that airline to a number of European destinations and to Hong Kong. In comparison, British Airways uses Gatwick somewhat reluctantly because of the cost penalties, largely in aircraft maintenance, in

operating from two London airports, and the unattractiveness for transit
passengers of transferring between airports. This factor of economies in aircraft
maintenance in operating from one major airport was an important consideration
in implementation of the Edwards Plan for a second-force airline. The UK
Department of Trade has also been quite successful in making use of Gatwick a
condition of new services to additional 'gateway' airports in the United States.
However, there is still reluctance by current American operators into Heathrow —
Pan-American and Trans-World Airlines — to move operations to Gatwick, an
attitude which is supported by the American government. The difficulty in
obtaining international recognition for Gatwick as an alternative to Heathrow is
a major factor in these plans for providing for London's air traffic needs. It also
indicates similar problems for London's Third Airport.

Central government can influence traffic growth at London's airports in a
secondary way by influencing the landing fee charges of the British Airports
Authority: for example, in 1980, as part of the overall policy for the public
sector regarding cash-limits and borrowing requirements, central government
required the British Airports Authority over the next three years to increase its
return on assets employed and its financing of airport development out of
revenue; the response of the British Airports Authority has been to increase
landing fees at all its seven airports except Stansted, with a 40 per cent increase
at Heathrow and a 20 per cent increase at Gatwick.

It is generally accepted that development of regional airports cannot make a
significant contribution to this problem of London's air traffic capacity. The
major function of regional airports, with the exception of developing
international services at Manchester, and important domestic services there and
at Glasgow, Edinburgh and Belfast, is provision for charter traffic,[34] largely
related to summer holidays for local catchment areas. Provision of a rail link,
and the introduction of Advanced Passenger Train services, will result in
Manchester Airport becoming an even more attractive 'alternative' airport to
Heathrow in times of bad weather conditions and/or capacity problems, but it is
difficult to envisage that these developments will make a serious contribution to
the problem of providing for the air transport demands of the London area.

The Structure of Civil Aviation

The structure of civil aviation in the United Kingdom has already been discussed
in section 2.6. An important element is British Airways, the state-owned airline.
The main arguments for a nationalised airline are the fundamental role of
governments in the regulation of international services, protection of domestic
aerospace manufacture, the advantages of having a 'flag-bearer' from the veiwpoint
of foreign relations and international trade, and the possible need to protect an
industry in its early stages of development. It is not always possible to satisfy
all these different criteria; for example, the aircraft purchasing policy of
British Airways is generally based on commercial considerations rather than a
distinct preference for buying British aircraft.

It is also understandable that there should be doubts about the need for a
nationalised airline when the second-force airline, British Caledonian, is

independent and operating successfully, and when there are no state-owned airlines in the United States; although it should be remarked that these enjoy the advantage of a very large domestic market. Such doubts found expression in the concept of a second-force airline; in principle, such an airline would provide a yardstick for the performance of its state-owned competitor, although no direct competition on individual routes takes place.[35] It is on the basis of this sort of comparison that British Airways is accused of having very high indirect costs. Practical considerations, such as the need to expand the use of Gatwick, and the diseconomies in operating out of two London airports, also supported the creation of a second-force airline as previously indicated.

Economic management of the United Kingdom by a monetarist policy in recent years is the latest factor in arguments for an element of denationalisation of British Airways. Such action would provide some relief on the Public Sector Borrowing Requirement regarding capital financing for British Airways.

6.7 Water Transport

This final section on national transport problems and policies considers inland waterways, ports and shipping.

6.7.1 Inland Waterways

As indicated in sections 2.7.4 and 3.4.4, inland waterways account for a very small proportion of domestic freight movement. This is concentrated over relatively short distances to and from the major estuaries, particularly the Humber. Freight movement by inland waterways has fallen by half in the past decade.

There are three main reasons for this small and declining contribution by inland waterways to domestic freight movement: the limited natural watercourses of the United Kingdom result in poor accessibility of inland waterways in terms of demand for freight movement and generally uneconomic short lengths of haul; the structure and location of modern industry is more suited for road transport; the relocation of ports downstream to deeper water facilities, as in the case of London and Bristol, has limited the distribution possibilities of inland waterways.

A basic problem with inland waterways is the expense of a transfer to and from road transport, unless industrial development by water courses and/or LASH shipping systems are used. It is also a slow form of transport, even though potentially cheap and energy-efficient for carriage of freight in bulk. These characteristics make it eminently suited for transport of heavy goods in bulk, where volume rather than speed of freight transfer is the main consideration.

There are three main problems with inland waterways: in view of their limited development potential and traffic trends, central government does not regard their investment needs with priority; union opposition to the use of innovative distribution systems such as LASH; and the increasing cost of maintaining the remaining canal system for recreational and water-supply purposes.

6.7.2 Ports

The 1980s are likely to be a period of consolidation for the port industry, unlike the times of severe rationalisation of manpower and modernisation in the 1960s, particularly at the largest ports.[36] Important trends are the continuing decline in throughput in volume terms at large and long-established ports like London and Liverpool, and the expansion of East Coast ports, like Felixstowe and Dover, on the increased trade with Europe, particularly in roll-on-roll-off (ro-ro) traffic. It is interesting that new developments in recent years have been concentrated at smaller ports. This partly reflects the attraction of expanding traffic on the basis of capital intensive facilities, so building up labour forces on the basis of new, rather than established, practices. In contrast, development at long-established ports is more likely to be problematic, with regard to rationalisation of labour forces, in any transition from conventional to specialised berths.

An important consideration for the ports industry is its future capacity, in terms of provision at individual ports for additional conventional and specialised berths, which is impossible to forecast with accuracy. The problem is made complex by a number of factors: future trends in the UK economy, particularly with regard to its structure, industrial location, and international trade; significant transport developments, such as completion of the M25 London Orbital Motorway and construction of the Channel Tunnel; and the frequency, capacity and location of shipping services.

Until the development of modern road transport, ports generally had fairly restricted hinterlands; this, of course, is still the case for some specialised traffics. However, development of containerisation and ro-ro traffics has introduced a degree of competition between ports; for example, the Hong Kong-based Orient Overseas Container Terminals transferred from Felixstowe to Southampton in 1976 because its ships were too big for the former, but will be returning its operations to Felixstowe on completion there of new deep draft vessel berths.

There is also some discussion of the future structure of the ports industry. Currently, ownership is vested in a wide range of interests, ranging from the British Transport Docks Board, a nationalised undertaking created by the 1962 Transport Act, and handling some 25 per cent of the throughput of the industry in volume terms at its nineteen ports, public trusts like the Port of London Authority, municipal undertakings as in the case of Preston Docks, which were closed in 1981, to private owners like European Ferries who control the Felixstowe Dock and Railway Company. Investment in the industry has been overseen by the National Ports Council, created by the 1964 Harbours Act, but to be disbanded by the present administration, a reflection of its lack of support for intervention in the market, particularly by non-representative bodies.

The British Transport Docks Board as a nationalised undertaking has to satisfy Treasury requirements on rate-of-return on assets employed, and must meet its investment needs under the cash-limits imposed by central government as part of public-expenditure plans. It is successful in financing its expenditure on investment internally but, like other profitable nationalised industries, is under pressure to seek private capital solutions to its investment needs, and so relieve central government partially of financial responsibility. As in the case of other nationalised transport undertakings not in a monopolistic position in their markets, the financial viability of privately owned ports is a strong argument for a measure of denationalisation.

Competition between ports for freight transport on the basis of price and quality of service is implicit, of course, in this viewpoint. However, in developing this line of argument it is essential to be confident that port dues do not reflect an element of cross subsidisation from passenger services, or from other activities of the owners, or from central government in the form of redundancy payments, or from local government through grants in connection with port development.

There is not a strong case for further rationalisation of ports, in as much as the majority are financially viable. However, if the large investments in capacity in recent years are not fully utilised as a result of future changes in economic structure, then the case for further rationalisation could become a real one.

6.7.3 Shipping

There have been five major developments in shipping since the Second World War

(1) a trend to larger and to specialised vessels

(2) containerisation

(3) increased competition from Communist Bloc countries, particularly Russia, the Trans-Siberian Railway, and Far East operators

(4) the demise of passenger and passenger-cargo liners under the competition of air transport.

(5) changes in operating practices and technical development in response to increasing oil prices.

As just indicated, ports have been modernised and deep-water facilities have been provided in response to technical developments. The most significant development in this context has been the very large reduction in turn-round times at ports, and consequential improvements in capacity and productivity.

There is a close relationship between shipping and shipbuilding activity. As previously discussed in sections 1.1, 1.2.2 and 3.5.1, increases in oil prices and the related economic recession of the 1970s resulted in surplus capacity in world shipping, particularly in oil tankers, attendant lowering of freight rates, and a decline in shipbuilding activity. However, the long-run trend has been an expansion of world shipping capacity with growth in world trade, and there are now signs that this underlying long-run expansion in trade is resulting in a revival of shipping activity, and a hardening of freight rates. However, this development is sensitive to political initiatives, like the US embargo on grain sales to Russia under the Carter administration, and to the degree of restraint shown by shipbuilders generally, but particularly the Japanese, the country with the largest shipbuilding capacity, in responding to these indications of a revival in shipping activity.

The capacity of the world's merchant fleet has expanded very significantly since 1945; for example, the gross registered tonnage of dry cargo ships was 66.7 million in 1950 and 162.7 million in 1974; corresponding figures for tankers were 18.6 and 132.7 million. However, the proportion accounted for by UK registered ships has steadily declined, from some 21 per cent over all in terms of gross registered tonnage in 1950, to some 10 per cent in 1974, even though the capacity of the UK merchant fleet has increased, albeit at a very modest rate. So far as the structure of the UK merchant fleet is concerned, numbers of liners, tramps and tankers have decreased with the trend to larger vessels, but only the capacity of liners has decreased in gross registered tonnage terms. In the case of tramps, one reason for the decline in numbers of vessels is the increasing proportion of trading activity being conducted by large specialised bulk carriers.

Increasing oil prices are a general problem for shipping in the world. Their indirect effects on world trade are more serious for shipping activity than such direct effects as substitution from other modes; for example, even though air transport accounts for a significant proportion of world freight activity in value terms, its substitution would only make a modest addition in overall shipping activity in volume terms, even though trends in fuel costs make this more likely. In the short run, fuel consumption can be reduced by operating at lower speeds, but such a practice is more acceptable as a response to a reduction in flow of a commodity, and/or as an alternative to laying vessels up at times of surplus capacity, as happened in the 1970s with oil tankers, rather than in the transport of general merchandise where journey time is likely to be a more important factor. Possible technical responses to increasing costs of oil include the following: the use of low-grade heavy oil fuels; lighter super-structures and more hydraulically efficient hulls; alternative power sources such as coal, even wind, and common use of nuclear power in large merchant ships.

Two possible problem areas for UK shipping activity are the liner trades and short sea ferries. Freight rates for liner trades are agreed by the various Shipping Conferences; an analogy may be drawn with the fixing of scheduled air fares by IATA.[37] Traditionally, the liner trades were dominated by the developed countries, and, by virtue of its colonial empire, particularly by the United Kingdom. However, this trade has increasingly suffered through developing countries setting up their own shipping lines (again an analogy may be drawn with air transport) and negotiating for a higher proportion of traffic, and from fleets based in the Far East, particularly in Hong Kong, Singapore and Taiwan. Another factor influencing competition on Europe—Far East trades is the Trans-Siberian Railway, which in recent years has been significantly improved. Communist Bloc countries consistently charge significantly lower freight rates, partly through subsidisation of capital costs, partly through a closer relationship between their export trades and their merchant-fleet capacity than is possible in the non-Communist world where, in general, shippers compete for freight business in the market, and partly to increase foreign exchange earnings. Far East operators benefit from lower labour costs. It is this increasing competition for liner trade traffic that has resulted in the decrease in liner capacity of the UK merchant fleet.

Such a development could have worrying implications for the important contribution by UK shipping to invisible trade, as discussed in sections 1.4.2 and 3.5.1. In principle, the government could take action under the 1974 United Kingdom Merchant Shipping Act against measures by other governments harming or threatening to harm British shipping or trading interests. A more recent development affecting the United Kingdom's position as a maritime nation has been loss of control of important sections of its shipping industry to foreign operators.

Another possible problem area for UK shipping is integration of a Channel Tunnel with existing ferry services. The general situation on short sea ferries is an expanding market for passengers, accompaned vehicles and ro-ro traffic, as discussed in section 3.3.2, although there is ample spare capacity with the present recession. Therefore, the effect of a Tunnel will depend upon the extent to which it serves this traffic. Present indications are that the UK government will favour a lower capital cost scheme, without facilities for road ro-ro traffic, and which is likely to provide competition with air transport for business passengers, rather than with existing ferries for holiday traffic.[38] Other considerations are possible opposition by ferry employees to through-rail operation, and the possible inconsistency of providing Tunnel facilities that will complete with existing ferry services with the suggestion by the present administration that British Rail sells its ferry operations to the private sector.

So we end with yet another example of questioning the role of nationalisation in transport, a problem which has been brought into relief by monetary management of the economy under a cash-limits system.

References

1. Department of Transport, *The Report of the Advisory Committee on Trunk Road Assessment* (HMSO, 1978)
2. K. M Gwillian, The Indirect Effects of Highway Investment, *Regional Studies*, **4** (1970) 167–76
3. M. J. Moseley, *Accessibility: The Rural Challenge* (Methuen, London, 1979)
4. D. Maltby, I. G. Monteath and K. A. Lawler, *Urban Transport Planning and Energy: A Quantitative Analysis of Energy Use*, University of Salford, Dept of Civil Engineering Working Paper 3 (Salford, 1976)
5. G. Leach *et al.*, *A Low Energy Strategy for the United Kingdom* (Science Reviews, London, 1979)
6. D. Maltby, I. G. Monteath and K. A. Lawler, *Urban Transport Planning and Energy: A Review*, University of Salford, Dept of Civil Engineering Working Paper 1 (Salford, 1975)
7. Department of Energy, *Energy Act 1976; Passenger Car Fuel Consumption Order* (HMSO, 1977)
8. The Treasury, *Financial Statement and Budget Report 1979–80* (HMSO, 1979)
9. Corporate plan for British Leyland Limited, submitted to UK Government, September 1979
10. Ministry of Transport, *Roads for the Future – The New Inter-Urban Road Plan for England*, Cmnd 4369 (HMSO, 1970)

11. *Design Flows for Motorways and Rural All-Purpose Roads*, Department of the Environment Technical Memorandum H6/74 (London, 1974)
12. *National Road Traffic Forecasts*, Department of Transport Memorandum (London, 1980)
13. The Treasury, *The Test Discount Rate and the Required Rate of Return on Investment*, Treasury Working Paper No 9 (HMSO, 1979)
14. Department of Transport, COBA — A Method of Economic Appraisal of Highway Schemes (HMSO, 1981)
15. Department of the Environment Road Research Laboratory, *Road Note 29 — A Guide to the Structural Design of Pavements for New Roads* (HMSO, 1970)
16. *Regional Highway Traffic Model Project Report: Volume 1* (Department of the Environment Directorate General Highways, London, 1976)
17. Department of Transport, *Trunk Road Proposals — A Comprehensive Framework for Appraisal* (HMSO, 1980)
18. Department of Transport, *Forecasting Traffic on Trunk Roads: A Report on the Regional Highway Traffic Model Project* (HMSO, 1980)
19. J. Tyme, *Motorways Versus Democracy: Public Inquiries into Road Proposals and their Political Significance* (Macmillan, London, 1978)
20. Select Committee on Nationalised Industries, *First Report — The Role of British Rail in Public Transport*, Session 1976–77, HC 305 (HMSO, 1977)
21. Transport Act 1980
22. A. D. W. Smith and R. K. Turner, *The 40 Tonne Lorry*, Informal Discussion Transportation Engineering Group, The Institution of Civil Engineers (London, 13 November 1978); Department of Transport, *Report of the Inquiry into Lorries, People and the Environment* (HMSO, 1980)
23. Department of the Environment, *Transport Policy — A Consultative Document, Volume 2, Paper 6* (HMSO, 1976)
24. Lorries and the Environment Committee Report on Transhipment (London, 1976)
25. H. Conway and H. P. White, Fixed Track Costs and Shifting Subsidies, University of Salford Discussion Paper in Geography No. 10 (Salford, 1979)
26. F. H. G. Wakefield, Lightweight DMU Could Cut Costs on Secondary Lines, *Railway Gazette International*, **136** (1980) 416–17
27. K. M. Gwilliam, J. D. C. A. Prideaux, *et al.*, *A Comparative Study of European Rail Performance* (British Railways Board, London, 1980)
28. S. Wheatcroft, *Air Transport Policy* (Michael Joseph, London, 1964)
29. John E. Allen, Have Energy, Will Travel, *Proceedings 15th Anglo-American Aeronautical Conference* (Royal Aeronautical Society, London, 1977)
30. Committee on the Problem of Noise, *Noise — Final Report*, Cmnd 2056 (HMSO, 1963, reprinted 1968)
31. P. S. Smith, *Air Freight: Operations, Marketing and Economics* (Faber, London, 1974)
32. R. Horonjeff, *Planning and Design of Airports* (McGraw-Hill, New York, 1962)
33. N. Ashford and P. H. Wright, *Airport Engineering* (Wiley, New York, 1979)
34. Department of Trade, *Airports Policy*, Cmnd 7084 (HMSO, 1978)

35. Department of Trade, *British Air Transport in the Seventies*, Cmnd 4018 (HMSO, 1969)
36. Ministry of Transport, *Reorganisation of the Ports*, Cmnd 3903 (HMSO, 1969)
37. S. G. Sturmy, *Shipping Economics: Collected Papers* (Macmillan, London, 1975)
38. Channel Tunnel Advisory Group, *Channel Tunnel and Alternative Cross-Channel Services* (HMSO, 1975)

Index